LANGUAGE IN SOCIETY 28

The English History of
African American English

Language in Society

GENERAL EDITOR
Peter Trudgill, Chair of English Linguistics,
University of Fribourg

ADVISORY EDITORS
J. K. Chambers, Professor of Linguistics,
University of Toronto

Ralph Fasold, Professor of Linguistics,
Georgetown University

William Labov, Professor of Linguistics,
University of Pennsylvania

Lesley Milroy, Professor of Linguistics,
University of Michigan, Ann Arbor

The English History of
African American English

Edited by

Shana Poplack

BLACKWELL
Publishers

First published 2000

2 4 6 8 10 9 7 5 3 1

Blackwell Publishers Inc.
350 Main Street
Malden, Massachusetts 02148
USA

Blackwell Publishers Ltd
108 Cowley Road
Oxford OX4 1JF
UK

Library of Congress Cataloging-in-Publication Data

The English history of African American English / edited by Shana
Poplack.
p.   cm. — (Language and society; 28)
Includes bibliographical references and index.
ISBN 0–631–21261–2 (hc.: alk. paper)
ISBN 0–631–21262–0 (pbk.: alk. paper)
1. English language—United States—History. 2. Black
English—United States—History. 3.
Afro-Americans—Language—History. 4. Americanisms—History. I.
Poplack, Shana. II. Series: Language and society (Blackwell
Publishers); 28.
PE3102.N42   E54   1999
427′.08996073—dc21   99–34522
                                       CIP

British Library Cataloguing in Publication Data

A CIP catalogue record for this book is available from the British Library.

Typeset in 10 on 12½ pt Ehrhardt
by Graphicraft Limited, Hong Kong
Printed in Great Britain by MPG Books Ltd, Bodmin, Cornwall

This book is printed on acid-free paper.

Contents

PART I   MORPHOPHONOLOGICAL VARIABLES

PART II   MORPHOSYNTACTIC VARIABLES

For Simon

List of Tables

List of Maps

List of Figures

Series Editor's Preface

This book is undoubtedly one of the finest pieces of work ever to emerge from the linguistic-variation-and-change enterprise. Here are articles by some of the leading scholars of our time in this field. Here are the results of some pioneering fieldwork in locations where no linguist has trod before. Here are meticulous analyses of carefully obtained and unique data from hitherto mostly ignored speech communities. These data turn out to have enormous consequences for the study of the linguistic history of African American English and constitute a validation for the importance to historical linguistics – if one were needed – of the secular linguistics paradigm which owes so much to William Labov.

The study of the origins of African American English is one of the most fascinating and controversial tales in the history of our science, and no doubt the full story remains to be told. But this volume, which is the result of brave, exciting and painstaking research by leading scholars, many inspired by Shana Poplack, will be the definitive work in this area for some considerable time to come and no worker in this most rewarding of empirical linguistic research fields will be able to afford to ignore it. This work, resulting as it does from a combination of research in social history, dialectology, geolinguistics, creolistics, historical linguistics, and sociolinguistics, makes a central and most welcome addition to this Blackwell series.

PETER TRUDGILL
University of Fribourg

Preface

The impetus for this volume came from an invitation to present, at the 26th Conference on New Ways of Analyzing Variation (NWAVE 26), the results of a long-term research effort aimed at shedding light on the origins of African American Vernacular English (AAVE) through analysis of the language of African Americans in the diaspora. It has been supported since 1988 by grants from the Social Sciences and Humanities Research Council of Canada (1988, 1990, 1995), the Institute of Social and Economic Research, Memorial University of Newfoundland (1990), and University and Faculty of Arts Research Funds from the University of Ottawa (1992, 1998), gratefully acknowledged here. But it actually began well before, when David Sankoff and I, at the urging of Dominican colleagues, first traveled to the peninsula of Samaná in 1981, and collected data there. It was expanded in 1990, when in conjunction with Sali Tagliamonte, I obtained funding to validate our accumulating findings on Samaná, by extending the research to other diaspora communities in Nova Scotia. At about the same time, Guy Bailey and associates invited us to participate in their project on the Ex-Slave Recordings, and furnished the reel-to-reel recordings of interviews made with former slaves in the 1930s. This was the birth of our focus on "Early" African American English (AAE).

The NWAVE 26 symposium, entitled *Objectivity and Commitment in the Study of Early Black English*, originated as a showcase for the work of project members, who had been discovering many striking linguistic parallels among the three varieties of Early African American English, and between them and older, regional and nonstandard varieties of English. Meanwhile, corroborative evidence of a purely sociohistorical nature was being uncovered by other colleagues, and I invited them to help us place the linguistic results in perspective. Lesley Milroy contributed a talk on 'The Pan-Atlantic African Speech Community in the Eighteenth and Nineteenth Centuries: A Sociohistorical Reconstruction' (not included here). A much expanded version of Salikoko Mufwene's 'Notes on the Ecology of the Development of AAVE' appears as chapter 8. Gunnel Tottie agreed to collaborate with Dawn Harvie in replicating her original presentation of relativization strategies in the Ex-Slave Recordings on the diaspora varieties. The new study appears as chapter 7. Sali Tagliamonte, Ejike Eze and myself contributed a synthesis of our work on pluralization patterns in Early African American English and Nigerian Pidgin English (chapter 3).

I am grateful to Diane Vincent for offering us the forum for the symposium. Sali Tagliamonte, my co-investigator and collaborator on the larger projects from which these studies emerged, co-ordinated the data collection effort in Nova Scotia, and conceived and oversaw the data manipulation and handling protocols for all of the Early AAE corpora, which are fully computerized. Her imprint on the research presented here is unmistakable. David Sankoff not only collected the Samaná English data with me in 1981 and 1982, he has been instrumental in its analysis ever since. His influence and example, evident throughout this volume, are gratefully acknowledged.

The contributions of many colleagues working on other varieties of African American English also appear in each of these chapters. Our sometimes heated debates on the occasion of numerous presentations of these materials have never been less than stimulating, and have incited us all to greater efforts to understand the materials.

The research projects on 'Contextualizing Language Contact', 'A Historical and Comparative Study of Black English in Canada' and 'From Synchrony to Diachrony in the Evolution of African American English' have been among the most exciting and stimulating I have worked on, due in no small part to the dynamic group of students and colleagues who have been associated with them over the years in my Sociolinguistics Lab. I thank them for their enthusiasm and perspicuity, especially James Walker and Dawn Harvie, to whose intellectual, organizational, and material contributions this volume owes so much.

I am particularly indebted to the late Mr Moses Shepherd and his family for guidance and help with the fieldwork in Samaná. The support and collaboration of friends and colleagues in Nova Scotia were indispensable. Special thanks go to Henry Bishop, Curator of the Black Cultural Centre; Rosie Fraser, Lisa George-Worth, Wayn Hamilton, Anne Johnson-McDonald, and David States for their help in the initial stages of the Nova Scotia project.

These chapters are dedicated to the African Americans in the diaspora who so generously shared their time, experiences and language with us. It is our sincere hope that they will contribute in some small measure to the understanding of their linguistic heritage.

Shana Poplack
University of Ottawa

List of Abbreviations

A	adjective/adverb
AAE	African American English
AAVE	African American Vernacular English
ADJ	predicate adjective
ANSE	African Nova Scotian English
AUX/aux	auxiliary verb
BCK	Buckie, Scotland
BE	Barbadian English
C	consonant *or* number of contracted copula tokens
D	number of deleted copula tokens
Det	determiner
EBC	English-based Creole
ESR	Ex-Slave Recordings
F	number of full copula tokens
GYE	Guysborough Enclave, Nova Scotia
GYV	Guysborough Village, Nova Scotia
I/IP	intonational phrase
JC	Jamaican Creole English
LOC	locative
LSE	Liberian Settler English
ME	Middle English
ModE	Modern English
N	noun
NEG/Neg	negation
NP	noun phrase
NPE	Nigerian Pidgin English
NPR	North Preston, Nova Scotia
NSVE	Nova Scotian Vernacular English
NWNE	Northern White Nonstandard English
OE	Old English

OED	*Oxford English Dictionary*
PPh/φ	phonological phrase
PWd/ω	prosodic Word
Q	quantifier
SE	Samaná English
StdE	Standard English
SWNE	Southern White Nonstandard English
TC	Trinidadian Creole English
U/UP	utterance phrase
V	verb *or* vowel
V-ing	progressive participle
VP	verb phrase
WNBE	White Nonstandard British English
WPA	Works Progress Administration

List of Contributors

Ejike Eze, Department of Linguistics, University of Ottawa.

Dawn Harvie, Department of Linguistics, University of Ottawa.

Darin M. Howe, Department of Linguistics, University of British Columbia.

Salikoko S. Mufwene, Department of Linguistics, University of Chicago.

Shana Poplack, Department of Linguistics, University of Ottawa.

Jennifer Smith, Department of Language and Linguistic Science, University of York.

Sali Tagliamonte, Department of Language and Linguistic Science, University of York.

Gunnel Tottie, English Seminar, University of Zurich.

Gerard Van Herk, Department of Linguistics, University of Ottawa.

James A. Walker, Department of Linguistics, University of Ottawa.

1

Introduction

Shana Poplack

1.1 Preamble

African American Vernacular English (AAVE) ranks among the most widely documented varieties in the sociolinguistic literature, yet its structure and status remain most controversial. The key – and as yet unresolved – question concerns the differences between AAVE and other dialects of English. Are they the legacy of an earlier widespread creole which has since decreolized, or reflexes of the acquisition of contemporaneous regional Englishes to which its early speakers were first exposed, followed by internal differentiation and divergence? The "creole-origins" position, based on suggestive parallels between features of AAVE and certain English-based creoles, has until quite recently been the dominant view. The papers assembled in this volume support an alternative hypothesis, that the grammatical core of contemporary AAVE developed from an English base, many of whose features have since disappeared from all but a select few varieties (African American *and* British-origin), whose particular sociohistorical environments have enabled them to retain reflexes of features no longer attested in Standard English (StdE). This scenario suggests that the many grammatical distinctions between contemporary varieties of AAVE and American and British English are relatively recent developments, possibly initiated during the post-Civil War period, as suggested by Mufwene in chapter 8, in a social context highly propitious to racial segregation and divergence. This does not of course preclude cultural, lexical, onomastic and other distinctly African and/or creole contributions to the current physiognomy of AAVE. But the research in this volume shows that the details of the grammatical core were acquired from earlier English models.

The papers assembled here all represent new work, but are at the same time the fruits of almost twenty years of research into the origins of AAVE, using evidence from enclaves of African American speakers outside the United States.

Poplack and Sankoff's first reports (Poplack 1982a, 1982b; Poplack and Sankoff 1980, 1981) suggesting that earlier stages of African American English were more similar to some British-origin varieties than contemporary AAVE, and not reflective of a more creolized state, were met with disbelief, and provoked extensive replication by ourselves and others. While our approach and conclusions are still the focus of debate, many scholars, erstwhile proponents of the creole-origin hypothesis included (e.g. Winford 1998), have today come to accept our view that the grammar of AAVE originated largely from the regional and nonstandard Englishes to which the early African Americans were exposed, and not from any widely-spoken creole.

Of course this line of research is not the first to stress the English history of AAVE (see, for example, Bailey 1997; Montgomery 1997; Schneider 1989). But the methodological and analytical basis of its conclusions is quite different from that of the older "anglicist" or "dialectologist" tradition (e.g. D'Eloia 1973; Krapp 1924; Kurath 1949; McDavid and McDavid 1951). In particular the linguistic studies assembled here all analyze the same unique body of data on the language of the African American diaspora, which is argued in what follows to represent a precursor of contemporary AAVE. Each focuses on the distribution and conditioning of a linguistic variable, some of which have figured prominently in the origins debate (the copula, negation, plural), others hardly invoked in this connection at all (relativization strategies, question formation, *was/were* variation). Each employs the same rigorous variationist methodology to operationalize and scientifically test competing hypotheses about the origins of AAVE. Finally, building on techniques of historical/comparative reconstruction, they systematically confront the results with those for candidate sources, of both African and British origin. A major focus on *older* and *nonstandard* varieties of English furnishes a diachronic perspective on the relevant features.

This volume also explores a number of theoretical and methodological issues pertinent to the debate about the origins of AAVE: inferring diachronic processes from synchronic evidence, the relationship between surface form and underlying function, and appropriate diagnostics for membership of forms in a linguistic system. The contributions in chapters 2–7 document grammatical variability in three varieties of English spoken in the African American diaspora, and compare them with the Ex-Slave Recordings, English-based creoles, and contemporary AAVE with respect to variability in six distinct areas of the grammar. Chapter 8 situates the findings within the sociocultural and historical contexts in the United States in which the variety we will call *Early African American English* (Early AAE) developed.

1.2   The Diachrony Problem

Although this has not been explicitly recognized in most of the relevant work, espousal of any position on the origins debate inevitably implies a comparison of AAVE with some earlier form: creolization, decreolization, convergence and divergence all involve linguistic change, and neither the existence nor the direction of change can be assessed without examining at least two discrete stages of the language. But reliable data on the precursor(s) of AAVE are notoriously elusive. The last two decades have seen an increased interest in the few historical representations available, mainly compendia of transcribed interviews conducted in the early part of the twentieth century with elderly former slaves, taken to reflect African American English as spoken in the mid-nineteenth century. Best documented among these are the "Works Progress Administration Ex-Slave Narratives" (e.g., Brewer 1974, 1979, 1986; Pitts 1981, 1986; Schneider 1979, 1982, 1989). The Hyatt Corpus, and the Hoodoo texts, collected around the same time and representative of approximately the same period, have been exploited by Viereck (1988, 1989) and Ewers (1996). Collections of personal correspondence of eighteenth- and nineteenth-century African Americans are currently being unearthed and mined for the light they can shed on earlier stages of African American English (Kautzsch 1998; Montgomery in press; Montgomery, Fuller and DeMarse 1993; Van Herk 1998, 1999).

But detractors cast doubt on the validity of such historical sources (and the analyses based upon them) for many reasons, not least of which is the difficulty of disentangling the linguistic system of the transcribers from that of the speakers (e.g. Wolfram 1990; Dillard 1993). Nor do all vernacular forms characteristic of informal African American English speech appear in writing (e.g. Montgomery in press; Van Herk 1998). This is one of the reasons why most of the evidence contributing to the origins debate continues to be based on inferences drawn from contemporary speech data, often simply assuming that the forms currently in use were also present in the past.

The ideal evidence would come from a historically authentic *and* linguistically faithful representation of Early AAE, as would be obtained from appropriately collected audio recordings from an earlier point in time. A corpus which partially satisfies these criteria in fact exists. The Ex-Slave Recordings – mechanically recorded interviews with former slaves born in five Southern states between 1844 and 1861: see Bailey, Maynor and Cukor-Avila (1991a) – constitute a bona fide variety of earlier African American English, although here as elsewhere, questions have been raised as to their stylistic, social, and geographical representativeness (e.g. Rickford 1991; Schneider 1994). In any event, the Ex-Slave Recordings consist of only a few hours of audible speech, insufficient for the systematic quantitative study of most grammatical structures of interest, albeit invaluable for comparative purposes.

1.3   The African American Diaspora

Partially as a response to the problems characterizing earlier records of AAVE, researchers have begun focusing on the language of the "African American Diaspora" – synchronic recordings of *transplanted* varieties of African American English – as a means of reconstructing the diachronic status of AAVE. This volume presents analyses of two such varieties, spoken to this day in widely separated destinations to which escaped slaves and freedmen emigrated by the thousands in the late eighteenth and early nineteenth centuries: the Samaná peninsula of the Dominican Republic in the Hispanic Caribbean, and two communities on the Atlantic coast of Nova Scotia.[1] The speech of their descendants can furnish historical insight into the current structure of AAVE, providing we can establish its relationship to the language spoken by the original input settlers of these regions, and the relationship of that language in turn to other varieties spoken by African Americans some two centuries ago. Though language-internal evolution is of course a factor, it is the existence of *external* influences on the enclave varieties, whether from adjacent local (Spanish- or English-speaking) populations or from contacts with non-local varieties of African American English, which most threatens to invalidate them as evidence about an earlier stage of AAVE. In what follows we sketch the characteristics of these varieties that substantiate their use in the reconstruction of contemporary AAVE.

1.3.1   Communities and varieties

The three diaspora varieties examined in this volume have in common that the ancestors of current speakers were resident in the United States in the late eighteenth and early nineteenth centuries, before dispersing to diverse locations (map 1.1).

1.   *Guysborough, Nova Scotia* (see map 1.2) was settled in 1783 by the first wave of Black Loyalists, mainly freedmen from the North and house slaves with

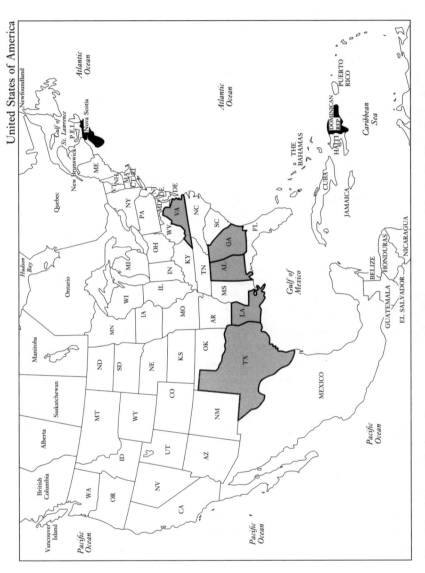

Map 1.1 African American diaspora communities and states represented in the Ex-Slave Recordings

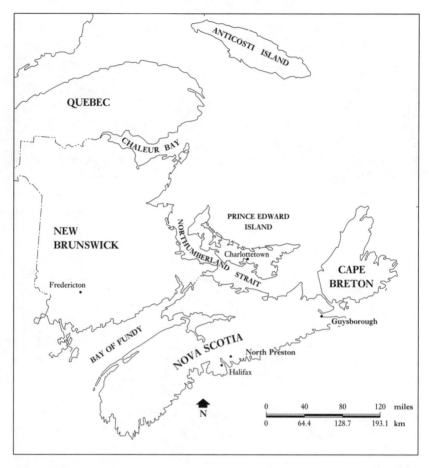

Map 1.2   African American diaspora communities in Nova Scotia: Guysborough and
North Preston

service-related skills (e.g. domestics, waiters, messengers). The settlers were
located outside the districts populated by white settlers, in communities of their
own. Unlike North Preston (see below), Guysborough was unaffected by the
mass exodus to Sierra Leone and by the subsequent influx of refugees. Nowadays, Guysborough figures among the most socioeconomically disadvantaged
counties in Nova Scotia, and the African Nova Scotians residing there have
little contact with neighboring white communities (Poplack and Tagliamonte
1991a: 307–9).

2. *North Preston, Nova Scotia* (see map 1.2) was initially settled at the same time as Guysborough (1784) by a mixture of White and Black Loyalists. By 1792, most if not all of the Black Loyalists had left the community in the exodus to Sierra Leone. A group of 500–600 Jamaican Maroons was exiled to the area in 1796 but was relocated to Sierra Leone in 1800. The current residents of North Preston descend from the immigration to the area of refugee slaves in 1815. The input settlers were predominantly field slaves, characterized as having no specific training or skills, traced to Maryland and Virginia and, to a lesser extent, Louisiana and Georgia. Today, North Preston, more densely populated than Guysborough and the largest African Nova Scotian community, is still topographically and socially isolated from nearby Dartmouth-Halifax (Poplack and Tagliamonte 1991a: 309–10).

3. *Samaná*, a peninsula largely separated from the rest of the Dominican Republic (see map 1.3), was settled at approximately the same time as North Preston (1824), by ex-slaves or their descendants, who immigrated to Santo Domingo via arrangements between its Haitian rulers and church and philanthropic agencies in the US. The exact provenance of the immigrant settlers to Samaná is unclear: although nearly all those interviewed in 1981–2 cited Philadelphia, New Jersey, and New York as their ancestors' place of origin, many of the escaped slaves who boarded at these Northern US ports probably originated from the Southern states. Newspaper articles contemporary with the settlement period reported manumission of entire plantations to Haiti, suggesting that both field and house slaves were among the original settlers. Although the community has been characterized since its inception by increasing bilingualism with Spanish, especially in the younger generations, English was the primary language for all those interviewed. Contact with other varieties of English appears to have been restricted and spread out over several generations (Poplack and Sankoff 1987).[2]

Use of the diaspora varieties as evidence of an earlier form of AAVE is validated through comparison with the real-time data of the Ex-Slave Recordings. As detailed in Bailey et al. (1991a, 1991b), the ex-Slaves presumably acquired their language some four to five decades after the ancestors of the diaspora informants and subsequently remained in the five Southern states in which they were born (map 1.4).

The speakers whose varieties are analyzed in ensuing chapters, amply described elsewhere (e.g. Bailey et al. 1991a; Poplack and Tagliamonte 1991a, and forthcoming), all figured among the oldest and most insular members of their respective communities.

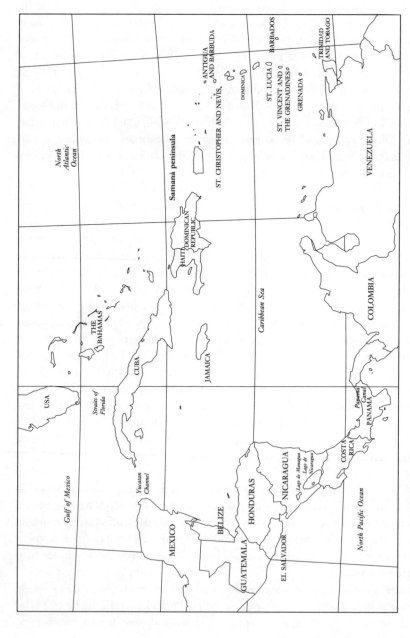

Map 1.3 African American diaspora community in the Dominican Republic: Samaná peninsula

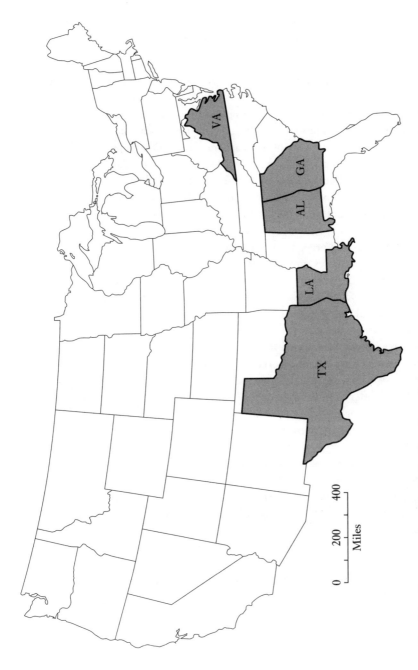

Map 1.4 States represented in the Ex-Slave Recordings

1.4   Validating the Diaspora Data as Evidence of an Earlier Form of AAVE

A number of criticisms may be leveled against the use of the diaspora materials as evidence of an earlier form of AAVE. The first concerns the extent and direction of linguistic change each has undergone subsequent to the split between them and metropolitan varieties of African American English (e.g. Rickford 1998). The sociogeography of the diaspora communities is pertinent here, since two of the migrations resulting in their formation led African Americans to the Canadian Maritimes, where no significant creole influence is known to have existed,[3] while the other led them to the Caribbean, where, in the vicinity of the Hispanic environment of the Dominican Republic, a number of English-based creoles are spoken, e.g. on the islands of Turks and Caicos, the Bahamas, the Virgin Islands and other Leeward Islands, and Jamaica.

Travelers, teachers and merchant sailors from these places have of course visited Samaná from the earliest times, and some may have remained there permanently. The question is how much creole influence they could have imparted to the established English-speaking enclave living in scattered hamlets and farms and proudly resisting assimilation by their Dominican neighbors. Similarly, there have been a number of church emissaries, entrepreneurs from the US as well as returning workers and students, all speaking American English or AAVE or having been influenced by these varieties.

These differences in settlement patterns may be used to assess the extent to which the varieties spoken by their descendants result from contact-induced linguistic change. If contact were a viable explanation for the current form of the diaspora varieties, its traces should be reflected in substantive differences between the Nova Scotian and Samaná varieties (the latter showing more Spanish and/or English – or even Haitian creole – features), as well as between the diaspora varieties and the Ex-Slave Recordings, whose speakers had never been transplanted. If, on the other hand, they display common features, and those features can be identified as *diagnostic* (in the sense discussed below) rather than circumstantial, we may infer that the varieties descend from a common stock. Assessment of which of these scenarios provides the best explanation of the linguistic facts has been a major goal of the long-term research project from which chapters 2–7 emerge.

1.4.1   The role of the enclave in resisting contact-induced grammatical change

Poplack and Sankoff (1980, 1987) and Poplack and Tagliamonte (1991a, and forthcoming) have documented the sociohistorical circumstances enabling Samaná English and African Nova Scotian English to resist contact-induced change at the core grammatical level. Key among them are the social, psychological, geographic, and in some cases, religious separation of their speakers from surrounding local populations. Linguistic confirmation comes from the dearth in Samaná of evidence of grammatical convergence. External influence was shown in Poplack and Sankoff (1987) to be limited to a small set of calques and integrated loanwords which do not alter the grammar of the recipient language (see Poplack and Meechan 1998), and the occasional case of code-switching or interference. Wide-ranging post-settlement influence of adjacent varieties on African Nova Scotian English is argued against by differences among them in constraint hierarchies conditioning variable grammatical processes (chapter 4; Poplack and Tagliamonte 1995, 1996), though they, of course, share a common stock of English features.

Indeed, the enclave conditions under which these varieties developed offer the strongest *external* evidence that in many ways they reflect a precursor of contemporary AAVE, despite the independent internal evolution each has undergone. The conservative role of the linguistic isolate in resisting external influence is corroborated by examining other English-speaking enclaves which, through like configurations of circumstances, have fortuitously retained the same variable structures as those attested in these African American varieties. Tagliamonte and Smith show in chapter 5 that non-concord *was* in African Nova Scotian English is conditioned by the same Northern British constraint currently operative in a British-origin enclave in northern Scotland, legacy of the erstwhile Northern British English model to which both were exposed.

1.4.2   Tapping the vernacular

A second critique – voiced most recently by Hannah (1997) and Rickford (1998) – concerns the possibility of informant accommodation to the standardizing influences of the interviewers, obscuring their (more creole- or AAVE-like) vernacular. Since the African Nova Scotian English interviews were carried out solely by community members within social networks of their peers, accommodation is not an issue here. For Samaná English, however, the possibility of such

an "interviewer effect" must be considered. None of the scholars who collected
data there (DeBose 1983; Hannah 1997; Poplack and Sankoff 1981; Vigo 1986)
is a community member, and to the extent that the Samaná informants accom-
modated at all, such accommodation could be expected to any interviewer from
outside the community. Whether toward StdE, AAVE or English-based creoles,
the result of accommodation would be equally artifactual.

There are several reasons why an interviewer effect, if one exists, does not
affect the results presented in chapters 2–7. First, despite the unfortunate use
of terminology contrasting the "standard English" characteristics of Samaná
English with contemporary AAVE in Poplack and Sankoff (1987), a plethora of
more recent publications (Poplack and Tagliamonte 1989, 1991b, 1994, and
forthcoming; Tagliamonte 1991; Tagliamonte and Poplack 1993) has made it
clear that the relevant comparison is between Samaná English and archaic,
regional and nonstandard varieties of English, not the English spoken by the
interviewers in 1981. Even if the interviewers had had a standardizing effect
on the speakers, it leaves unexplained the provenance of the specific Samaná
English patterns, which are not evinced in the decidedly standard speech of
the interviewers. Indeed, accommodation towards the interviewers would only
have obscured the effects clearly found, for example, in the chapters of the
present volume.

More important, were there accommodation, speakers could conceivably control the overall rates of variant usage, but could not be expected to alter the
deeper grammatical conditioning of linguistic forms (as recently pointed out
again by Rickford and McNair-Knox (1994)). It is this conditioning which is
the crucial evidence for the historical origins of Samaná English.

Finally, in each of Samaná, Nova Scotia and the Southern US states, speech
data were collected under quite different circumstances: by individuals whose
status in the community ranged from member (Nova Scotia) to outsider (Samaná,
most of the Ex-Slave Recordings), at time periods ranging from the 1930s to
the 1990s, and in exchanges including "sociolinguistic interviews" (Samaná,
Nova Scotia), group interactions (Nova Scotia), and formal interviews. Such
discrepancies in data collection make the many linguistic parallels across varieties, detailed in ensuing chapters, all the more unexpected and compelling.

1.4.3   Speaker representativeness

Another critique of these data sources as evidence of an earlier form of AAVE
concerns the lack of representativeness of the speakers who provided them
(Hannah 1997; Singler 1998). Indeed, the informants (or their forebears) hailed

from different parts of the US; one of the drawbacks associated with use of diaspora varieties in reconstructing contemporary AAVE is that in most cases their exact provenance is impossible to reconstruct.

Some of these problems have no doubt affected to some extent the results presented in this volume. However, none of them, in and of itself, could be responsible for the complex hierarchies of conditions on grammatical variability *shared* by the diaspora varieties and the Ex-Slave Recordings, documented in these chapters. The fact that pattern after pattern is reproduced across the communities is the power of the comparative method and the essence of our argument that they share a grammatical system pre-dating the split among them. Thus, whatever the methodological flaws, when the same analytical methodology is applied to data on the diaspora varieties, creoles, and British-origin varieties, the diaspora varieties are seen to pattern alike, and their patterns parallel the British-origin varieties rather than the creoles.

1.5   A Note on Nomenclature: "Early" AAE

By the criteria of historical and comparative linguistics, features shared by varieties are considered likely to have been present in the grammar of their ancestor. We stress that is the *aggregate* of these commonalities in the diaspora varieties and the Ex-Slave Recordings to which we refer, following Brewer (1973), as *Early* AAE. Clearly, none of these varieties represents, in and of itself, the earliest African American English (cf. Dillard 1993; Schneider 1989, 1993: 217f). They are descendants, arguably conservative descendants, of late eighteenth- to mid-nineteenth-century vernaculars.

The role of these vernaculars in giving rise to contemporary AAVE is detailed in chapter 8. Independent evidence of their linguistic details, some of which are described in this volume, comes from comparing the results of chapters 2–7 with studies of other types of sources representative of approximately the same period. There are many distributional parallels, particularly evident when like quantitative methodology is used, between these Early AAE varieties and sources as disparate as the WPA Ex-Slave Narratives (Schneider 1989), the Hoodoo Texts (Ewers 1996), and the early letters studied by Kautzsch (1998) and Montgomery (in press; Montgomery et al. 1993). They may differ in terms of the frequency of occurrence of particular variants, but many of the more revealing details of grammatical conditioning are in evidence. For example, the Early AAE patterning of non-inversion in questions, choice of relative markers, and the distribution of *ain't* detailed in chapters 4, 6 and 7, all find parallels in the WPA Ex-Slave Narratives (Schneider 1989). Kautzsch's (1998) study of negation in the Virginia Narratives supports Howe's (1995, 1997) and Howe and Walker's (chapter 4) findings on *ain't* and negative postposing. The effects of pronominal subject and following V-*ing*/*gonna* on zero copula in the Hoodoo texts (Ewers 1996) parallel those in Early AAE (chapter 2) – and other varieties of AAVE.

1.6   A Variationist Perspective

The studies assembled here make use of the variationist enterprise, not only in its methodological aspect – the construction, statistical analysis and linguistic interpretation of a suitable corpus – but crucially, in its *critical* role in deciding among linguistic hypotheses. The focus is on identifying and operationalizing empirical criteria capable of distinguishing competing models, and testing them to determine their goodness of fit with the data. The point is not so much to describe the variation (e.g. to observe that zero copula is favored by a following predicate adjective), although this is a *sine qua non* of all the work we report, but to explain and motivate it.

1.6.1   *Rates versus conditioning*

An important distinction we draw here is between rates and conditioning of the variable occurrence of variant forms. Much discussion relating to the origins of AAVE has revolved around frequencies. For example, Hannah (1997) recently adduced her finding that rates of zero copula in her Samaná English data were double what had been found in Poplack and Sankoff (1987) as evidence that she had succeeded in tapping a more creole-like variety. As pointed out in chapter 2, however, the constraints conditioning the choice of zero copula in her data are essentially identical to those attested in the earlier study. Differences in overall rate of variant occurrence may be due to any number of (non-linguistic) factors, and can only be used with caution to infer differences among data sets which are already disparate in terms of collection procedures, interviewer technique, and a host of other factors. But the conditioning of variability (i.e. the configuration of factors affecting the occurrence of the variant forms), as well as the direction of their effects, are deeper constraints, remaining constant regardless of the extralinguistic circumstances.

Nowhere is the distinction between rates and conditioning more evident than in chapter 7: Tottie and Harvie document distinct preferences for the relative markers *that*, *what* and zero in each variety of Early AAE, but the major constraints on choice of the latter are shared by all. Likewise, though rates of non-concord *was* vary widely in the four communities studied by Tagliamonte and Smith (see chapter 5), examination of their conditioning shows which share the same set of constraints. Indeed, since most of the analyses in this volume deal with variants attested in both English and creoles, the configuration of factors conditioning their occurrence assumes primary importance in revealing their source.

1.7 Comparative Reconstruction

Work aimed at establishing the origins of AAVE has often invoked coincidental similarities with creoles and African languages, on the one hand, and differences from Standard English on the other. Inexplicably rare, with a few notable exceptions, are systematic comparisons with varieties approximating the older, regional and/or nonstandard forms of English to which the Africans were likely to have been first exposed. This lacuna is at the root of much of the controversy over the status of variables that has figured so prominently in the origins debate. For example, it is the source of early characterizations of verbal *-s* as a hypercorrect intrusion when it occurred in persons other than third singular (e.g. Fasold 1972; Labov et al. 1968; Wolfram 1969). In fact, research on older varieties of English shows that *-s* not only appeared variably throughout the verbal paradigm, but more important, its occurrence is still conditioned by the same hierarchy of constraints in Early AAE (Montgomery in press; Poplack and Tagliamonte 1989, and forthcoming; Tagliamonte and Poplack in press). Likewise, in this volume, Van Herk shows that non-inversion in questions, often characterized as a creole feature, stems from the replacement in Middle English of lexical verb inversion by *do-* support, and is variably conditioned in Early AAE by the same factors operative then, now extended to the auxiliary system. Tottie and Harvie also detail how the frequency of the zero relative in specifically subject position underscores the character of the Early AAE relativization system as deriving from an English vernacular, despite its superficial identity to the zero relatives attested in some creoles.

Chapters 2–7 share an explicit emphasis on cross-variety comparison – insofar as pre-existing claims about the behavior of variables in the relevant varieties are sufficiently explicit to permit such comparison from a variationist perspective. Chapter 3 showcases this comparative method by first operationalizing constraints on variable plural marking in both English and English-based creoles,

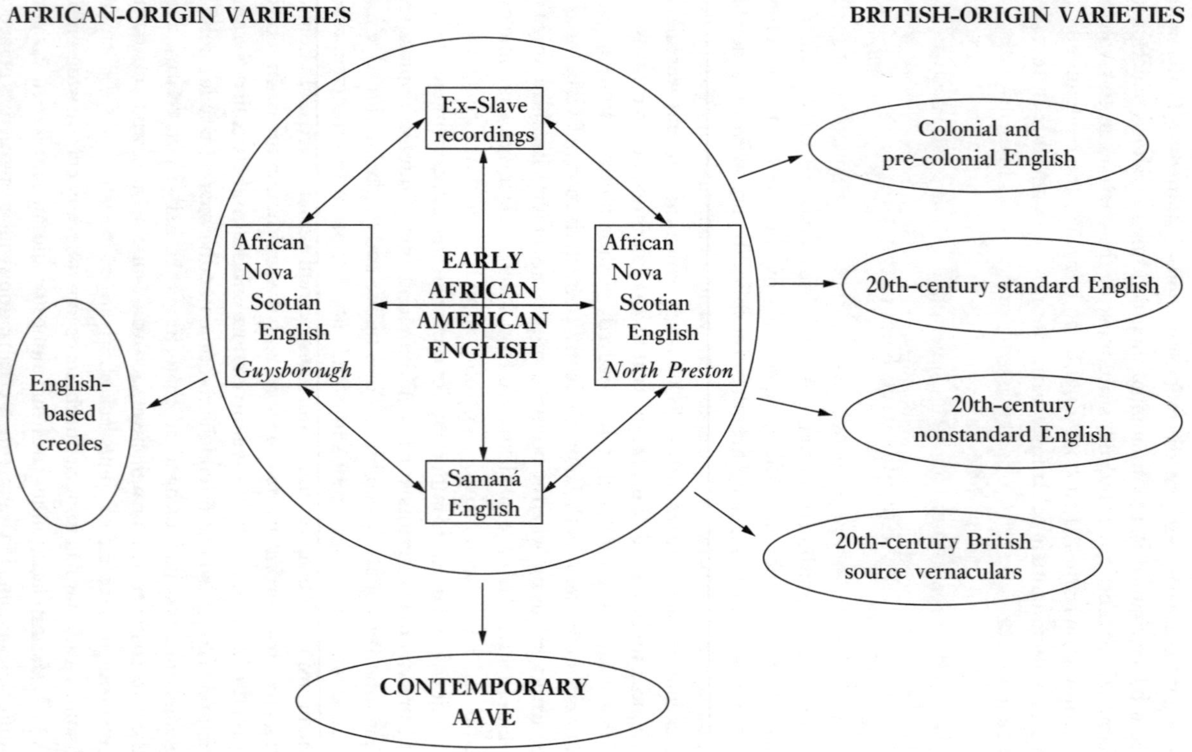

BRITISH-ORIGIN VARIETIES

Colonial and pre-colonial English

20th-century standard English

20th-century nonstandard English

20th-century British source vernaculars

AFRICAN-ORIGIN VARIETIES

African Nova Scotian English *North Preston*

Ex-Slave recordings

EARLY AFRICAN AMERICAN ENGLISH

Samaná English

African Nova Scotian English *Guysborough*

English-based creoles

CONTEMPORARY AAVE

Figure 1.1   Cross-variety comparison

and testing them on Early AAE. Though the predictions associated with each may overlap to a large extent, the effect of the diagnostic explanatory factor – generic reference – is clear. Successive testing and discarding of analyses that obscure the relevant distinctions among putative source varieties pinpoints the differences between the constraints conditioning this phenomenon in Early AAE and in creoles.

Thus, in substantiating claims for the origins of an AAVE feature in a particular source variety, the research assembled here seeks to establish that the feature functions in a non-trivial way as it does in that source, while simultaneously differing from its behavior in the other putative source(s). Where neither of these proofs is possible, the conclusion is that the feature is consistent with both, i.e. not *diagnostic*, as detailed below. Figure 1.1 highlights the appeal to nonstandard, historical or regional varieties of English appropriate to the period and the locale, since these tend to be relatively well-documented.

Factoring contemporary AAVE into the equation provides evidence not only of whether change has taken place, but also of its direction. Thus Howe and Walker (chapter 4) show that current frequent or categorical uses of both negative concord and the use of *ain't* for *didn't* are recent and spectacular developments. In contrast, chapter 3 reveals that the current near-categorical preference for inflecting plural nouns with -*s* was far more variable in Early AAE (as indeed it was in colonial English). Such results provide valuable evidence for the *divergence* hypothesis (Bailey 1985; Bailey and Maynor 1989; Butters 1989; Labov 1985; Rickford 1992): they suggest that contemporary varieties of AAVE and English are evolving away from each other at a rate sufficient to explain by itself the current degree of difference between them.

On the other hand, cross-variety comparison is often hindered by the dearth of quantitative studies of variability in English-based creoles and especially African languages. More such studies would provide a better basis for comparison than the impressionistic claims about these varieties which are often used as metrics for creole origin, without scientific proof as to whether the claims obtain.

A recurrent result of the comparative effort undertaken here is that the same variant forms tend to be attested in each of the putative source varieties: colonial English, contemporary nonstandard English, and English-based creoles. Thus neither the existence of a form, nor even its overall rates of occurrence, can suffice to determine its provenance. This lack of privative association between variants and source varieties has important repercussions for reconstructing the origins of AAVE. It graphically illustrates that the prior and current status of a form can only be ascertained by examining its distribution in the language, as evidenced by the hierarchy of variable constraints conditioning its occurrence. The variationist approach to language use is uniquely suited to resolving such questions.

1.8 The Principle of "Diagnosticity"

Cross-variety comparison is only as revealing as the *diagnosticity* of the item compared, i.e. the extent to which it entertains a unique association with a source variety, and surprisingly few linguistic features turn out to be strongly diagnostic in the sense of distinguishing among the varieties of interest to us. On the contrary, these chapters reveal that most variant forms are shared by all the putative sources. Much controversy in the field results from invocation of coincidental or superficial similarities, as opposed to systematic conditioning of variable occurrences. For example, absence of suffix markers, consonant cluster simplification, "*r*-dropping" and lack of subject–verb agreement were all cited by Dillard (1971) as pidgin or decreolized features of African Nova Scotian English, though these are widely attested in all of the source varieties. Indeed, chapters 2, 4 and 6 reveal that even some of the enshrined frontrunners for creole status, e.g. negative concord, non-inversion in questions, and zero copula are not, in and of themselves, diagnostic of creole origin.

The studies assembled in this volume each make an explicit effort to establish diagnosticity through reliance on deeper similarities, as may be inferred from comparison across varieties of the *conditioning* of their variable occurrence in discourse. The examination in chapter 6 of the "creole" feature of non-inversion in questions graphically demonstrates the pitfalls of failure to assess the diagnosticity of a linguistic feature. After systematic weeding out from an initial dataset of over 3,300 questions those ineligible for inversion (because they contained a non-operator auxiliary or no overt auxiliary at all), Van Herk's pertinent data are reduced by two-thirds. Among the remaining theoretically eligible tokens, the class of yes/no questions, said not to invert in creoles, is found to admit non-inversion in (early and contemporary) English as well. This renders the yes/no context equally non-diagnostic as a metric for assessing creole origins, further reducing the relevant data to under 18 percent of the original corpus. Only the *Wh-* context, in which non-inversion is excluded in contemporary Standard (though not Early Middle) English, is truly diagnostic in this sense. And when rates of non-inversion are examined, they are now found to occur in only a minority of such contexts, rather than categorically, as studies which fail to make these distinctions have assumed (DeBose 1996).

1.9   Non-Independence of Explanatory Factors

A problem related to diagnosticity is the lack of independence among explanatory factors. Variable rule analysis starts with the working hypothesis that the effects of linguistic factors are orthogonal, but close inspection reveals that, as often as not, this is not the case. Recoding and further analysis may be in order. If the interaction is not factored out, one apparent effect may actually be an epiphenomenon of another. As detailed in chapter 2, this appears to be the case for the type of grammatical category following the copula and its prosodic structure. Thus even the occurrence of zero copula before a predicate adjective, widely considered African or creole in origin, may in fact be inextricable from the prosodic structure of sentences containing predicate adjectives. Similarly, in attempting to disentangle the effects of some of the factors said to be responsible for variability in plural marking, variously attributed to creoles and non-standard English, chapter 3 reveals that they overlap: nouns delimited by [+numeric, +individuating] or [−numeric, +individuating] quantifiers fall into the category of indefinites, while those with no determiner tend to be generics; in turn, nouns delimited with [+numeric, +individuating] quantifiers are by definition disambiguated as to number. This means that the presumed polar predictions made by the creole-origins and English-origins hypotheses are much the same. It also entails that the factors of nominal reference, individuation and number disambiguation cannot be incorporated into a single multivariate analysis without causing erratic results, possibly explaining why factors relevant to a creole origin were not revealed to be significant predictors of plural marking in Gullah (Rickford 1990). Interaction is also hidden in explanatory hypotheses for the choice of relative markers, as described in chapter 7: subjects tend to be human, objects do not. Humanness of the antecedent thus cannot be distinguished from the syntactic function of the relative marker in its clause as explanatory factors for relative choice.

This volume is divided into four parts. The first three, all associated with University of Ottawa research projects, deal respectively with Early AAE morphophonological, morphosyntactic and syntactic variables. The goal of these chapters is twofold: to provide linguistically sound descriptions of features of the diaspora varieties (many for the first time) and to assess the usefulness of the materials in shedding light on an earlier stage of AAVE. All are unified by a common theme – assessment of the evidence for origins in creole or English structure – and a common method – the variationist framework of sociolinguistic analysis. Each explicitly enunciates the hypotheses relevant to the diverse scenarios, operationalizing specific predictions as factors in a quantitative (where practicable, variable rule) analysis, and testing them against a large, often exhaustive, body of Early AAE data.

The linguistic developments detailed in chapters 2–7, however compelling, would remain ultimately unconvincing without some understanding of the broader sociohistorical context in which they were enabled. Salikoko Mufwene, though not associated with the Ottawa projects, graciously accepted my invitation to help situate the questions and empirical findings of our research group in such a context. His meticulously researched contribution details how the historical, demographic, social and economic conditions in which African Americans evolved conspired, over time, first to result in a variety like Early AAE, and subsequently to give rise to contemporary AAVE.

1.10   Morphophonological Variables

Chapter 2, by **James Walker**, focuses, appropriately enough, on what Rickford and associates (Rickford et al. 1991) have termed the "showcase" variable, and what Walker calls one of the "most studied but least understood variables in sociolinguistics" – contracted and zero copula.

Zero copula has been attested in older forms of English, but was apparently a restricted literary phenomenon, occurring largely in appositional contexts (Visser 1970). It remains minor in the nonstandard varieties of English in which it is attested (e.g. Feagin 1979; Wolfram 1974), in contrast with its robustness in contemporary AAVE. Indeed, zero copula is perhaps the only variant studied in this volume which cannot be identified as a legacy of English, except perhaps as an additional strategy, complementary to contraction, for reducing prosodic complexity. Nevertheless, Walker's results argue against a creole origin for this variant. For one thing, it was fairly infrequent in Early AAE; for another, there are substantial parallels between contraction and zero. Most relevant for the diagnosticity of zero copula as a creole inheritance, however, is his discovery that the copula is not solely a grammatical variable, as has been assumed until now.

This is most evident in the role of what has come to be known as the "following grammatical category." This context has been accorded pride of place in copula studies, probably due to Holm's widely cited (1984) argument that the association of zero copula with a following predicate adjective was evidence of African language ancestry. Yet Walker points out that the effects of the following grammatical category that have emerged from the many replications of Labov's seminal study (1969) are notoriously inconsistent, while the more consistent effect of subject type tends to be neither highlighted nor explained. Making use of recent models of prosodic structure, he demonstrates that both preceding and following grammatical categories correspond to – and are inextricable from – different prosodic configurations. This results in two types of interaction: the first is between subject type and preceding prosodic constituent (personal pronoun subjects are always proclitics, nominal subjects are virtually always prosodic "words" or phrases, other pronominal subjects are never prosodic phrases). The following grammatical category likewise overlaps almost completely with the following prosodic constituent (e.g. *gonna* occurs in complex prosodic phrases while phrase-final function words are almost exclusively locatives). Crucially, the ordering of the contentious categories, adjective and locative, is sometimes reversed, depending on whether they occur in a complex or a simple prosodic phrase. Walker concludes that the "following grammatical category" is not a well-defined factor: its constituents represent an amalgam of syntactic, semantic and prosodic structure, and its apparent effects are likely epiphenomena of constraints dictated by prosody. This reduces its diagnosticity in assessing the origins of AAVE.

While the proliferation of zero copula and its stereotypical association with contemporary AAVE seems to be a recent and endogenous development, zero plural, reportedly quite rare in AAVE, was once a good deal more frequent. Is the current preference for marking the plural with -*s* a case of approximation, decreolization, or convergence of AAVE to StdE? In chapter 3, **Shana Poplack, Sali Tagliamonte** and **Ejike Eze** try to clarify the direction of the change by pinpointing the source of Early AAE variability. Exploiting the comparative method, they identify and test constraints operating on plural marking in each of the source varieties. The varieties share a plural-marking system which appears to owe its main lines to contemporaneous English models. Further comparison reveals detailed similarities amongst West African creoles, particularly on the diagnostic creole characteristic of generic reference, patterns that differ profoundly from those operative in Early AAE. The authors relate the NPE generic effect to West African substrate influence, and the Early AAE effects to lack thereof.

Chapter 3 shows how the existence of prior variability in both English and Early AAE plural marking has been obscured by the (parallel?) development in both Standard English *and* AAVE of a plural marking system in which -*s* is the norm. This points up the problems involved in exclusive reliance on contemporary StdE as a comparison point, without also considering the details of its development. Once these are factored in, Early AAE plural-marking patterns can be understood as retentions of an earlier variable system, rather than imperfect acquisition of a categorical English system.

1.11   Morphosyntactic Variables

In chapter 4, prompted by observations of Winford (1991) and DeBose (1994) that the creole origins of AAVE were evident in its negation system, **Darin Howe** and **James Walker** systematically examine four Early AAE negation types: *ain't*, negative concord, negative inversion, and negative postposing, three of which have been associated with a creole origin for AAVE. As in the case of the zero plural marker examined by Poplack et al. and the zero copula studied by Walker, evidence from contemporary AAVE for at least some of these constructions appears consistent with a creole-origins scenario. However, the negative constructions are not equally "diagnostic" in the sense discussed above, again requiring recourse to the conditioning of their occurrence in discourse. Typifying the approach of chapter 4 is the analysis of *ain't*, whose robustness in each of Early and contemporary African American English, colonial and contemporary nonstandard English, as well as English-based creoles, makes it particularly suitable for comparative reconstruction. The authors test DeBose's (1994) and DeBose and Faraclas's (1994) hypothesis that AAVE *ain't* functions as a creole universal negator, occurring indifferently regardless of verb type or tense. The virtual restriction of Early AAE *ain't* specifically to the present tense and to the auxiliaries *be* and *have* reveals this usage to have originated in (nonstandard) English. The frequent or near-categorical use in contemporary AAVE of *ain't* for *didn't*, and negative concord, result from relatively recent, and what the authors term "spectacular," innovations made by African Americans to the system they originally acquired. Even patterning revealed by comparison to be consistent with what is reported for creoles (as for negative concord), can be seen, by the same method, to be likewise consistent with (nonstandard) English. They conclude that the negation system of Early AAE displays no *distinct* creole behavior, only the details of the colonial English negation system African Americans were exposed to.

Chapter 5, by **Sali Tagliamonte** and **Jennifer Smith**, highlights the role of the enclave in retaining older features by unveiling vigorous and unexpected parallels between the conditioning of *was/were* variation in African Nova Scotian English and a likely Northern British source dialect. Focusing on contexts in which StdE prescribes *were*, they examine the variable usage of *was* in four speech communities, distinguished according to the African or British ancestry of their residents, the status of their variety as source or transplanted, and the degree of general isolation from mainstream developments.

Variable-rule analysis of constraints on *was/were* variation – some attested in the English language since the Middle English period – reveals that the prominent "Type of Subject" constraint associated with British dialects in general is operative in all varieties in the expected direction (full noun phrase subjects favor *was*). Two other constraints, including one (favoring *was* in second person singular) specifically associated with Northern British dialects only, are shared in the Northern Scottish and African Nova Scotian enclaves. They are surprisingly absent from the British-origin Guysborough Village neighboring the African Guysborough Enclave. The authors invoke settlement histories to explain this finding. The input settlers to the African Nova Scotian enclaves hailed mainly from US colonies which had largely been settled by emigrants from the northern areas of Scotland, Ireland and England; the English models presented to them should therefore have contained features of Northern British dialects. The founders of Guysborough Village, on the other hand, originated from locations settled by migrants from the southern regions of Britain, explaining the absence, in their variety, of the Northern feature.

This distinction between the neighboring African- and British-origin communities in Nova Scotia militates against the possibility of wholesale post-migration contact-induced change in the language of the former, and supports the suggestion that early African Americans adopted not only features, but also their variable conditioning, from the models available to them.

1.12 Syntactic Variables

A well-known though less well-documented syntactic feature of AAVE said to evince its creole origins (DeBose 1996) is the non-inversion of auxiliaries in question formation. Although traditional descriptions of both StdE and creoles describe inversion (or lack thereof) as categorical, **Gerard Van Herk**'s contribution in chapter 6 notes pervasive variability in both. Here again the history of English provides a variable model, in the adoption in Early Middle English of *do* support, a form of non-inversion of lexical verb + subject. Van Herk tests the applicability of five Middle English constraints on non-inversion of lexical verbs to Early AAE questions. The detailed hierarchy of constraints that emerges bears close parallels to the complex system of Early Middle English question formation. Van Herk concludes that it was acquired from English and subsequently extended by Early AAE speakers to auxiliaries, as part of a unitary process of regularization of word order in questions. The extension of lexical verb inversion to auxiliaries qualifies as another innovation of AAVE, based not on creole heritage, but on its own internal evolution.

Relativization is another area of the grammar that has received little attention in the origins debate, despite characterizations of its zero variant as typical of

AAVE (Dillard 1972) and creoles (Bickerton 1981; Dillard 1972), particularly in
subject position, which Martin and Wolfram (1998) consider to distinguish
such languages from other varieties of English. Observing, however, that each
of the three major variants, *that*, *what* and zero, are again well established in the
relative paradigms of British and American English, **Gunnel Tottie** and **Dawn
Harvie** investigate whether their use in Early AAE is the legacy of a creole or
an English relative system.

   In contrast to the other variables studied in this volume, whose variants tend
to show parallel distributions across the Early AAE varieties, preferences for
relative pronouns are quite distinct. African Nova Scotian English, though
arguably the most vernacular, favors standard *that*, Samaná English prefers
what, and zero predominates in the Ex-Slave Recordings. Though their comparative endeavor is hampered by the rarity of relative contexts, the lack of
accountable studies of relativization in creoles and AAVE, and pervasive interaction between explanatory factors proposed in the literature, the authors show
that both in terms of the variant pool among which they alternate as well as in
their distribution, the Early AAE varieties parallel each other and other varieties of standard and nonstandard English, especially with regard to the effects
of type of antecedent and adjacency of antecedent and relative marker. Category
membership is a determining factor in two out of the three varieties. These
results highlight the distinction between overall rates of occurrence, which
differ substantially from variety to variety, and conditioning of that occurrence,
which is substantially the same. Much like the situation for *was/were* variation,
in which regional distinctions in the original British models were seen to
be translated into different preferences in the offshoot varieties studied by
Tagliamonte and Smith, here too the different variant preferences evidenced by
the Early AAE varieties are explained by Tottie and Harvie as relating to a more
general lack of vernacular "norm" for relative markers in either British or
American English. In this area of the grammar as well, then, variant preferences
in the contemporaneous local dialects which served as models are the likely
source of the Early AAE patterns.

1.13   Sociohistorical Considerations

The final contribution to this volume deals with the sociohistorical context in
which the linguistic features described in the preceding six chapters could have
arisen. Tracing the historical, demographic, and socioeconomic circumstances
surrounding the development of African American English, **Salikoko Mufwene**

argues that the socioeconomic history of the United States does not support the existence of an erstwhile creole out of which AAVE would have developed. As he rightly observes, a common mistake has been to compare the emergent varieties with *Standard* English rather than with the nonstandard Englishes, both present-day and colonial, that developed concurrently with African American English. While not ruling out either Caribbean or African-language influence, Mufwene stresses the central role of colonial English as target language during the development of African American English.

Mufwene adduces crucial demographic evidence that distinct socioeconomic situations in the colonies resulted in different linguistic outcomes. Thus the socioeconomic ecology of the coastal rice fields of South Carolina and Georgia, which was similar to that of the Caribbean, led to the development of Gullah. In other colonies, such as Virginia and North Carolina, the emergence of a Gullah-like basilect was less likely, since tobacco plantations were small and Africans were rarely in the majority, leading in turn to increasing contact between Africans and Europeans. The low proportion and sparse distribution of Africans deterred the development of a distinct African American variety of English. Indeed, Mufwene provides evidence for the existence of a "founder population" of locally born and seasoned slaves, in place by the end of the seventeenth century, who "presumably spoke the same kind of English as the Europeans with whom they regularly interacted." It was their English which served as the linguistic model for newly arriving slaves in the eighteenth century. Mufwene notes that the colonial varieties were themselves highly heterogeneous and variable. I would add that insufficient understanding of their nature, now being addressed (e.g. Kytö 1991), no doubt underlies the misidentification of specific nonstandard English features of AAVE as distinctly African or creole.

By the early nineteenth century, much of the foundation of today's AAVE had stabilized, following two centuries of parallel development of African and European vernaculars, which ended with the Civil War (1861–5). This provided the first socioeconomic ecology favorable to linguistic divergence between the two varieties. The subsequent migrations of African Americans to the North and West in the late nineteenth and early twentieth centuries, and their segregation in urban ghettos, enabled them to consolidate the distinctive features of the speech variety they had developed in the South. Thus chapter 8, along with Bailey (1993) and Labov (1998), characterizes urban varieties of AAVE as a twentieth-century phenomenon. Many of the features stereotypically associated with them – probably including some of the recent and spectacular developments referred to in the following chapters – would have emerged and/or spread since the last quarter of the nineteenth century. If Mufwene is correct, the diaspora materials analyzed in this volume figure among the last extant speech evidence representing Early AAE pre-dating the onset of rapid divergence. The similarities between AAVE and nonstandard British-origin varieties detailed in chapters 2–7 are thus explicable in terms of the shared history Mufwene describes; the differences between contemporary AAVE and other varieties of American English can be attributed in large measure to more recent independent (and in some cases divergent) development.

In sum, the studies assembled here confirm the usefulness of Samaná English and African Nova Scotian English in reconstructing an earlier stage of AAVE. The parallels between them and the Ex-Slave Recordings are remarkable in view of the sociolinguistic and geographic disparities among the diaspora settlements, the conditions and time periods under which the data were collected, and nearly two centuries of independent development. They militate against the idea that the diaspora varieties feature substantial contact-induced structural change postdating the dispersal, and locate the similarities in a grammar shared by the ancestors of these speakers. These chapters marshal findings that dispute a creole origin for this grammar, bolstered by both sociohistorical and structural evidence.

Early studies of AAVE focused (perhaps understandably, given the climate of the time) on linguistic features which were most distinct from StdE. Indeed, their absence from StdE was what came to define AAVE (negatively), so that the features eventually assumed an "AAVE" identity. As a result, African American varieties of English appeared far more distinct from English than was warranted by the extent of actual differences. By the time AAVE began to receive serious scientific attention, the English origins of these features were obscured by their virtual elimination from mainstream varieties (cf. zero plural). This, in conjunction with the fact that African Americans were so instrumental in exporting the features to the North, surely bolstered their subsequent identification with AAVE, and compounded the tendency (already decried by Rickford 1998 and Winford 1998) to compare inappropriately these nonstandard structures with counterparts in Standard or literary English.

By identifying constraints on variable realizations and situating them in historical context, these chapters reveal just how far off the mark that association has been. It misses the parallels between Early AAE and the varieties of English early African Americans were likely to have been exposed to and apparently acquired. These parallels are equally evident in non-stigmatized and less noticeable features, such as negative postposing, expression of future time, and relativization strategies.

This research suggests that many of the features that have come to be associated with AAVE – e.g. *was* for *were*, *what* for *that*, zero plural, negative concord, non-inversion in questions – are not simply incorrect forms that have subsequently become fossilized, as would be expected from the scenario attributing them to imperfect acquisition (e.g. Winford 1998). On the contrary, they are regular, rule-governed parts of the grammar. In almost every case, quantitative variationist methodology has shown the system governing their use to be that attested in older forms of English. It has also shown them to differ systematically from creoles and, in one case, African languages. This lends strong confirmation to the idea that the structures, along with their variable conditioning, were already present in the English that the Africans first acquired, supporting the founder effect posited by Mufwene (1996).

These facts suggest that AAVE originated as English, but as the African American community solidified, it innovated specific features. Among them were the spread of *ain't* to past-tense contexts, the proliferation of zero copula, and the extension of lexical verb inversion to auxiliaries, as well, no doubt, as many others not treated here. While the impetus for the selection of some of these features may conceivably have come from English-based creoles or African languages, this must have postdated the period we deal with, since wherever this could be explicitly tested, no evidence emerged that such influences played a role at an earlier time. Contemporary AAVE is the result of evolution, by its own unique internal logic, from a system like the one described here.

Notes

1 Liberia, another diaspora locale, has been extensively documented by Singler (1986, 1988, 1989a, 1989b, 1989c, 1991a, 1991b, 1991c, 1993).
2 The fact that the vast majority of original input settlers was decimated by typhus shortly after their arrival in the Dominican Republic makes the task of determining the geographic provenance of the few survivors sisyphean. This lacuna is unfortunate, but does not detract from the linguistic evidence in ensuing chapters showing numerous and non-trivial parallels between Samaná English and the other two varieties whose original speakers are better documented (*pace* Singler 1998).
3 The passage of the Jamaican Maroons through North Preston (1796–1800) was too early and too brief in duration to have had a lasting effect on the language of the input settlers.

References

Bailey, G. (1985) The divergence of Black and White Vernaculars. Paper presented at NWAVE 14, Georgetown University.

Bailey, G. (1993) A perspective on African-American English. In D. R. Preston (ed.), *American Dialect Research,* Amsterdam / Philadelphia: John Benjamins, 287–318.

Bailey, G. (1997) Southern American English: A prospective. In C. Bernstein, T. Nunnally, and R. Sabino (eds), *Language Variety in the South Revisited,* Tuscaloosa: University of Alabama Press, 21–31.

Bailey, G., and Maynor, N. (1989) The divergence controversy. *American Speech,* 64 (1): 12–39.

Bailey, G., Maynor, N., and Cukor-Avila, P. (eds) (1991a) *The Emergence of Black English: Texts and Commentary.* Amsterdam and Philadelphia: John Benjamins.

Bailey, G., Maynor, N., and Cukor-Avila, P. (eds) (1991b) Introduction. In *The Emergence of Black English: Texts and Commentary,* Amsterdam and Philadelphia: John Benjamins.

Bickerton, D. (1981) *Roots of Language.* Ann Arbor: Karoma.

Brewer, J. (1973) Subject concord of *be* in early Black English. *American Speech,* 48 (1/2): 5–21.

Brewer, J. (1974) The verb *be* in Early Black English: A study based on the WPA Ex-Slave Narratives. Ph.D. dissertation, University of North Carolina at Chapel Hill.

Brewer, J. (1979) Nonagreeing *am* and invariant *be* in Early Black English. *The SECOL Review,* 3: 81–100.

Brewer, J. (1986) Durative marker or hypercorrection? The case of *-s* in the WPA Ex-Slave Narratives. In M. B. Montgomery and G. Bailey (eds), *Language Variety in the South: Perspectives in Black and White,* Alabama: University of Alabama Press, 131–48.

Butters, R. (1989) *The Death of Black English: Divergence and Convergence in Black and White Vernaculars.* Frankfurt: Peter Lang.

DeBose, C., and Faraclas, N. (1994) An Africanist approach to the linguistic study of Black English: Getting to the roots of the tense-aspect-modality and copula systems in Afro-American. In S. Mufwene (ed.), *Africanisms in African American Language Varieties,* Athens: University of Georgia Press, 364–87.

DeBose, C. E. (1983) Samaná English: A dialect that time forgot. In *Proceedings of the Ninth Annual Meeting of the Berkeley Linguistics Society,* 47–53.

DeBose, C. E. (1994) A note on *ain't* vs. *didn't* negation in African American Vernacular. *Journal of Pidgin and Creole Languages,* 9 (1): 127–30.

DeBose, C. E. (1996) Question formation in Samaná English. Paper presented at NWAVE 25, Las Vegas, Nevada.

D'Eloia, S. G. (1973) Issues in the analysis of Nonstandard Negro English: A review of J. L. Dillard's *Black English: Its History and Usage in the United States. Journal of English Linguistics,* 7: 87–106.

Dillard, J. L. (1971) The West African day-names in Nova Scotia. *Names,* 19 (4): 256–61.

Dillard, J. L. (1972) *Black English: Its History and Usage in the United States.* New York: Random House.

Dillard, J. L. (1993) The value (linguistic and philological) of the WPA Ex-Slave Narratives. In S. S. Mufwene (ed.), *Africanisms in Afro-American Language Varieties,* Athens, Georgia: University of Georgia Press, 222–31.

Ewers, T. (1996) *The Origin of American Black English:* Be-*forms in the HOODOO Texts.* New York: Mouton de Gruyter.

Fasold, R. (1972) *Tense Marking in Black English: A Linguistic and Social Analysis.* Washington DC: Center for Applied Linguistics.

Feagin, C. (1979) *Variation and Change in Alabama English: A Sociolinguistic Study of the White Community.* Washington DC: Georgetown University Press.

Hannah, D. (1997) Copula absence in Samaná English: Implications for research on the linguistic history of African-American Vernacular English. *American Speech*, 72 (4): 339–72.

Holm, J. (1984) Variability of the copula in Black English and its creole kin. *American Speech*, 59 (4): 291–309.

Howe, D. M. (1995) Negation and the History of African American English. Unpublished MA thesis, University of Ottawa.

Howe, D. M. (1997) Negation and the history of African American English. *Language Variation and Change*, 9 (2): 267–94.

Kautzsch, A. (1998) Liberian letters and Virginian narratives: negation patterns in two new sources of Earlier AAVE. Paper presented at NWAVE 27. Athens, Georgia.

Krapp, G. P. (1924) The English of the Negro. *American Mercury*, 2: 190–5.

Kurath, H. (1949) *A Word Geography of the Eastern United States.* Ann Arbor: University of Michigan Press.

Kytö, M. (1991) *Variation and Diachrony, with Early American English in Focus.* Frankfurt: Peter Lang.

Labov, W. (1969) Contraction, deletion, and inherent variability of the English copula. *Language*, 45 (4): 715–62.

Labov, W. (1985) The increasing divergence of Black and White vernaculars: Introduction to research reports. Unpublished manuscript.

Labov, W. (1998) Co-existent systems in African-American vernacular English. In S. Mufwene, J. Rickford, G. Bailey, and J. Baugh (eds), *African-American English: Structure, History and Use*, London and New York: Routledge, 110–53.

Labov, W., Cohen, P., Robins, C., and Lewis, J. (1968) *A Study of the Non-standard English of Negro and Puerto Rican Speakers in New York City*, Co-operative Research Report 3288, vol. I. Philadelphia: US Regional Survey.

Martin, S., and Wolfram, W. (1998) The sentence in African-American Vernacular English. In S. Mufwene, J. Rickford, G. Bailey, and J. Baugh (eds), *African-American English: Structure, History and Use*, London and New York: Routledge, 11–36.

McDavid, R. I., Jr, and McDavid, V. (1951) The relationship of the speech of American Negroes to the speech of Whites. *American Speech*, 26 (1): 3–17.

Montgomery, M. (1997) Language variety in the South: A retrospective and assessment. In C. Bernstein, T. Nunnally, and R. Sabino (eds), *Language Variety in the South Revisited*, Tuscaloosa: University of Alabama Press, 3–20.

Montgomery, M. (in press) Eighteenth-century Sierra Leone English: Another exported variety of African American English. In J. Lipski (ed.), *African American English and its Congeners*, Amsterdam and Philadelphia: John Benjamins.

Montgomery, M. B., Fuller, J. M., and DeMarse, S. (1993) "The black men has wives and sweet harts [and third person plural -*s*] jest like the white men": Evidence for verbal -*s* from written documents on 19th-century African American speech. *Language Variation and Change*, 5 (3): 335–57.

Mufwene, S. S. (1996) The founder principle in creole genesis. *Diachronica*, 13 (1): 83–134.

Pitts, W. (1981) Beyond hypercorrection: The use of emphatic -*z* in BEV. *Chicago Linguistic Society*, 17: 303–10.

Pitts, W. (1986) Contrastive use of verbal -*z* in Slave Narratives. In D. Sankoff (ed.), *Diversity and Diachrony*, Amsterdam and Philadelphia: John Benjamins, 73–82.

Poplack, S. (1982a) Black American English in the Hispanic Caribbean. Paper presented at the Department of Spanish, University of Massachusetts at Amherst.

Poplack, S. (1982b) Resultados del contacto inglés-español en Samaná. Paper presented at VIIIth Symposium on Caribbean Dialectology, Universidad de Puerto Rico.

Poplack, S., and Meechan, M. (1998) How languages fit together in codemixing. *International Journal of Bilingualism: Instant Loans, Easy Conditions: The Productivity of Bilingual Borrowing*; Special Issue, 2 (2): 127–38.

Poplack, S., and Sankoff, D. (1980) El inglés de Samaná y la hipótesis del origen criollo. *Boletín de la Academia Puertorriqueña de la Lengua Española*, VIII (2): 103–21.

Poplack, S., and Sankoff, D. (1981) The Philadelphia connection in the Spanish Caribbean. Paper presented at NWAVE 10, University of Pennsylvania.

Poplack, S., and Sankoff, D. (1987) The Philadelphia story in the Spanish Caribbean. *American Speech*, 62 (4): 291–314.

Poplack, S., and Tagliamonte, S. (1989) There's no tense like the present: Verbal -*s* inflection in Early Black English. *Language Variation and Change*, 1 (1): 47–84.

Poplack, S., and Tagliamonte, S. (1991a) African American English in the diaspora: The case of old-line Nova Scotians. *Language Variation and Change*, 3 (3): 301–39.

Poplack, S., and Tagliamonte, S. (1991b) There's no tense like the present: Verbal -*s* inflection in Early Black English. In G. Bailey, N. Maynor, and P. Cukor-Avila (eds), *The Emergence of Black English: Texts and Commentary*, Amsterdam and Philadelphia: John Benjamins, 275–324.

Poplack, S., and Tagliamonte, S. (1994) -*S* or nothing: Marking the plural in the African American diaspora. *American Speech*, 69 (3): 227–59.

Poplack, S., and Tagliamonte, S. (1995) It's black and white: the future of English in rural Nova Scotia. Paper presented at NWAVE 24, University of Pennsylvania, Philadelphia, USA.

Poplack, S., and Tagliamonte, S. (1996) The grammaticization of gonna in six varieties of English: a cross-linguistic comparison. Paper presented at NWAVE 25, University of Nevada, Las Vegas, USA.

Poplack, S., and Tagliamonte, S. (forthcoming) *African American English in the Diaspora*. Oxford: Blackwell.

Rickford, J. R. (1990) Number delimitation in Gullah: A response to Mufwene. *American Speech*, 65 (2): 148–63.

Rickford, J. R. (1991) Representativeness and reliability of the ex-slave narrative materials, with special reference to Wallace Quarterman's recording and transcript. In G. Bailey, N. Maynor, and P. Cukor-Avila (eds), *The Emergence of Black English: Text and Commentary*, Amsterdam and Philadelphia: John Benjamins, 191–212.

Rickford, J. R. (1992) Grammatical variation and divergence in Vernacular Black English. In M. Gerritsen and D. Stein (eds), *Internal and External Factors in Syntactic Change*, Berlin: Mouton de Gruyter, 175–200.

Rickford, J. R. (1998) The creole origins of African-American Vernacular English: Evidence from copula absence. In S. Mufwene, J. R. Rickford, G. Bailey, and J. Baugh (eds), *African-American English: Structure, History, and Use*, London: Routledge, 154–200.

Rickford, J. R., Ball, A., Blake, R., Jackson, R., and Martin, N. (1991) Rappin on the copula coffin: Theoretical and methodological issues in the analysis of copula variation in African American Vernacular English. *Language Variation and Change*, 3 (1): 103–32.

Rickford, J. R., and McNair-Knox, F. (1994) Addressee and topic-influenced style shift: A quantitative sociolinguistic perspective. In D. Biber and E. Finegan (eds), *Sociolinguistic Perspectives on Register*, New York: Oxford University Press, 235–76.

Schneider, E. W. (1979) The diachronic development of the Black English perfective auxiliary phrase. *Journal of English Linguistics*, 13 (1): 55–64.

Schneider, E. W. (1982) On the history of Black English in the USA: Some new evidence. *English World Wide*, 3 (1): 18–46.

Schneider, E. W. (1989) *American Earlier Black English*. Tuscaloosa, Alabama: University of Alabama Press.

Schneider, E. W. (1993) Africanisms in Afro-American English Grammar. In S. Mufwene (ed.), *Africanisms in Afro-American Language Varieties*, Athens: University of Georgia Press, 209–21.

Schneider, E. W. (1994) Review of Bailey, Maynor and Cukor-Avila (eds) 1991. *American Speech*, 69: 191–6.

Singler, J. V. (1986) Liberian Settler English. Paper presented at Workshop on Creoles in Time, Space and Society, LSA Summer Institute, CUNY, New York.

Singler, J. V. (1988) Topics in Liberian English modality. In P. Newman and R. Botne (eds), *Current Issues in African Linguistics*, Dordrecht: Foris, 253–66.

Singler, J. V. (1989a) An African American linguistic enclave. In H. Aertsen and R. J. Jeffers (eds), *Historical Linguistics 1989: Papers from the 9th International Conference on Historical Linguistics*, Amsterdam and Philadelphia: John Benjamins, 457–65.

Singler, J. V. (1989b) *Do, de* and *be* in Settler and Non-Settler Liberian English: who gave what to whom? Paper presented at NWAVE 18, Duke University.

Singler, J. V. (1989c) Plural marking in Liberian Settler English. *American Speech*, 64 (1): 40–64.

Singler, J. V. (1991a) Copula variation in Liberian Settler English and American Black English. In W. F. Edwards and D. Winford (eds), *Verb Phrase Patterns in Black English and Creole*, Detroit: Wayne State University Press, 129–64.

Singler, J. V. (1991b) Liberian Settler English and the Ex-Slave Recordings: A comparative study. In G. Bailey, N. Maynor, and P. Cukor-Avila (eds), *The Emergence of Black English: Texts and Commentary*, Amsterdam and Philadelphia: John Benjamins, 249–74.

Singler, J. V. (1991c) Social and linguistic constraints on plural marking in Liberian English. In J. Cheshire (ed.), *English Around the World: Sociolinguistic Perspectives*, Cambridge: Cambridge University Press, 545–61.

Singler, J. V. (1993) An African-American linguistic enclave: Tense and aspect in Liberian Settler English. In H. Aertsen and R. Jeffers (eds), *Historical Linguistics 1989. Papers from the 9th International Conference on Historical Linguistics*, Amsterdam and Philadelphia: John Benjamins, 457–65.

Singler, J. V. (1998) The African-American Diaspora: who were the dispersed? Paper presented at NWAVE 27, Athens, Georgia.

Tagliamonte, S. (1991) A matter of time: Past temporal reference verbal structures in Samaná English and the Ex-Slave Recordings. Ph.D. dissertation, University of Ottawa.

Tagliamonte, S., and Poplack, S. (1993) The zero-marked verb: Testing the creole hypothesis. *Journal of Pidgin and Creole Languages*, 8 (2): 171–206.

Tagliamonte, S., and Poplack, S. (in press) Back to the present: Verbal -s in the (African American) English Diaspora. In J. Lipski (ed.), *African American English and its Congeners*, Amsterdam and Philadelphia: John Benjamins.

Van Herk, G. (1998) Don't know much about history: letting the data set the agenda in the Origins-of-AAVE Debate. Paper presented at NWAVE 27, Athens, Georgia.

Van Herk, G. (1999) "We was very much Oppress": 18th-century AAVE texts and the origins debate. Paper presented at Society for Pidgin and Creole Linguistics, Los Angeles.

Viereck, W. (1988) Invariant *be* in an unnoticed source of American Early Black English. *American Speech*, 63 (4): 291–303.

Viereck, W. (1989) A linguistic analysis of recordings of 'Early' American Black English. In U. Fries and M. Heusser (eds), *Meaning and Beyond*, Tübingen: Gunter Narr Verlag, 179–96.

Vigo, J. (1986) Language maintenance in Samaná: the case of the Americanos. Paper presented at the Ist International Conference on the Dominican Republic, Rutgers University.

Visser, F. T. (1970) *An Historical Syntax of the English Language*. Leiden: E. J. Brill.

Winford, D. (1991) Back to the past: The BEV/Creole connection revisited. Paper presented at NWAVE 20, Georgetown University.

Winford, D. (1998) On the origins of African American Vernacular English – A creolist perspective, Part II: Linguistic features. *Diachronica*, 15 (1): 99–154.

Wolfram, W. (1969) *A Sociolinguistic Description of Detroit Negro Speech*. Washington DC: Center for Applied Linguistics.

Wolfram, W. (1974) The relationship of White Southern speech to Vernacular Black English. *Language*, 50 (3): 498–527.

Wolfram, W. (1990) Re-examining vernacular Black English. *Language*, 66 (1): 121–33.

Part I
Morphophonological Variables

2

Rephrasing the Copula: Contraction and Zero in Early African American English*

James A. Walker

2.1 Introduction

The copula is probably the most studied but least understood variable in socio-linguistics. Despite almost thirty years of research, no conclusive evidence has yet been provided for the origin and conditioning of its variability, especially in terms of its role in the controversy over the history of African American Vernacular English (AAVE). All dialects of English show variability between full and contracted forms, but the existence in AAVE of an additional zero variant, as well as the factors hypothesized to condition its occurrence, have led some researchers to conclude that it results from a rule of copula deletion in AAVE, an extension of English copula contraction. Others have argued that zero copula is evidence that AAVE derives from a prior creole, since English-based creoles (EBCs) have zero in some copula environments.

Resolving the origins debate on the basis of zero copula has been hampered by several methodological factors: different definitions of the variable context and methods of calculation; continued replication of the factors originally proposed by Labov (1969), often without justification of their role or of the hypotheses they are supposed to test; the incomplete basis of comparisons between AAVE, EBCs, and other varieties of English; and finally, the major focus of this chapter, the interpretation of the significance of the "following grammatical category" factor, which (in retrospect, curiously) has played a key role in arguing for a creole origin for AAVE (e.g. Baugh 1980; Holm 1984; Rickford et al. 1991; Rickford 1996; Weldon 1996; Winford 1992), despite the inconsistency of constraint hierarchies between AAVE and creoles, and even within AAVE.

While this study cannot claim to resolve all of these issues, the analysis presented here is intended to make two key contributions to our understanding of the copula. First, my synthesis of the vast and conflicting literature shows that there has been an unjustified focus on the following grammatical category, while another factor also selected as significant in every study, subject type, has received little attention. A second and more important contribution is to draw attention to those properties of the copula that have until now gone uninvestigated: the ensuing analysis of copula variability in three varieties of early AAE makes use of recent phonological theory (e.g. Nespor and Vogel 1986; Selkirk 1984) to show that prosodic considerations are just as significant as (and, indeed, inseparable from) the following grammatical category, and in fact offer a more meaningful *linguistic* explanation for the variability. These findings also have consequences for the use of zero copula as a metric in the origins debate.

2.2   Zero Copula and the Creole-Origins Controversy

Ideally, determining the origins of zero copula in AAVE first requires a thorough understanding of copula behavior in other varieties of English and in EBCs. We could then determine, as the other contributions to this volume do, whether the factors conditioning copula variability in AAVE resemble one or the other of the comparison varieties. However, the tendency in published reports about the copula has been to compare rates of variability in AAVE not with rates in comparison varieties, but rather with statements about the copula in (idealized) "Standard English" (StdE) and "creole." Such comparisons, often invoking isolated example sentences from different languages without regard to their linguistic patterning, are insufficient to resolve the origins problem. Recent empirical variationist analysis of the copula in EBCs has begun to address this gap (see section 2.2.4), but studies on demonstrably non-creolized varieties of English are still relatively few in number (Fasold and Nakano 1996; Labov 1969; McElhinny 1993; Meechan 1996; Walker and Meechan 1998). I therefore confine my review of the literature to comparisons of AAVE with EBCs.

2.2.1   *AAVE and the creole-origins controversy*

In his seminal study of the copula in AAVE, Labov (1969) noted that zero can occur prior to a noun phrase (NP), a predicate adjective (ADJ), a locative (LOC), negation (NEG), a progressive participle (V-*ing*), or the future *going to/ gonna*, and found the following hierarchy of deletion (most > least):

Table 2.1 Rates of zero copula in Jamaican and Gullah according to following grammatical category (Holm 1984)

Jamaican		Gullah	
Adjective	66%	*Gonna*	88%
Gonna	32%	Adjective	62%
NP	22%	V-*ing*	28%
V-*ing*	17%	Locative	22%
Locative	17%	NP	11%
Total N = 343		**Total N = 189**	

goin'/gonna > V-*ing* > ADJ/LOC > NP

Although he suggested parallels in copula absence between AAVE and both creoles and child language (Labov 1972: 68; 1995: 31), it was Holm's 1976 study (published in 1984) which made the first explicit comparison between AAVE and EBCs. Comparing transcribed Gullah texts with folktales told by a Jamaican speaker, he arrived at the results shown in table 2.1 (Holm 1984: 293).

Based on the high rates of zero before ADJ, supposedly obscured by Labov's (1969) combining of ADJ and LOC, Holm argued that had Labov separated the two categories (as Holm does in table 2.1), he would have found a similar pattern in his data, which would in turn indicate a creole origin for AAVE. Holm's explanation for the hierarchy is as follows: *gonna* is a calque for a protocreole preverbal irrealis marker, V-*ing* is a calque for a protocreole verb and its preverbal progressive/iterative marker, ADJ was a subclass of verb in the protocreole, and LOC and NP require copulas because of protocreole locative and equative copulas, respectively (Holm 1984: 298). Holm's explanation implicitly predicts higher rates of zero before *gonna*, V-*ing* and ADJ and lower rates before LOC and NP. Drawing on selections from *Teach Yourself Yoruba* (Rowlands 1969), he argued further that this hierarchy reflects a common, African ancestry for both AAVE and EBCs (Holm 1984: 301). Observing the variety of copulas used in different semantic and syntactic contexts in Yoruba, he argued that Yoruba speakers learning English would have carried these contextual distinctions into English, where they are not relevant (Holm 1984: 297).

Baugh's (1980) re-analysis of Labov's data, shown in table 2.2, followed on Holm's study. Unlike Labov, Baugh found that, although both *gonna* and V-*ing* favored contraction, neither category particularly favored zero, less so even than ADJ, LOC, *and* Det + NP. When LOC and ADJ were separated, Baugh found

Table 2.2   Factors contributing to the occurrence of contracted and zero copula in Harlem AAVE (adapted from Baugh 1980)

		Contracted	Zero
Preceding Segment	Consonant	0.000	0.061
	Vowel	0.408	0.000
Following Segment	Consonant	0.522	0.322
	Vowel	0.000	0.000
Subject Type	Pronoun	0.856	0.714
	NP	0.000	0.000
Following Grammatical Category	Adjective	0.116	1.000
	Det + NP	1.000	0.741
	Locative	1.000	0.682
	gon(*na*)	1.000	0.601
	V-*ing*	1.000	0.402
Total N = 578[a]	NP	0.000	0.000

[a] This is the total number of tokens in Baugh's dataset; he provides no totals for the individual variable-rule runs.

that ADJ favored zero more than LOC. Assuming some (unspecified) relationship between Jamaican and AAVE, Baugh (1980: 103) argued that originally there was no preadjectival copula in AAVE, and attributed this pattern to influence not from an African ancestry, as Holm did, but from West Indian creoles.

Interpreting these results as evidence for a creole origin meets with a number of problems. First, at least as far as the copula is concerned, there are no testable hypotheses or scenarios for creolization which make clear predictions about what linguistic evidence should be expected for each scenario (English origin, creole origin, West African origin). Secondly, there is no basis for the comparison of AAVE with either EBCs or English, since no explicit data either from other varieties of English or from EBCs is offered. Furthermore, the comparison with African languages with respect to copula usage provided by Holm is dubious at best: apart from the fact that pedagogical grammars are unreliable sources of evidence for naturalistic linguistic behavior, there is no one-to-one correspondence between copula categories in Yoruba, EBCs, and/ or AAVE (as Rickford [1998: 186] also notes). More important, neither study mentions Labov's original analysis of his data (Labov et al. 1968), in which separation of ADJ and LOC shows *different* orderings across groups of speakers

(Labov et al. 1968; Labov 1972: 86) who presumably should be on the same point in the creole continuum, if AAVE is a decreolized variety.

In addition, neither Holm nor Baugh provide an explanation for Labov's (1972: 85) and Baugh's (as shown in table 2.2) finding that a pronominal subject correlates more highly with *both* contraction and zero than does a full NP subject. In their focus on the following grammatical category, itself dictated by the (tenuous) parallels they adduced between it and an African origin, both Holm and Baugh neglected the significance of the subject-type effect.

2.2.2 Copula variability in the diaspora communities

To test claims about the early history of AAVE, several studies have investigated copula variability in the speech of African American *diaspora* communities, which have developed as enclaves, out of contact with the greater AAVE community and mainstream American English, and are assumed to have preserved older forms of AAVE which either have not participated in, or have lagged behind, linguistic changes in both AAVE and mainstream American English (see Poplack, this volume). Diaspora varieties in which the copula has been studied include Samaná English (SE; Hannah 1997; Poplack and Sankoff 1987), Liberian Settler English (LSE; Singler 1991), and African Nova Scotian English (ANSE; Poplack and Tagliamonte 1991). If AAVE did indeed descend from an earlier creole, copula variability in early AAE should more closely resemble that reported for EBCs than does AAVE. Table 2.3 compares contraction and zero in ANSE (Poplack and Tagliamonte 1991) and SE (Hannah 1997; Poplack and Sankoff 1987)[1] and table 2.4 shows the results for three speakers of LSE (Singler 1991).

As the figures in bold in table 2.3 indicate, many of the same factors that favor both contraction and zero are shared by the ANSE data and the two SE datasets, and in general parallel the findings for AAVE. Note that in the one factor group for which the SE and ANSE results do not parallel those of modern AAVE, the type of subject, the effect is shared by all three datasets: pronominal subjects such as *he/she* and *it/what/that* favor contraction, while NP subjects disfavor contraction and favor zero. With respect to the following grammatical category, V-*ing* and *gonna* favor both contraction and zero more than other categories in all three datasets. More important, ADJ consistently disfavors zero copula, the opposite of what Holm's explanation predicts. Furthermore, in ANSE, LSE (table 2.4), and Poplack and Sankoff's SE data, LOC favors zero copula more than ADJ. Even where this order does not obtain, as in Hannah's SE data, there is virtually no difference between these categories.

Table 2.3   Factors selected as significant to the occurrence of contracted and zero copula in Samaná English (Poplack and Sankoff 1987: 306–7; Hannah 1997: 356, 358) and ANSE (Poplack and Tagliamonte 1991: 320)

	Contracted			Zero		
	Samaná		ANSE	Samaná		ANSE
	P and S	Hannah	P and T	P and S	Hannah	P and T
Total N	489	502	545	384	443	462
Corrected mean	.89	.95	.94	.54	.26	.14
Factor group:						
Subject type						
I	.45	.32	.46	.06	.01	.16
he/she	**.93**	**.81**	.68	.28	.77	.52
it/what/that	**.85**	**.82**	.67	.06	.25	.29
you/we/they	.32	.62	.80	**.90**	**.86**	**.91**
those/them/these	.13	.04	.04	.43	.29	–
NP	.08	.04	.07	**.81**	**.81**	**.89**
here/there	.74	.15	.55	.53	.65	.37
Range	*85*	*78*	*76*	*84*	*85*	*75*
Following grammatical category						
gonna	**.90**	K/O	**1.00**	.59	**.93**	**.73**
V-*ing*	.48	**.92**	**.84**	.46	**.89**	**.69**
Adjective	.35	.54	.39	.19	.44	.46
Locative	.40	.52	.43	.23	.42	.49
NP	.24	.78	.37	.41	.12	.31
Wh-clause		.15		**.95**	.28	.79
Range	*66*	*85*	*63*	*76*	*81*	*33*
Preceding phonological environment						
Vowel	**.62**	**.65**	**.54**	[ ]	.41	.33
Consonant	.38	.16	.47	[ ]	**.90**	**.64**
Range	*24*	*49*	*7*		*49*	*31*
Following phonological segment						
Vowel	[ ]	[ ]	[ ]	.36	[ ]	[ ]
Consonant	[ ]	[ ]	[ ]	**.64**	[ ]	[ ]
Range				*28*		

Table 2.4 Factors contributing to the occurrence of contracted and zero copula in Liberian Settler English (adapted from Singler 1991)[a]

	Contracted		Zero	
	Carolina (%)	Albert and slim	Carolina (%)	Albert and slim
Total N	135	393	135	393
Subject				
I	0	.90	100	.24
he/she	0	.77	100	.51
we/you/they	4	.16	96	.51
NP (sg.)	0	.07	77	.43
NP (pl.)	0	.00	100	.89
it/what/that	33	.85	64	.22
here/there	0	.38	50	.63
Following grammatical category				
gon	0	.00	100	1.00
Locative	0	.17	100	.86
Participle	0	–	100	–
V-*ing*	3	.20	97	.72
Wh-comp	8	.45	92	.65
Adjective	0	.70	91	.35
Det + NP	56	.87	55	.13
NP	18	.60	28	.29

[a] Totals for Albert and Slim are from the percentage tables, since none are given for the variable-rule runs.

Although Hannah reports an overall rate of zero in her SE data (40%) twice that in Poplack and Sankoff's SE data (20%), it is clear that the factors *conditioning* the variability share more similarities than differences (note also that the corrected mean, indicating the overall tendency of zero to occur, is actually lower in Hannah's data than in Poplack and Sankoff's). Although Hannah makes much of the differences between her SE data and those of Poplack and Sankoff, asserting that her results show evidence of the creole nature of SE (Hannah 1997: 343, 363–4), table 2.3 reveals more similarities than differences. Indeed, the differences between her results and those of Poplack and Sankoff are consistent with findings (Rickford and McNair-Knox 1994: 252) that the level of speech style can affect the overall rate of zero without affecting the factors conditioning its variability.

As we have seen, a great deal of attention has been paid to the relative ordering of ADJ and LOC, which is subject to more fluctuation than that of any other categories (Rickford et al. 1991: 119). Poplack and Tagliamonte (1991: 323) have pointed out that while LOC and ADJ agree in most studies in showing comparable intermediate effects and being inconsistently ordered with respect to each other, "they should be showing widely consistent *divergent* effects, one highly favoring and one disfavoring," according to Holm's predictions. This close patterning is evident in table 2.3, in which the differences between ADJ and LOC, whatever their relative ordering, are very slight. In contrast, table 2.4 shows LOC to favor zero much more highly than ADJ, again disconfirming Holm's predictions.

In Singler's study of *Non*-Settler Liberian English, which he characterizes as representing several levels of the creole continuum, the LOC/ADJ ordering changes from the basilect, "where the rate of preadjectival deletion was far greater than the rate for the other two environments," to the mesolect and acrolect, where "the rate of preadjectival deletion is consistently lower than the rate of prelocative deletion" (Singler 1991: 156). This tendency is shown below, along with the rankings from the other varieties discussed above:

ADJ > LOC	*LOC > ADJ*
Basilectal/Lower Mesolectal Non-Settler Liberian English (Singler 1991)	Upper Mesolectal/Acrolectal Non-Settler Liberian English (Singler 1991)
Jamaican, Gullah (Holm 1984)	Samaná English (Poplack and Sankoff 1987)
AAVE (Harlem, Cobras) (Labov 1969/1972)	Liberian Settler English (Singler 1991)
AAVE (Harlem) (Baugh 1980)	ANSE, Ex-Slave Recordings (Poplack and Tagliamonte 1991)
	AAVE (Harlem, Jets) (Labov 1969/1972)

Singler's claim holds for the Liberian continuum, but the diaspora varieties (including the one he studied) show a more acrolectal pattern, which we would not expect if, as postulated above, they represent more creole-like varieties. In addition, two sets of Labov's AAVE data are divided as to ranking, despite the fact that both sets represent the same speech community.

Although not often emphasized in the literature, subject type is selected as significant in all the diaspora varieties, but with results that are not straightforward.

While the high correlation of *he/she* with both contracted and zero copula across all three datasets in table 2.3 suggests that the same finding for the subject-type effect noted above applies here as well, these studies include *is*, *am* and *are*, whereas Labov (1969) excluded *am* and Baugh (1980) studied only *is*. Since the differences among personal pronouns in table 2.3 could be attributed to confounding effects of the different morpholexical properties of each underlying form (*am/is/are*), separating these forms is an important analytical step.

2.2.3 *Decreolization?*

To explain the failure of following grammatical category to pattern according to the predictions of the creole-origins hypothesis, some have appealed to processes of decreolization. For example, Singler (1991) explains the LOC/ADJ reversal as a function of decreolization, though he notes (1991: 155) that the outcome of the ranking of grammatical constraints depends on the model of decreolization assumed, as shown in table 2.5.

In Singler's Model A, the basilect has overt copulas for LOC and NP and zero copula for ADJ, all of which are replaced with *is* in the acrolect. This model predicts that, even in decreolized varieties, ADJ occurs with the highest rate of zero (but note that it fails to predict zero variants for either LOC or NP). In Model B, all copulas are replaced with zero in the mesolect and *is* in the acrolect. This model predicts that the rate of zero mesolectally and acrolectally is roughly the same for all three environments (Singler 1991). Model B explains why there are zero forms in NP and LOC in decreolized varieties (since they are introduced in the mesolect), but if zero originates in the mesolect, then it also predicts a higher rate of zero for ADJ than for either NP or LOC (since non-zero forms are not introduced until the acrolectal stage). Yet in almost all studies, ADJ and LOC pattern more closely together than do LOC and NP.

Table 2.5 Singler's (1991) models of decreolization

	Model A		Model B				
	Basilect	Acrolect	Basiclect	Mesolect		Acrolect	
LOC	*de* →	*is*	*de* →	Ø	→	*is*	
NP	*be* →	*is*	*be* →	Ø	→	*is*	
ADJ	Ø →	*is*	Ø →	Ø	→	*is*	

Table 2.6 Factors contributing to the occurrence of contracted and zero copula in Trinidadian Creole (adapted from Winford 1992: 34, 46)[a]

	Contracted	Zero
Total N	1522	1522
Corrected mean	.03	.70
Factor group:		
Subject type		
we/they/you	–	.64
he/she	.61	.60
I	.64	.49
NP (Plural)	–	.46
NP (Singular)	.15	.42
it/that/what	.68	.39
RANGE	53	25
Following grammatical category		
goin	–	.88
V-*ing*	.38	.85
LOC	.33	.80
ADJ	.77	.64
NP	Ø	.00
RANGE	77	88

[a] Because the zero copula results are taken from the group-session data, I have included the contraction results only for the group-session data (Winford 1992: 46). The totals are from the entire dataset, since he provides no totals for the variable-rule runs. In addition, he excludes *goin* from the variable rule analysis of contraction.

Furthermore, there is no explanation for why LOC should consistently rank higher than NP, since neither model shows a difference between these two categories. Therefore, neither model's predictions are supported by the results of any studies.

Winford (1992) develops a more elaborate model of decreolization to explain the results of his analysis of Trinidadian Creole English (TC), shown in table 2.6. Criticizing previous analyses for comparing AAVE with basilectal creole varieties (since, in his view, AAVE represents a long-decreolized variety), he argues that the proper point of comparison is decreolized creoles "which have lost contact with an erstwhile basilectal variety" (1992: 29), such as TC.

Table 2.7 Winford's (1992) model of decreolization for Caribbean English Creoles

	Basilect		Lower Mesolect		Upper Mesolect		Acrolect
LOC	*de*	→	Ø	→	Ø/forms of *be*	→	inflected *be*
NP	*a*	→	invariant *is*	→	*is*/forms of *be*	→	inflected *be*
ADJ	Ø	→	Ø	→	Ø/forms of *be*	→	inflected *be*
Progressive	*a* + V	→	Ø V + *-ing*	→	(*be*) V + *-in*	→	*be* V + *-ing*
Future	*a go* + V	→	Ø *goin* + V	→	(*be*) *goin to* + V	→	*be goin to* + V

In TC, zero is favoured most by *goin*, V-*ing*, LOC and ADJ, though certainly not highly enough to warrant Winford's categorical statement (1992: 33) that "TC simply has no copula or auxiliary in such structures in present contexts." He argues that the high rate of zero with V-*ing* and *gonna* in both TC and AAVE demonstrates the lack of an underlying copula in such structures, and that the low rate of zero with NP in both languages (0–3.5% in TC) demonstrates that they *now* have a copula in such environments. To explain the different rates of zero with NP between the two languages, he argues that in TC the basilectal copula *a* was replaced by invariant *is* (1992: 35), whereas AAVE originally had no copula with NP, ADJ or LOC and has been incorporating an overt copula in such environments under the influence of StdE (1992). He argues that the differences in rates of zero between the following categories reflect the sensitivity of copula insertion to specific grammatical environments (1992: 45, 49). Table 2.7 summarizes his model of decreolization for Caribbean EBCs.

If zero is cumulative, persisting from the basilect into the upper mesolect, ADJ and LOC should favor zero most in mesolectal varieties. But Winford's model does not explain why V-*ing* and *gonna* favor zero copula so highly, more so even than ADJ and LOC, in both TC and AAVE. Nor does it explain why some grammatical environments should be more resistant (or amenable) to copula insertion than others, and in particular, why V-*ing* and *gonna* should be so resistant.[2] In addition, he offers no explanation for the fact that the effect of subject type for his contracted tokens is much more pronounced than that of following grammatical category (Winford 1992: 46).

The major problem with invoking decreolization to explain the inconsistent ranking of the following grammatical category is the lack of independent evidence (e.g. historical evidence, or comparison with other mesolectal varieties): the hypotheses formulated by these studies are not independent of their results and are thus impossible to test. Rather, they proceed under the assumption that the

Table 2.8 Factors contributing to the occurrence of contracted and zero copula in Barbadian English (BE; Rickford and Blake 1990),[a] Gullah (Weldon 1996 [2nd runs]),[b] and Jamaican Creole English (JCE; Rickford 1996)

		Contracted		Zero		
		BE	Gullah	BE	Gullah	JCE
Corrected mean		.86	.104	.88	.581	.52
Total N		522	403	385	403	368
Factor group:						
Subject type						
Personal Pronoun		.79	.75	.19	.65	.60
Other Pronoun		.58	.22	.45	.40	.23
NP		.16	.29	.84	.32	.70
	Range	*63*	*46*	*65*	*22*	*47*
Following grammatical category						
gonna		.91	.08	.77	.96	–
V-*ing*		.55	.29	.65	.75	.79
Locative		.54	.55	.54	.48	.12
Adjective		.40	.57	.42	.42	.75
V-*ed* (Participle)		–	–	–	–	.69
NP		.16	.72	.08	.23	.23
	Range	*75*	*64*	*69*	*73*	*56*
Underlying form						
am		.56				
is		.60				
are		.35				
	Range	*25*				
Following segment						
Vowel		.59				
Consonant		.41				
	Range	*18*				
Tense						
Past						.61
Present						.39
	Range					*22*

[a] I have not shown the factors not selected as significant or the speaker factor.
[b] Excluding *it/that/what*, *am* and collapsing *gon* and *gonna*.

varieties in question are (decreolized) EBCs and that their nonstandard features are relics of those creoles. Even this assumption fails to explain why the copula behaves differently depending on the following grammatical category, since the purported target of decreolization bears little resemblance to either StdE or basilectal creole varieties.

2.2.4 Copula variability in creoles

Because the use of the following grammatical category as a diagnostic of a creole origin requires a consensus on the proper analysis of copula behavior in EBCs, perhaps the greatest obstacle to a comparative study is the lack of such a consensus, as Holm's (1988: 174–9) overview (based on secondary sources) reveals. Although the literature surveyed by Holm is based on categorical rather than variable statements, it still does not support the claim that all EBCs have a single equative copula (preceding NP). Jamaican has one (*da/a*), but Sranan has two: *na*, distinguishing natural, inborn or permanent characteristics, and *de*, used for accidental, acquired or temporary characteristics. Similarly, many EBCs have a locative copula *de*, derived from English *there*, but Holm (1988: 177) notes that *de* is often ambiguous with the adverb *de* "*there*" and may even be omitted, suggesting that this copula is in fact ambiguous with the deictic adverb (as McWhorter 1997: 103–4 argues for early Saramaccan). Furthermore, Sranan distinguishes between existential/locative *de* and attributive *tan* (< "stand") ("to be a certain way") (Holm 1988: 178), and the uses of locative *de* and equative *da* overlap to some extent in Saramaccan (McWhorter 1997: 87–90), complicating the picture even further.[3] Even more controversial is the status of adjectives. While Holm (1988: 176) characterizes them as stative verbs, since they take preverbal markers in some EBCs, Seuren (1988) argues that some adjectives in Sranan take a copula and are therefore not verbs, and Winford (1990) draws a distinction in Guyanese Creole between "physical property" adjectives, which behave like true adjectives, and all others, which behave like verbs.

A further obstacle to a comparative analysis is the commensurability of the context of copula variability between EBCs and varieties of English. Although V-*ing* and *gonna* tend to favor zero highly, Winford (1990: 230) argues that such forms are not true copula contexts in EBCs: V-*ing* corresponds to a verb plus the preverbal marker *a* and *gonna* corresponds to future marker *gon*.

Despite these obstacles, there are several recent studies of copula variability in creole or creole-like varieties, such as Barbadian English (BE; Rickford and Blake 1990), Jamaican Creole English (JC; Rickford 1996) and Gullah (Weldon 1996). Their results are summarized in table 2.8.

As Rickford and Blake (1990) note, the main factors affecting contraction and zero in mesolectal BE are the type of subject, with pronouns favoring contraction and NP subjects favoring zero, and the following grammatical category, the hierarchy of which parallels both one of Labov's (1969) AAVE groups (Harlem Jets) and Poplack and Sankoff's (1987) SE data.

Rickford's (1996) study of JC re-analyzes the recordings on which the texts used by Holm (1976, 1984) were based and, following Winford (1992: 26), excludes *gon*, *de* and *a*, with the result that the rate of zero with V-*ing* is raised. Although LOC and NP do not correlate highly with zero, unlike other studies, LOC here favors zero even *less* than NP, a finding which Rickford (1996: 366) attributes to "the persistence of creole copula *de*." He argues that his re-analysis makes the following grammatical category hierarchy much more similar to that of AAVE, explaining the difference in patterning for some forms as due to a(n unelaborated) re-analysis process on the part of AAVE speakers. Since Rickford characterizes the JC speech as "replete with basilectal or 'deep creole' elements" (1996: 361), and bearing in mind Winford's caveat that mesolectal varieties are the proper point of comparison with AAVE, it seems odd that AAVE should in one study (Winford 1992) look mesolectal and in another (Rickford 1996) look basilectal.[4]

In Weldon's (1996) study of "mesolectal" Gullah, which also heeds Winford's caveats, the pattern of following grammatical category is identical to that found for (one variety of) AAVE (Weldon 1996: 17; Rickford et al. 1991), a finding she uses to support Stewart's (1973) claim that AAVE is a slightly decreolized form of Gullah and hence derives from a common creole origin. She argues that the low rate of zero with adjectives supports Winford's (1992) claim that "high adjectival" is not characteristic of mesolectal varieties. Recall that the creole origins hypothesis was originally made on the basis of a high rate of zero with adjectives (Holm 1984); here a low rate of zero in this context is being used to argue for the same thing. Although the similarities between Gullah and AAVE may be indicative of a genetic relationship, I submit that it is premature to infer from these similarities that they represent two points along a cline of decreolization. Before concluding that the features shared by Gullah and AAVE have a creole origin, we need evidence that they show systematic similarities to some other, demonstrably creole, variety and that they differ from other, demonstrably *non*-creole varieties. This consideration is especially important since Weldon's Gullah results look nothing like Rickford's JC results, where we would expect a resemblance if creoles shared constraints on copula variability.

Indeed, although these studies of BE, JC and Gullah represent a methodological step forward in the study of the copula in EBCs and creole-like varieties, they have not succeeded in uncovering a single, consistent pattern of copula behavior in EBCs with respect to the following grammatical category.

2.2.5   Summary

The above review of the literature on copula variability in AAVE and EBCs over the last thirty years has revealed a number of recurring themes, some of them interrelated. Most frustrating is the lack of a comparative base, since no single model of copula behavior in EBCs has emerged. The few creole studies reveal no clear relationship between them, at least with respect to following grammatical category. There is also the unanswered question of the variable context of the copula in EBCs. Thus, it is difficult to substantiate arguments for similarity of AAVE to EBCs. All of these reasons are responsible for the absence of clear hypotheses about the nature of the linguistic consequences of prior creolization, at least as far as the copula is concerned. While the creole-origins hypothesis initially predicted a high correlation of zero with following adjectives, this prediction was not confirmed by studies of any of the diaspora varieties. This discrepancy was then explained as a function of decreolization in the case of LSE, but subsequent examination of this explanation revealed it to be *post hoc* and unmotivated by independent linguistic evidence. Most strikingly, much attention has been given to the following grammatical category, whose effects are notoriously inconsistent, while the more consistent effect of subject type has never been highlighted or explained. The remainder of this chapter puts forward an alternative explanatory factor that the recurring reliance on the following grammatical category as a diagnostic of creole origin has obscured: prosodic structure.

2.3   An Unexplored Explanation: Prosody

Given that the variable contraction of unstressed auxiliaries has been a feature of English for several hundred years (see, e.g., Saxon 1737/1979: 25), and given the similarities between contraction and the more general phenomenon of vowel elision (Selkirk 1984), which is uncontroversially conditioned by prosody, it seems surprising that an explanation of copula variability (at least for contraction) has never been explored in prosodic structure. While stress did figure in Labov's (1969) early analysis, subsequent work has never attempted to operationalize prosodic structure as factor groups in a variationist analysis. Prosodic and syntactic structure are crucially not isomorphic, but the former does encode information about the latter (Nespor and Vogel 1986: 171; Selkirk 1986: 373; 1990: 180), which suggests that the effects of the grammatical factors might in fact be epiphenomena of constraints dictated by prosody. This section outlines the model of prosodic structure which will be used in my analysis.

For the purposes of this analysis, I adopt the prosodic hierarchy outlined in Nespor and Vogel (1986), as shown in (1) below.[5]

(1)   *The Prosodic Hierarchy*

Utterance Phrase (U/UP)
|
Intonational Phrase (I/IP)
|
Phonological Phrase (ϕ/PPh)
|
Prosodic Word (ω/PWd)

The levels that concern us are the Prosodic Word (PWd or ω) and the Phonological Phrase (PPh or ϕ). Selkirk (1986: 385) argues that these levels are defined in terms of the edges of syntactic constituents: in English, it is the right edge of a lexical category (N, V or A) and the right edge of its maximal projection that define the edges of the PWd and the PPh, respectively, as demonstrated in (2) (structural details adapted from Selkirk 1986: 387; 1990: 193): (2a) is the syntactic structure of the sentence, while (2b) shows the edges relevant to the mapping of the prosodic structure in (2c).

(2)   The   dog   licked   the   man.

a.   [[[Det] [Noun]]$_{NP}$ [[Verb] [[Det] [Noun   ]]$_{NP}$]$_{VP}$]$_S$

b.   ]$_X$]$_X$]$_X$
                            ]$_{Xmax}$]$_{Xmax}$

c.   (   )$_\omega$ (   )$_\omega$ (   )$_\omega$
      (   )$_\phi$ (   )$_\phi$

While lexical words map to PWds, the mapping of function words (e.g. auxiliaries, modals, complementizers) depends on their syntactic position (Selkirk 1995: 440). Function words that are not emphasized and do not occur phrase-finally become a prosodic clitic to the following PWd (1995), as shown in (3).[6]

(3)   [*function-word* (*lexical-word*)$_{PWd}$]$_{PPh}$

Since the copula is a function word, its prosodic behavior follows from its position and its interaction (syntactic, phonological and prosodic) with adjacent elements. As a function word, the copula has a number of "strong" and "weak" allomorphs (Inkelas and Zec 1993: 208):

	Full	Reduced	Clitic
is	ɪz	ɪz	z
am	ɛm/æm	əm	m
are	ar	ər	r

Full forms occur only when the copula is mapped to a PWd – that is, phrase-finally or emphatically (Selkirk 1984: 400), but since these cases are invariant, I do not consider their prosodic structure here. Following (3), the reduced form is incorporated into the following PPh:

(4)   [(Tom)$_\omega$]$_\phi$ [ɪz (complaining)$_\omega$]$_\phi$ (Inkelas and Zec 1993: 218)

The contracted form is *en*clitic, subcategorizing for a PWd on its left (Inkelas 1989; Inkelas and Zec 1993: 243; McElhinny 1993: 383), and cliticizes to the *preceding* PWd, entailing resyllabification, as in (5).

(5)   a.   [(Tom)$_\omega$]$_\phi$ ['z (complaining)$_\omega$]$_\phi$
                        ⇓
      b.   [(Tom'z)$_\omega$]$_\phi$ [(complaining)$_\omega$]$_\phi$

I hypothesize that the structure of the preceding prosodic constituent accounts for the effect previously attributed to the subject type. The phonological literature on English auxiliaries makes several predictions about the effect of the preceding prosodic constituent (e.g. Selkirk 1984; Inkelas and Zec 1993), but it has little to say about the effect of the following prosodic constituent. Nevertheless, given the apparent significance of the following grammatical category, I hypothesize that the prosodic structure of the following constituent is also relevant to the choice of variant, and may serve to explain this significance. I discuss the operationalization of these assumptions in my analysis of copula variability in more detail in section 2.4.3.5 below.

2.4   Contraction and Zero Copula in Early African American English

2.4.1   Data

The data used in this study were extracted from three corpora representing early AAE: two diaspora varieties (African Nova Scotian English [Poplack and Tagliamonte 1991] and Samaná English [Poplack and Sankoff 1987]) and one baseline variety (the Ex–Slave Recordings [Bailey et al. 1991]), distributed as in table 2.9.

Table 2.9 Distribution of Early African American English speakers and data

	ANSE	SE	ESR
Number of speakers	22	16	11
Total number of tokens	997	941	155

2.4.2   The variable context

The variable context is every present-tense declarative sentence in which the verb *be* was used or could have been used as a copula or an auxiliary. As in previous studies, I do not consider environments in which neither contraction nor zero can occur (Labov 1972: 69–73; Blake 1997). I also disregard past-tense contexts, as in (6), as well as ambiguous temporal reference, as in (7), since it is impossible to tell whether the full form of the verb would be *is* or *was*.

(6)   And then uh- we thought we's in big city.   (ANSE/053/065)[7]

(7)   When Mama was gone, that's when Papa used to take over.

(ANSE/040/241)

Restricting the context to declaratives avoids the issue of variable non-inversion in questions (Blake 1997: 66–7; DeBose 1996; Van Herk, this volume). For example, in (8), because it is impossible to tell what position the full form would occupy, some of the factors cannot be coded.

(8)   What we going to do?   (SE/003/427)
       = What *are* we going to do?
       = What we *are* going to do?

In addition, I do not consider *it/ that/ what* subjects (as in (9–11)), since such forms tend to be almost invariably contracted in AAVE (Labov 1972: 69–70) and thus may distort the overall rate of contraction (Meechan 1996; Weldon 1996).

(9)   And when you are old *it's* something else.   (SE/003/229)

(10)   Old aspirin, *that's* all they got.   (ANSE/040/362)

(11)   This is *what's* all the trouble.   (ANSE/033/263)

Finally, I do not consider neutralization contexts (where contraction and zero are indistinguishable), as illustrated in (12–13) for *is* and *are*.

(12) He(*'s*) civil engineer, navy engineer.   (SE/001/125)

(13) They(*'re*) ransacking all the time.   (ANSE/063/842)

2.4.3 Coding

In addition to noting whether the copula occurred as full, contracted or zero, each token was coded for several factors, each representing a hypothesis about the linguistic constraints on variability.

2.4.3.1 *Type of subject*
The subject was coded as a personal pronoun (e.g. *he/she, we/you/they*), other pronoun (*there/here, this/these*) or NP, because of the subject-type effect noted above.

2.4.3.2 *Following grammatical category*
As noted in section 2.2, the predictions of this factor are not clear. For example, if early AAE is a more creole-like variety, we expect higher rates of zero before adjectives. Given the contradictory findings in various studies, this prediction cannot be maintained. Nevertheless, I adopted the traditional coding of this factor (V-*ing*, *gonna*, ADJ, LOC, NP) and, following recent studies (e.g. Meechan 1996; Poplack and Sankoff 1987; Rickford 1996), I separated participles (14) from "true" adjectives (15).[8]

(14) The children today *are* **blessed**.   (ANSE/008/208)

(15) The cotton root'*s* **good** for plenty medicines.   (SE/002/721)

Further distinctions (such as *wh*-clauses [Poplack and Tagliamonte 1991]) were not justified by the distribution of the data.

2.4.3.3 *Phonological environment*
Labov (1969, 1995) notes that the effect of contraction is to reduce a CVVC sequence to CVC, unless the result would be a consonant cluster, which AAVE simplifies at a higher rate than many other dialects. In the latter case, zero is favored (Labov 1972: 106; 1995: 44–5). The following phonological segment was coded only as a consonant or vowel, but the preceding segment was coded as [r], a sibilant, any other consonant, or a vowel, since Fasold and Nakano

Table 2.10 Cross-tabulation of overt forms of *be* with personal pronouns

	I	*he/she*	*we/you/they*
ANSE			
am/'m	206	0	0
is/'s	0	79	6
are/'re	0	0	165
Agreement:	**100%**	**100%**	**96%**
SE			
am/'m	167	0	0
is/'s	0	170	29
are/'re	0	0	34
Agreement:	**100%**	**100%**	**54%**
ESR			
am/'m	66	0	0
is/'s	0	2	2
are/'re	0	0	8
Agreement:	**100%**	**100%**	**80%**

(1996) found [r] highly favorable to contraction in StdE and sibilants strongly disfavorable to contraction in both StdE and AAVE. Thus, we expect preceding vowels and [r] to favor contraction, and following consonants, especially sibilants, to favor zero.

2.4.3.4 *Underlying form of the copula*

Previous studies have shown that the morpholexical properties of each underlying form of the copula (*is/'s*, *am/'m* and *are/'re*) have different effects: in Poplack and Sankoff's (1987: 307) SE data, *is* contracts more than *am*, which contracts more than *are*; in Labov's (1969) AAVE data, *am* contracted so much that he did not consider it part of the variable context. I coded every token, whether overt or zero, for its corresponding full standard form. However, in varieties with nonstandard subject–verb agreement (see Poplack and Tagliamonte 1991: 327–31), zero forms are ambiguous between underlying *is* and *are*. Table 2.10, in which overt forms are cross-tabulated with personal pronoun subjects, shows categorically standard agreement for all pronouns except *we/you/they*. ANSE and ESR (Ex-Slave Recordings) have very high rates of agreement for these pronouns (96% and 80%, respectively), and thus justify the decision to code for the standard underlying form, but the lower rate of agreement in SE

(54%) suggests that this factor could cause problems for the analysis if the different underlying forms are not separated, a point to which I return in section 2.5.

2.4.3.5 *Prosodic environment*

While the foregoing factors replicate those of previous studies, the prosodic factors are an innovation, at least as far as the copula is concerned. Operationalizing these factors in copula analysis is difficult because of the limited number of structures in which the variants appear. Unlike other variables whose prosodic effects have been investigated within the variationist framework (e.g. Poplack and Tagliamonte 1993; Silva 1994), the copula is restricted to one morphosyntactic environment: the left edge of a VP, which maps to the left edge of a PPh (as in (2)). If copula tokens were coded in the prosodic environments in which they appear on the surface (e.g. (4) and (5b)), there would be no variation, since the contracted form would always occur with a preceding PWd. Therefore, I have assumed that the choice of variant occurs at a point after the mapping of prosodic structure, but before resyllabification.

Under the Strict Layer Hypothesis (Nespor and Vogel 1986: 7; Selkirk 1984: 26), the preceding constituent is always a PPh (except for pronouns, as I explain below). Since my hypothesis is that the effects of the preceding prosodic environment are related to the complexity or branchingness of the PPh, I coded each PPh as either "simple" (a single PWd, as in (16)) or "complex" (a PWd plus additional functional elements or other PWds, as in (17)).

(16) [(Tansy)$_\omega$]$_\phi$'s really good. (ANSE/014/293)

(17) [(The milk)$_\omega$ in (town)$_\omega$]$_\phi$ is fifteen. (SE/003/69)

Subject pronouns are syntactic NPs, but prosodically, they behave like function words (Inkelas and Zec 1993: 206; Selkirk 1984: 346; Selkirk 1995) and procliticize to the following PPh (18).

(18) [(You)$_{cl}$'re (going)$_\omega$ in (debt)$_\omega$]$_\phi$ for what you want. (ESR/006/015)

I coded all subject pronouns, as well as subjects that normally do not receive primary stress, such as expletive *there*, as proclitic. Constituents longer than a PPh, such as nonrestrictive relative clauses and parentheticals, as in (19), were coded as a preceding IP (Nespor and Vogel 1986: 188; Selkirk 1984; Taglicht 1998).

(19) A vision, [you know]$_{IP}$, *is* not like a dream. (ANSE/008/536)

The following prosodic constituent was more difficult to operationalize. Since the copula always surfaces at the left edge of a PPh, the following constituent is always internal to that PPh. I coded the PPh as simple if the following constituent was a lexical category, as in (20), and as complex if it was a functional category (e.g. *gonna*, determiner, quantifier), as in (21).

(20)   but tomorrow the tourist boat $_\phi$[Ø $_\omega$(coming)].   (SE/010/767)

(21)   You have a feeling when something $_\phi$['s gonna $_\omega$(happen)].

(ANSE/046/668)

One exception to this coding was clause-final function words, as in (22).

(22)   Through the field there where Doug $_\phi$[Ø $_{fnc}$(at)].   (ANSE/032/042)

Although such words are phrase-final and bear stress (Inkelas and Zec 1993: 221; Nespor and Vogel 1986: 179), they do not otherwise qualify as PWds (cf. Selkirk 1995: 454–5) and were coded separately. A number of tokens did not fit the other categorizations, such as parentheticals, slight interruptions, hesitations and prolongations, as in (23).

(23)   The weight $_S$[*is-*—$_{IP}$[pulling them down.   (ANSE/039/516)

Despite the fact that these junctures differ from the characterization of preceding IPs, in that they are truncations (what Taglicht 1998: 183 refers to as "IP breaks") arising from performance errors and thus do not constitute well-formed prosodic boundaries, I classed all such tokens as following IPs.

The first prediction made by these factors is that preceding elements which are prosodically simple (i.e. nonbranching: proclitics and simple PPhs) favor contraction more than those which are prosodically complex (complex PPhs, IPs). Although the theoretical literature makes no claims about prosodic constraints on zero, the second prediction is that zero is an additional strategy for avoiding prosodic complexity where contraction is disfavored; in other words, complex preceding and following prosodic constituents favor zero more than simple ones.

2.4.4   *Choosing the method of calculation*

I analyzed all factors first individually and then together using GoldVarb 2 (Rand and Sankoff 1990). Table 2.11 shows the overall distribution of copula occurrence by underlying form. Because *am* contracts so highly, especially in ANSE and the ESR, it does not figure in the ensuing analysis.

Table 2.11 Overall distribution of the realization of the copula by verb form

	Full (%)	Contracted (%)	Zero (%)	Total N
ANSE				
am/ 'm	1	98	1	208
is/ 's	31	48	20	486
are/ 're	8	53	39	303
Overall %	18	60	22	997
SE				
am/ 'm	13	77	10	186
is/ 's	48	38	13	582
are/ 're	20	10	71	173
Overall %	36	41	23	941
ESR				
am/ 'm	1	96	3	68
is/ 's	46	30	24	37
are/ 're	10	12	78	50
Overall %	15	53	32	155

Recently it has been argued (Rickford et al. 1991) that the method of calculation affects the results obtained, and that the choice of method is determined by the analyst's assumptions about the linguistic processes giving rise to surface variability. For example, since the environments in which deletion can occur are a subset of those of contraction, Labov (1972: 88; 1995) regarded contraction and zero as related and thus chose the following method of calculation:[9]

(24) a. *Labov Contraction:*   b. *Labov Deletion:*

$$\frac{C + D}{F + C + D} \qquad\qquad \frac{D}{F + C + D}$$

"Labov Contraction" includes both contracted and zero tokens, while "Labov Deletion" can only operate on those tokens which have already contracted.

Rickford et al. (1991) contrast Labov Contraction/Deletion with Straight Contraction/Deletion, in which contracted and zero tokens are calculated out of all possible environments:

(25)   a. *Straight Contraction:*   b. *Straight Deletion:*

$$\frac{C}{F + C + D}$$ $$\frac{D}{F + C + D}$$

They show that the ordering for the following grammatical category in (Palo Alto) AAVE is reversed depending on which method is used (Rickford et al. 1991: 114; cf. Labov 1969: 732–3), and outline three possible rule orderings for contraction, deletion and insertion (Rickford et al. 1991: 120–4; cf. Labov 1969: 728):

Case 1: Phonological	*Case 2: Grammatical*	*Case 3: Insertion*
1. Contraction	1. Deletion	1. Insertion
əz → z / ...	əz → Ø / ...	Ø → əz / ...
2. Deletion	2. Contraction	2. Contraction
z → Ø / ...	əz → z / ...	əz → z / ...

In Case 1, zero results from contraction feeding deletion (Labov Contraction and Deletion). In Case 2, contraction applies to forms which have not first been deleted (Straight Contraction and Deletion). In Case 3, consistent with the creole-origins hypothesis, there is no underlying copula: full forms are first inserted, then contracted. (Rickford et al. 1991: 123 erroneously formulate the insertion rule as Labov Contraction, but the correct formula is as in (26a), while the Case 3 contraction rule corresponds to what they call Romaine Contraction (26b).)

(26)   a. *Insertion*   b. *Romaine Contraction:*

$$\frac{F + C}{F + C + D}$$ $$\frac{C}{F + C}$$

As Rickford et al. (1991) correctly point out, the method of calculation and the results differ depending on which case the analyst assumes.

However, I cannot agree with some of this reasoning. First, Labov's (1972: 69–73; 1995: 39) observation that zero is restricted to environments of contraction, which led him to view them as aspects of the same process, may in fact have more to do with universal requirements of phrase structure (Ferguson 1971; Winford 1992: 50) or, as I argue, prosody (see Nespor and Vogel 1986: 168), rather than with a specific relationship between contracted and zero forms. Secondly, there is no one-to-one mapping of methods of calculation to hypotheses about rules or their ordering: a large number of linguistic analyses can correspond to a small number of possible statistical analyses (Sankoff and Rousseau

1989: 6). Since the three cases posited by Rickford et al. do not exhaust the number of possible linguistic assumptions behind the different methods of calculation, there is no guarantee that obtaining the results the analyst expected justifies his/her theoretical assumptions. Thirdly, the creole-origin hypothesis as it has appeared in the literature makes the assumption that there is underlyingly either an overt or no copula, the former associated with English and the latter with EBCs. We have already seen that the latter part of this assumption is premature, given the lack of consensus on copula behavior in EBCs. Moreover, such assumptions do not reflect recent semantic theory, which argues that, even in English, the copula is only introduced to satisfy tense/agreement require-ments of non-verbal predicates and is not underlyingly present (e.g. Bouchard 1995: 470; Hengeveld 1992: 32–3; Mufwene 1989; 1990: 790–1). In environ-ments of non-verbal predication, English varieties with a zero variant have three options (a full copula, a contracted copula, or nothing), whereas other varieties have only two.

For these reasons, I determined the method of calculation by statistical rather than theoretical means. Following Sankoff and Rousseau (1989: 4–7), I per-formed a series of calculations on the data with the same set of conditions, obtaining results for every possible method of calculation (Labov, Straight, Romaine, Insertion), and compared the log likelihoods for each run. For this dataset, the greatest log likelihood was consistently that of the sum of the log likelihoods of {{F}, {C, D}} and {C, D}, indicating that a rule ordering F → (C → D) was the most likely. On this basis, I chose Labov Contraction and Deletion as the most appropriate method of calculation.

2.4.5 *Interaction*

A first important finding is that, regardless of the labels attached to the factors, they correspond to different prosodic configurations. This correspondence, which I suggest stems from the close relationship between certain syntactic categories and certain prosodic structures, resulted in two types of interaction which initially made it impossible to obtain valid results with GoldVarb's multiple-regression feature. The first is between the subject type and the pre-ceding prosodic constituent: as table 2.12 shows, personal pronoun subjects are always proclitics, and nominal subjects are virtually always simple or complex PPhs, while other pronominal subjects (*there*, demonstratives) can be either proclitics or simple PPhs, but not complex PPhs. To factor out this interaction, I combined these two factors as one. Further cross-tabulation revealed interac-tion between this new factor and that of the preceding phonological segment: as

James A. Walker

Table 2.12 Cross-tabulation of subject type by preceding prosodic constituent

	NP	Personal pronoun	Other pronoun
Proclitic subject	0	778	234
Simple PPh	333	0	22
Complex PPh	235	2	3
Intonational phrase	19	2	2

Table 2.13 Cross-tabulation of preceding segment by prosodic status of subject

	Proclitic (pronoun)	Proclitic (other)	Simple PPh (noun)	Simple PPh (other)	Complex PPh	IP
[r]	0	102	17	20	26	4
Vowel	778	27	67	2	37	9
Sibilant	0	69	55	18	42	4
Other Consonant	0	17	191	1	136	6

Table 2.14 Cross-tabulation of following prosodic constituent by following grammatical category

	Phrase-final function word	Prosodic word	Complex PPh	Intonational phrase
V-*ing*	2	303	34	4
gonna	0	0	113	0
Locative	26	37	153	1
Adjective	1	213	99	3
Participle	1	64	36	1
NP	3	407	116	12

table 2.13 shows, the most serious effect is that proclitic pronouns end exclusively in vowels.

Using a series of runs to determine whether any factors patterned similarly, I first collapsed the two factors internally, to obviate the problem of low representation evident in many of the cells in table 2.13: the preceding segment was reduced to two values, vowels/[r] and consonants/sibilants, and all proclitics were grouped together. I then combined the factors with each other, and classed preceding IPs, whatever the phonological segment, as one category.

The second type of interaction was between the following grammatical category and the following prosodic constituent. As shown in table 2.14, *gonna* correlates highly with a complex PPh, and phrase-final function words are almost exclusively locatives. To take this interaction into account, I combined these two factors, and grouped phrase-final function words with complex PPhs.

2.4.6 Multivariate analysis

Although the underlying form of the copula was selected as significant in initial runs, I found in separate runs for *is* and *are* that contracted and zero *are* occur only when the preceding segment is a proclitic ending in a vowel or [r]. Because of this restricted distribution, I consider here only the results for *is*, although I will return to the question of *are* in section 2.5.

The results of multivariate analysis for *is* are shown in table 2.15 for ANSE and in table 2.16 for SE.[10] Once the analysis was restricted to *is*, the ESR data contained insufficient data (N = 37) to perform multivariate analysis.

In both ANSE and SE, the preceding context was selected as significant, both for contraction and for zero. For contraction, two trends can be observed, one prosodic and one phonological. Prosodically complex elements tend to disfavor the contracted form: a preceding IP disfavors contraction highly, while proclitic personal pronouns favor contraction almost categorically, and all other categories disfavor. The conspicuous "no data" gaps in the table demonstrate the impossibility of extricating the effects of prosodic and grammatical factors from those of phonological factors. Nevertheless, a robust phonological effect is evident in those categories in which a comparison is possible, with a preceding vowel or [r] favoring contraction more than a preceding consonant.

Zero shows complementary results, not only in the preceding phonological segment but also in the preceding prosodic/grammatical constituent: those categories that favor contraction disfavor zero, and vice versa. Phonologically, zero is favored more by a preceding consonant than by a preceding vowel or [r]. Thus, the argument that contraction and zero arise from different historical processes because they are subject to significantly different constraints (e.g. Rickford et al. 1991: 124–7) misses the point: the difference in results between the two forms is a result of the complementary nature of their application. While contraction is a means of reducing prosodic complexity, zero copula, however it originated, appears to have developed in Early AAE as an additional means of reducing prosodic complexity in contexts where contraction is disfavored.

As the bottom halves of tables 2.15 and 2.16 show, the following prosodic/ grammatical constituent was also selected as significant in both ANSE and SE,

Table 2.15 Factors contributing to the occurrence of contracted and zero *is* in ANSE, using Labov Contraction ($\frac{C}{F+C+D}$) and Deletion ($\frac{D}{C+D}$)

	Contracted	Zero
Corrected mean	.874	.241
Total N	465	334

Factor-group:

Preceding prosodic/grammatical context and phonological segment

	Vowel/[r]	Consonant	Vowel/[r]	Consonant
Proclitic, Personal Pronoun	.97	*no data*	.33	*no data*
Proclitic, Other Pronoun	*no data*	.04	*no data*	**.94**
Simple ɸ, Other Pronoun	100%	*no data*	.24	*no data*
Simple ɸ, Noun	.42	.04	**.66**	**.68**
Complex ɸ	.22	.12	**.63**	**.85**
IP		.01		–
RANGE		*96*		*70*

Following grammatical category and prosodic context

	Simple ɸ	Complex ɸ	Simple ɸ	Complex ɸ
gonna	*no data*	**.94**	*no data*	.64
Verb-*ing*	.76	100%	.75	.94
Adjective	.41	.44	.67	.24
Locative	.38	.70	0%	.51
Participle	.28	.43	.19	0%
NP	.27	**.62**	.35	.30
IP		.05		*no data*
RANGE		*89*		*75*

Following phonological segment

Consonant	[ ]		[ ]
Vowel	[ ]		[ ]

Table 2.16 Factors contributing to the occurrence of contracted and zero *is* in SE, using Labov Contraction ($\frac{C}{F+C+D}$) and Deletion ($\frac{D}{C+D}$)

	Contracted	Zero
Corrected mean	**.564**	**.166**
Total N	**556**	**287**

Factor-group:

Preceding prosodic/grammatical context and phonological segment

	Vowel/[r]	Consonant	Vowel/[r]	Consonant
Proclitic, Personal Pronoun	.91	*no data*	.39	*no data*
Proclitic, Other Pronoun	.45	.21	0%	.97
Simple ϕ, Other Pronoun	.48	*no data*	.93	*no data*
Simple ϕ, Noun	.41	.10	.64	.78
Complex ϕ	.21	.07	.73	.88
IP	0%		*no data*	
RANGE		*71*		*58*

Following grammatical category and prosodic context

	Simple ϕ	Complex ϕ	Simple ϕ	Complex ϕ
gonna	*no data*	.97	*no data*	.94
Verb-*ing*	.83	.89	.92	.90
Adjective	.54	.20	.65	.45
Locative	.66	.46	.45	.23
Participle	.33	.42	.81	.54
NP	.36	.47	.21	.53
IP	K/O [0%]		*no data*	
RANGE		*77*		*73*

Following phonological segment

Vowel	.62	*excluded*[a]
Consonant	.45	
RANGE	*17*	

[a] In the SE data, following phonological segment interacted so much with the other two factors that it was impossible to obtain a valid result. It was excluded for comparability with the ANSE findings.

although an interpretation of the results is not immediately apparent. As in previous studies, V-*ing* and *gonna* favor both contraction and zero, while NP disfavors and ADJ and LOC have intermediate effects. When these categories are separated according to the complexity of the following PPh, as I have done, different rankings emerge, even within the same dataset. Some grammatical categories are associated exclusively with certain prosodic constituents: for example, *gonna* and complex PPhs. More notably, the ordering of the contentious categories, ADJ and LOC, is sometimes *reversed* according to whether they occur in a simple or a complex PPh, as in table 2.15. Thus, the hierarchy of the following grammatical category depends not only on grammatical structure, but also on the complexity of the prosodic environment, further evidence that contraction and zero are strategies for reducing prosodic complexity. The remaining effect of the following grammatical category within each type of prosodic structure remains to be investigated, with better-defined syntactic and semantic factors. For now, these findings reveal the problematic nature of the following-grammatical-category factor: the fluctuating rankings noted in many studies may have less to do with processes of decreolization than with the interaction between grammatical and prosodic structure.

2.5   Discussion

These findings entail a number of consequences for the methodology and theory of the copula, as well as for the creole–origins debate.

2.5.1   *Methodological consequences*

First, *am*, *is* and *are* should be separated in future analysis. The high rate of contraction of *am* in AAVE (Labov 1969; Rickford et al. 1991) suggests that *I'm* has become a single entry in the speaker's lexicon. While the findings for SE and LSE, in which *am* is not more favorable to contraction than *is* or *are*, suggest that this lexicalization is a more recent development, the near-categorical figures of *I'm* in ANSE and ESR make the hypothesis of recent lexicalization difficult to justify. Furthermore, Meechan's (1996) finding of near-categorical *am*-contraction in disparate Canadian English dialects suggests that lexicalization is proceeding at different rates in different varieties of English and does not appear to be an innovation of AAVE.

Future analysis should also distinguish *is* from *are*. As McElhinny (1993: 392) points out, most copula research concerns *is*, whose contracted form ([z])

has few syllabic restrictions. In contrast, contracted *are* ([r]) is restricted to postvocalic environments: in other environments, it becomes syllabic to satisfy English phonotactics and thus is not, strictly speaking, contracted. Phonotactics may also explain why phonological considerations are consistently selected as significant. In addition, the restriction of zero *are* to postvocalic environments could be related to the fact that at least one of these varieties (ANSE) has a high rate (60%) of (r)-lessness (Walker 1995). Because the environment of *are*-contraction is exactly that in which postvocalic (r)-deletion occurs, many tokens of zero *are* may in fact be *are*-contractions that have undergone (r)-deletion. Since we cannot distinguish *are*-deletion from (r)-deletion, *are* should be excluded from future analysis of zero copula.

2.5.2 Consequences for the origins debate

Is Labov's contention that deletion is an extension of contraction correct? Yes and no: contraction and zero are both sensitive to phonological and prosodic effects, but these effects are different and impossible to extricate from each other. Contraction is favored by proclitics ending in a vowel or [r] and disfavored by all other forms, while zero is favored by all forms but proclitics and non-nominal simple PPhs ending in a vowel or [r]. This correlation is understandable whether we regard it as evidence that clitics (contracted elements) prefer to pattern with elements that are also clitic or as evidence of lexicalization (of pronoun and contracted auxiliary) and phonotactics. These results do not support the creolist claim (e.g. Rickford et al. 1991: 124–7) that contraction and zero are subject to significantly different constraints originating from different historical processes. However, zero is not exactly an *extension* of a contraction rule, as Labov (1969) hypothesized, since it is favored only by factors which disfavor contraction.

A more telling argument against the creolist hypothesis is the similarity of hierarchies of constraints conditioning contraction and zero in the following grammatical category. In general, both forms are favored by complex PPhs over simple PPhs, lending further support to the hypothesis that contraction and zero are strategies for reducing prosodic complexity. Within each type of PPh, we see the same tendency of V-*ing* and *gonna* to favor both contraction and zero, NP to disfavor, and LOC and ADJ to have intermediate effects that we have seen in other studies. Separating the prosodic structures reveals the inconsistent nature of the effects of the following grammatical category, the most striking result being the reversal in ordering of ADJ and LOC in ANSE. The fluctuating ordering of these two categories, a finding noted in many studies, is therefore straightforwardly explained by the interaction between grammatical and prosodic structure, independent of processes of decreolization. I argue that this interaction is an inherent property of language, which, despite its extremely pervasive and perhaps universal nature, has until now gone uninvestigated. Although it is frustrating to be unable to extricate the effects of different parts of the linguistic system on the variation (after all, we like our questions to have clear-cut answers), this interaction is itself a significant finding.[11] Thus, the copula is not primarily a *grammatical* variable, as the (disproportionate) focus of creolists on the following grammatical category would imply.

2.6   Conclusion

The preceding discussion leaves a couple of questions to be answered. The first is why V-*ing* and *gonna* favor contraction and zero, and NP disfavors so consistently in every study. The most obvious answer is that this pattern reflects a distinction between the auxiliary and copular functions of *be*. In auxiliary contexts, *be* functions only to convey tense or aspect (see, e.g., Bouchard 1995: 470; Langacker 1991: 65; Li and Thompson 1977: 436; Mufwene 1989; Napoli 1989: 9) and, since this information can be conveyed in a number of other ways in discourse (via adverbs, sequencing, discourse context, etc.), it can be omitted. In contrast, *be* with NP predicates has been argued (e.g. Bouchard 1995: 470; Hengeveld 1992: 74; Napoli 1989: 16) to convey several semantic functions: thus, it has a higher "semantic load" and is less easily omitted. In fact, the category "NP" designates a syntactic constituent, but this designation matches completely neither the prosodic structure to which it is mapped, nor the range of semantic functions it serves.

Another, related question is exactly what the variable context of the copula actually is. Perhaps the problem is not that these contexts in EBCs and in English are incommensurable, as some would have it, but rather that we have conflated two variable contexts: verbal aspect, marked by auxiliaries in English and by preverbal markers in creoles; and non-verbal predication, marked by a true copula in all varieties. Thus, future studies should investigate the semantics of the copula/auxiliary distinction. Rickford et al.'s (1991) argument that StdE shows only this distinction, while AAVE shows a more fine-grained distinction of grammatical function, is belied by the consistent opposition of auxiliary V-*ing* and *gonna* to all other categories. In addition, McElhinny (1993: 378) found *gonna* to *dis*favor contraction in Standard American English, and Meechan (1996) found no clear copula/auxiliary distinction in Canadian English. Even Labov (1969) was careful to note that grammatical differences between the two uses were still significant (1969: 721). Separating these contexts might not only solve the problem of comparing variable contexts, but might also contribute to explaining the inconsistency of results for following grammatical category. This task should figure prominently in the agenda for future work on the copula.

Thus, I conclude that the following grammatical category is not a well-defined factor: its constituents represent an overlap of syntactic, semantic and prosodic structures. If the variable ranking of its constituents is better explained by interaction with prosodic structure than by decreolization, it is not surprising that the use of this factor as a tool in the creole-origins debate has not met with any lasting success. The analysis in this chapter has demonstrated that many of the purported grammatical effects are due to prosody. Future analysis should investigate the further possibility that the prosodic structure of the *entire* sentence conditions the form of the copula (as Inkelas and Zec [1995: 544] suggest and Walker and Meechan [1998] illustrate) and should operationalize a semantic factor separate from the following grammatical category.

Finally, I hope that these findings will encourage future studies to move beyond AAVE and EBCs to the larger question of the development of copula variability in English. Although zero copula has been attested in older forms of English, it seems to have been more of a restricted, perhaps literary construction, rather than a productive process: the examples cited by Visser (1970: 190–1) in Old and Middle English occur almost exclusively in appositional contexts with following NPs and in inversion contexts. Regardless of the lack of historical examples, zero copula does exist in other nonstandard varieties of English, in locales such as Alabama (Feagin 1979), Mississippi (Wolfram 1974) and Yorkshire (Tagliamonte, p.c.), although the fact that it has not become so highly developed there as it has in AAVE makes zero copula another spectacular and relatively recent innovation of AAVE (see Howe and Walker, this volume). Given the complementarity of contraction and zero, it is likely that zero represents the exploitation in AAVE of an additional possibility of reducing prosodic complexity that was inherent in the English language once contraction developed. Studies as diverse as Jacobs' (1994) (non-variationist) work on clitic placement in Brazilian and European Portuguese, Cedergren's (1986, 1990; Cedergren and Simoneau 1985) on rhythmic differences between Québécois and Parisian French, and Yoneda's (1993) on intergenerational changes in pitch accent in Japanese demonstrate that varieties of the same language can and do differ prosodically, and that these differences have grammatical consequences. Therefore, there is no need to posit a creole origin for zero copula: the differences we see between AAVE and other varieties of English are the kind we see elsewhere among dialects of the same language. In order for the rethinking (or "rephrasing") of copula variability presented in this chapter to serve a larger purpose in the origins debate, it must now be extended to other varieties of English (as Walker and Meechan 1998 have done). This extension could form the basis of a truly comparative approach, one that might provide reliable evidence for the origins of zero copula in AAVE.

Notes

* Portions of earlier versions of this paper were presented at NWAVE 26 in Québec City and the SPCL in New York. I thank Tracey Weldon, David Silva, and Draga Zec for sending me copies of papers that weren't readily available. I especially thank Henrietta Cedergren for helping to sort out the prosodic factor groups, David Sankoff for advice on statistical techniques, and William Labov for many valuable suggestions. Any remaining errors of theory, methodology or interpretation are of course my own responsibility. Financial support was provided by the Social Sciences and Humanities Research Council of Canada in the form of doctoral fellowship #752-97-1759.

1 For comparability, I include Hannah's calculations that most closely match the variable context and method of calculation used by Poplack and Sankoff.
2 Winford has more recently reinterpreted his decreolization model as a process of "shift" resulting from imperfect second-language acquisition (SLA) (1998: 111–12), but the same objections apply to this reinterpretation. In addition, as Rickford (1998: 180) notes, patterns of zero copula in SLA do not appear to parallel those in AAVE.
3 Note that none of these observations appears to be based on systematic analysis of spoken language.
4 Since Rickford's re-analysis of Holm's study is based on less than two hours of recorded speech of one speaker of JC, it is unclear whether the findings can be generalized to the language as a whole.
5 Nespor and Vogel (1986) include a clitic group between ω and φ, but recent analyses (e.g. Booij 1996; Selkirk 1995) argue against such a level.
6 This structure violates the Strict Layer Hypothesis (SLH; Nespor and Vogel 1986: 7; Selkirk 1984: 26), which prohibits both the "nesting" and the "skipping" of prosodic levels, but recent work (e.g. Booij 1996; Dresher 1994; Ladd 1986; Selkirk 1995) suggests that the SLH can be minimally violated to satisfy other requirements.
7 Numbers in parentheses identify the corpus, speaker and location of the utterance in the transcription. Corpora include:

ANSE: African Nova Scotian English (Poplack and Tagliamonte 1991).
SE: Samaná English (Poplack and Sankoff 1987)
ESR: Ex-Slave Recordings (Bailey et al. 1991)

8 Following participles such as *gone, growed,* and *changed* (intransitives involving a change of state or location) were not considered because contraction here is

ambiguous between *is* and *has*, reflecting an earlier stage in the grammaticization of the perfect tense in English (Tagliamonte 1996).

9   C = number of contracted tokens, D = number of zero tokens, F = number of full tokens.

10   Within each table, there is one variable-rule run for contraction and one for zero. To illustrate the different effects of the interacting factors, within each factor group I have separated the original factors along different axes.

11   One evident drawback of this interaction is that it is difficult to determine the true effect of prosody. It is for this reason that I have elsewhere (Walker and Meechan 1998) disregarded grammatical factors.

References

Bailey, G., Maynor, N., and Cukor-Avila, P. (eds) (1991) *The Emergence of Black English: Texts and Commentary*. Amsterdam: Benjamins.

Baugh, J. (1980) A reexamination of the Black English copula. In W. Labov (ed.), *Locating Language in Time and Space*, New York: Academic Press, 83–106.

Blake, R. (1997) Defining the envelope of linguistic variation: The case of "don't count" forms in the copula analysis of African American Vernacular English. *Language Variation and Change*, 9 (1), 57–79.

Booij, G. (1996) Cliticization as prosodic integration: The case of Dutch. *The Linguistic Review*, 13: 219–42.

Bouchard, D. (1995) *The Semantics of Syntax: A Minimalist Approach to Grammar*. Chicago: University of Chicago Press.

Cedergren, H. J. (1986) Metrical structure and vowel deletion. In D. Sankoff (ed.), *Diversity and Diachrony*, Philadelphia: Benjamins, 293–300.

Cedergren, H. J. (1990) Rhythm and length in phonological variation. In C. Kirschner and J. DeCesaris (eds), *Studies in Romance Linguistics*, Philadelphia: Benjamins.

Cedergren, H. J., and Simoneau, L. (1985) La chute des voyelles hautes en français de Montréal: As-tu entendu la belle syncope? In *Tendances dynamiques du français de Montréal, vol. I*, Montréal: Office de la langue française, 57–144.

DeBose, C. (1996) Question formation in Samaná English. Paper presented at NWAVE 25, Las Vegas.

Dresher, B. E. (1994) The prosodic basis of the Tiberian Hebrew system of accents. *Language*, 70 (1): 1–52.

Fasold, R., and Nakano, Y. (1996) Contraction and deletion in vernacular Black English: Creole history and relationship to Euro-American English. In G. R. Guy, C. Feagin, D. Schiffrin, and J. Baugh (eds), *Towards a Social Science of Language, vol. 1: Variation and Change in Language and Society*, Amsterdam and Philadelphia: Benjamins, 373–95.

Feagin, C. (1979) *Variation and Change in Alabama English: A Sociolinguistic Study of the White Community*. Washington: Georgetown University Press.

Ferguson, C. A. (1971) Absence of copula and the notion of simplicity: A case study of normal speech, baby talk, foreigner talk, and pidgins. In D. Hymes (ed.), *Pidginization and Creolization of Languages*, Cambridge: Cambridge University Press, 141–50.

Hannah, D. (1997) Copula absence in Samaná English: Implications for research on the linguistic history of African-American Vernacular English. *American Speech*, 72 (4): 339–72.

Hengeveld, K. (1992) *Non-verbal Predication: Theory, Typology, Diachrony*. Berlin and New York: Mouton de Gruyter.

Holm, J. (1976) Copula variability on the Afro-American continuum. Paper presented at SCL, Georgetown, Guyana.

Holm, J. (1984) Variability of the copula in Black English and its creole kin. *American Speech*, 59 (4): 291–309.

Holm, J. (1988) *Pidgins and Creoles, vol. 1: Theory and Structure*. Cambridge: Cambridge University Press.

Inkelas, S. (1989) Prosodic constituency in the lexicon. Ph.D. dissertation, Stanford University. (Published in 1990, New York: Garland Publishing.)

Inkelas, S., and Zec, D. (1993) Auxiliary reduction without empty categories: A prosodic account. *Working Papers of the Cornell Phonetics Laboratory*, No. 8, 205–53.

Inkelas, S., and Zec, D. (1995) Syntax–phonology interface. In J. A. Goldsmith (ed.), *The Handbook of Phonological Theory*, Oxford: Basil Blackwell, 535–49.

Jacobs, H. (1994) An optimality-theoretic analysis of phonological and syntactic aspects of enclisis and proclisis in Old French, Brazilian and European Portuguese. Paper presented at ABRALIN.

Labov, W. (1969) Contraction, deletion, and inherent variability of the English copula. *Language*, 45 (4): 715–62.

Labov, W. (1972) *Language in the Inner City: Studies in the Black English Vernacular*. Philadelphia: University of Pennsylvania Press.

Labov, W. (1995) The case of the missing copula: The interpretation of zeroes in African-American English. In L. R. Gleitman and M. Liberman (eds), *An Invitation to Cognitive Science (Second Edition), Volume 1: Language*, Cambridge, MA: MIT Press, 25–54.

Ladd, D. R. (1986) Intonational phrasing: The case for recursive prosodic structure. *Phonology Yearbook*, 3, 311–40.

Labov, W., Cohen, P., Robins, C., and Lewis, J. (1968) A study of the Nonstandard English of Negro and Puerto Rican speakers of New York City. Final Report, Co-operative Research Project no. 3288, United States Office of Education.

Langacker, R. W. (1991) *Foundations of Cognitive Grammar, vol. II: Descriptive Application*. Stanford, CA: Stanford University Press.

Li, C. N., and Thompson, S. A. (1977) A mechanism for the development of copula morphemes. In C. N. Li (ed.), *Mechanisms of Syntactic Change*, Austin and London: University of Texas Press, 419–44.

McElhinny, B. S. (1993) Copula and auxiliary contraction in the speech of White Americans. *American Speech*, 68 (4): 371–99.

McWhorter, J. H. (1997) *Towards a New Model of Creole Genesis*. New York: Peter Lang.

Meechan, M. (1996) In search of the missing link: Copula contraction in Canadian English. Unpublished manuscript, University of Ottawa.

Mufwene, S. S. (1989) How many *be*'s are there in English? Paper presented at SECOL, Norfolk, VA.

Mufwene, S. S. (1990) Creoles and universal grammar. *Linguistics*, 28: 783–807.

Napoli, D. J. (1989) *Predication Theory: A Case Study for Indexing Theory.* Cambridge: Cambridge University Press.

Nespor, M., and Vogel, I. (1986) *Prosodic Phonology.* Dordrecht and Riverton: Foris.

Poplack, S., and Sankoff, D. (1987) The Philadelphia story in the Spanish Caribbean. *American Speech*, 64 (2): 291–314.

Poplack, S., and Tagliamonte, S. (1991) African American English in the diaspora: The case of old-line Nova Scotians. *Language Variation and Change*, 3 (3): 301–39.

Poplack, S., and Tagliamonte, S. (1993) "They talks with grammar, with -*s*": Phono-prosodic vs. grammatical influences on word-final -*s* variability in African Nova Scotian English. Paper presented at NWAVE 22, Ottawa, Ontario.

Rand, D., and Sankoff, D. (1990) *GoldVarb: A Variable Rule Application for the Macintosh*, version 2. Montreal: Centre de recherches mathématiques, University of Montreal.

Rickford, J. R. (1996) Copula variability in Jamaican Creole and African American Vernacular English: A reanalysis of DeCamp's texts. In G. R. Guy, C. Feagin, D. Schiffrin, and J. Baugh (eds), *Towards a Social Science of Language, vol. 1: Variation and Change in Language and Society*, Amsterdam and Philadelphia: Benjamins, 357–72.

Rickford, J. R. (1998) The creole origins of African-American Vernacular English: Evidence from copula absence. In S. S. Mufwene, J. R. Rickford, G. Bailey, and J. Baugh (eds), *African-American English: Structure, History, and Use*, London: Routledge, 154–200.

Rickford, J. R., Ball, A., Blake, R., Jackson, R., and Martin, N. (1991) Rappin on the copula coffin: Theoretical and methodological issues in the analysis of copula variation in African American Vernacular English. *Language Variation and Change*, 3 (1): 103–32.

Rickford, J. R., and Blake, R. (1990) Copula contraction and absence in Barbadian English, Samaná English and Vernacular Black English. *Berkeley Linguistics Society*, 16: 257–68.

Rickford, J. R., and McNair-Knox, F. (1994) Addressee- and topic-influenced style shift: A quantitative sociolinguistic study. In D. Biber and E. Finegan (eds), *Socio-linguistic Perspectives on Register*, New York and Oxford: Oxford University Press, 235–76.

Rowlands, E. C. (1969) *Teach Yourself Yoruba.* London: English Universities Press.

Sankoff, D., and Rousseau, P. (1989) Statistical evidence for rule ordering. *Language Variation and Change*, 1 (1): 1–18.

Saxon, S. (1737) *The English Scholar's Assistant*, 2nd edn. Republished 1979, Menston, UK: Scolar's Press.

Selkirk, E. O. (1984) *Phonology and Syntax: The Relation Between Sound and Structure.* Cambridge: MIT Press.

Selkirk, E. O. (1986) On derived domains in sentence phonology. *Phonology*, 3: 371–405.

Selkirk, E. O. (1990) On the nature of prosodic constituency: Comments on Beckman and Edwards's paper. In J. Kingston and M. E. Beckman (eds), *Papers in Laboratory Phonology, I: Between the Grammar and Physics of Speech*, Cambridge: Cambridge University Press, 179–200.

Selkirk, E. O. (1995) The prosodic structure of function words. *University of Massachusetts Occasional Papers in Linguistics*, 18: 439–69.

Seuren, P. A. M. (1988) Adjectives as adjectives in Sranan: A reply to Sebba. *Journal of Pidgin and Creole Languages*, 1 (1): 123–34.

Silva, D. (1994) The variable elision of unstressed vowels in European Portuguese: A case study. *UTA Working Papers in Linguistics*, 1: 79–94.

Singler, J. V. (1991) Copula variation in Liberian Settler English and American Black English. In W. F. Edwards and D. Winford (eds), *Verb Phrase Patterns in Black English and Creole*, Detroit: Wayne State University Press, 129–64.

Stewart, W. (1973) Continuity and change in American Negro dialects. In *Black Language Reader*, Glenview, IL: Scott, Foresman, and Co., 45–55.

Tagliamonte, S. (1996) Has it ever been "perfect"? Uncovering the grammar of early Black English. *York Papers in Linguistics*, 17: 351–96.

Taglicht, J. (1998) Constraints on intonational phrasing. *Journal of Linguistics*, 34: 181–211.

Visser, F. Th. (1970) *An Historical Syntax of the English Language, Part One: Syntactical Units with One Verb*. Leiden: E. J. Brill.

Walker, J. A. (1995) The (r)-ful truth about African Nova Scotian English. Paper presented at NWAVE 24, Philadelphia, PA.

Walker, J. A., and Meechan, M. E. (1998) The decreolization of Canadian English: Copula contraction and prosody. Paper presented at CLA, Ottawa.

Weldon, T. L. (1996) Copula variability in Gullah: Implications for the creolist hypothesis. Paper presented at NWAVE 25, Las Vegas.

Winford, D. (1990) Copula variability, accountability, and the concept of "polylectal" grammars. *Journal of Pidgin and Creole Languages*, 5 (2): 223–52.

Winford, D. (1992) Another look at the copula in Black English and Caribbean Creoles. *American Speech*, 67 (1): 21–60.

Winford, D. (1998) On the origins of African American Vernacular English – A creolist perspective. Part II: Linguistic features. *Diachronica*, 15 (1): 99–154.

Wolfram, W. (1974) The relationship of white southern speech to vernacular black English. *Language*, 30, 498–527.

Yoneda, M. (1993) Survey of standardization in Tsuruoka City, Japan: Comparison of results from three surveys conducted at twenty-year intervals. Paper presented at Methods 8, Victoria, BC.

3

Reconstructing the Source of Early African American English Plural Marking: A Comparative Study of English and Creole*

Shana Poplack, Sali Tagliamonte, and Ejike Eze

3.1 Introduction

The morphological expression of the category of plural has been considered a robust, if variable, feature of African American English (AAE) grammar at least since the nineteenth century (Harrison 1884), largely on the basis of the consistent independent finding that the plural suffix -s is virtually always realized (Kessler 1972; Labov et al. 1968: 161; Wolfram 1969: 143) in contemporary vernaculars. In Early AAE, however, -s was often absent from nouns with plural reference, as shown in (1) below.

(1) a.   That man had two *trunks*. Two *trunkØ* full of all kind of gold and silver and everything. Two *trunkØ*, big *trunks*. Full of gold and silver.   (ANSE/30/1323)[1]

     b.   Now, walk – walking with the *mules*, them there *mules* an' one man a-riding – riding between two *muleØ*, . . .   (ESR/005:12)

     c.   All them die away *ya* [. . .] and the young *oneØ* never take practise.   (SE/005/663–5)

     d.   And the *ones* who come behind, they don't practise theirself to that.   (SE/005/669–70)

This is intriguing since in other areas of the grammar, notably the verb phrase, Early AAE appears consistently more conservative than contemporary AAVE in featuring higher rates of *overt* morphological marking (Poplack and Tagliamonte forthcoming). The apparent approximation of contemporary AAVE to Standard English (StdE) in this area of the grammar looks very much like a case of structural convergence, one consistent with the process of decreolization. In this chapter, we assess the viability of this explanation by investigating the source of the earlier variability. In particular, are the zero plurals common in Early AAE the legacy of prior creole marking of nouns with non-individuated referents, or do they result from phonetically or functionally motivated reduction of an English plural affix?

An interesting property of the facts illustrated in (1), as of many of the other variable phenomena examined in this volume, is that informal inspection is insufficient to reveal the nature of the underlying grammar that gave rise to the overt and zero variants, since the same forms appear in all the putative source varieties. The type of evidence we appeal to in this chapter therefore emerges from the *organization* of these forms in discourse. The prototypical creole is said to mark plural, morphologically or otherwise, according to criteria like nominal reference, individuation, and disambiguation within the NP headed by the noun in question. In StdE, on the other hand, plural is basically always marked morphologically, at least on the semantically plural individuated count nouns on which we focus here.

By means of comparative reconstruction, this study aims to uncover the system giving rise to the plural-marking facts depicted in (1). We first review what is known of plural marking in English-based creoles (section 3.2) and in contemporary AAVE (section 3.3). In section 3.4 we trace the development of plural formation through the history of English. Making use of multivariate analysis, we test the contribution of factors selected to capture the origins of the variant forms (section 3.6), and compare the patterning of plural marking amongst the three varieties of Early AAE (section 3.7). Section 3.9 tests the predictions for English-based creoles on Nigerian Pidgin English (NPE), and compares and contrasts its patterns of plural marking with those discovered for Early AAE. Section 3.11 offers our conclusions.

3.2   Plural Marking in English-based Creoles

In English-based creoles, nouns are generally pluralized by adding the third person plural pronoun (*dem* or similar), either postnominally (Jamaican, Gullah), prenominally (Saramaccan, Sranan), or both (Krio, Guyanese) (Alleyne 1980a: 100). Definite nouns are morphologically marked, while indefinite nouns "usually have unmarked plurals," patterns that Alleyne suggests were inherited from West African languages (1980a: 101). Dijkhoff (1983) also links the variable occurrence of the Papiamentu plural marker *-nan* with the referential status of its head. Abstracting from Bickerton's (1975) classification, she divides NPs into *existentially presupposed*, basically corresponding to definite NPs, which are overtly marked, *existentially asserted*, overtly marked only if plurality has not been otherwise indicated within the clause, and *existentially hypothesized*, corresponding roughly to *generic* or *nonspecific* NPs. Nouns in this context are never marked morphologically.

The sole attempt to test these predictions empirically in an English-based creole revealed that they did not hold. Rickford (1986) analyzed the variable occurrence of *-s* and zero on 128 semantically plural regular nouns in the speech of Mrs Queen, an elderly speaker of mesolectal Sea Island Creole (Gullah), according to nominal reference and the existence in the NP of a plural quantifier or demonstrative. Neither was selected as significant to the probability of plural marking, leading Rickford to conclude that the plural marking constraints [said to be] representative of basilectal creoles were not operative in the mesolect.

Mufwene (1986) contested his conclusion, asserting that the primary factors determining the presence of the English plural marker *-s* in Gullah were semantic, and suggesting that they were operative in English as well. He distinguished two axes of number delimitation: singular versus non-singular and individuated versus non-individuated. The first contrasts the number of the referent; the second, the speaker's perception of it as denumerable or not. The classes distinguished by these axes also differ in terms of the kinds of determiners with which they combine: only individuated nouns may co-occur with numerals and individuating quantifiers. In contemporary StdE, with the exception of irregular forms, individuated nouns with plural reference are morphologically marked with *-s*, while non-individuated nouns (i.e. mass nouns and count nouns in noncount uses) remain unmarked, as in the italicized portions of (2).

(2) a. You couldn't buy over two pound of *rice*, *sugar*, *salt* or anything.
(SE/1/343–5)

b. You got *trouble* on your hand. (ANSE/38/155A)

c. And we jus' turned out like lot of *cattle*. You know how they turn *cattle* out in a pasture? (ESR/8/104–5)

Apparently virtually any noun can alternate freely between individuated and non-individuated uses in creoles, with individuated nouns receiving an overt mark (as in English), and non-individuated nouns remaining "bare." Accordingly, Mufwene (much like Alleyne 1980a; Bickerton 1975, 1979; Dijkhoff 1983; and others) proposed that plural individuated nouns should be delimited with the postnominal pluralizer, which in turn must co-occur with a possessive or the definite article. Individuated nouns delimited with other determiners require no morphological mark. In addition, the plural marker *dem* should only be affixed to a noun which is both individuated and not otherwise disambiguated for number within the NP it heads.

3.3   Plural Marking in Contemporary AAVE

Early attempts to account for the variable, albeit infrequent, absence of plural -*s* in contemporary AAVE have appealed to three types of linguistic factors: (i) the principle of "non-redundant pluralization," whereby nouns would remain bare in the environment of a numeral or some other determiner indicating plurality (e.g. Dillard 1972: 61; Stewart 1966: 64), (ii) phonetic conditioning, operating to delete or conserve an underlying plural suffix (Labov et al. 1968), and (iii) individual lexical preferences for certain nouns traditionally classified as count in English to be "reanalyzed" in AAVE as mass (Labov et al. 1968; Wolfram 1969). However, the findings on which these explanations were based do not support them in detail.

For example, although Wolfram's (1969) analysis of plural marking in Detroit AAVE provided (at least weak) support for the non-redundant pluralization effect, Kessler's (1972) study of Washington DC could not replicate it. Similarly, while Labov et al. (1968: 163) reported a favorable effect of following consonantal segment on plural -*s* absence in New York City, Wolfram (1969: 145) found only a minor phonological effect in Detroit, involving a different environment. Kessler (1972: 234) also invoked a "weak" phonological effect, but it did not replicate previous findings either. Finally, there have been various reports (e.g. Labov et al. 1968: 164; Wolfram 1969: 145; Kessler 1972: 233; and section 3.7.4) on the tendency of specific lexical items to occur with no plural marker, though these vary across studies.

In sum, although the same (few) factors are recurrently cited as constraining variability in plural -*s* inflection in contemporary AAVE, the effects reported have not been consistent, perhaps due to the paucity therein of zero-marked plurals (ranging from 2 percent to 11 percent depending on the variety studied). Nonetheless, as we show in what follows, these factors also account for variability in plural marking in earlier forms of English and AAE.

3.4 The Development of Plural Formation in English Nouns

The contemporary English pattern of plural formation via affixation of -*s* is the sole productive legacy of what, at earlier stages of the language, was a rich and complex morphology of number marking. Old English nouns fell into 10 distinct declensional classes which were variously inflected for case, number and gender (Mossé 1952: 50; Wardale 1937: 72). By the Early Middle English period the nominal declension system began to be radically simplified, with the result that forms once associated with particular nominal cases and classes began to merge (Curme 1977: 144).

Only three of the original plural types persist in Modern English. *Weak* plurals are formed by affixing -*en* to the noun stem (e.g. *oxen*, *brethren* and *children*, the sole survivors of this type). *Mutation* plurals (e.g. *feet, men, women, mice, teeth,* about half of which are preserved in modern StdE) are derived from vowel fronting in certain Old English nominative and accusative plurals. A class of Old English neuter nouns (including *word, thing, leaf* and *year*), which bore no overt plural inflection in the nominative and accusative, as well as a number of names of domestic animals (including *horse, swine, deer, sheep*), is said to have provided the model for the contemporary option of *zero* inflection in collectives and nouns of weight and measure (Curme 1977; Ekwall 1975; Mossé 1952: 51; Wyld 1927: 245). We shall have no more to say about the first two plural types, as they do not participate in the "variable context" defined in section 3.5.1. We return to the zero plurals below.

With the exception of the small set of irregular vestiges of Old English plural types listed above, and a somewhat larger set of nouns in which morphological singular and plural are not fully isomorphic with semantic singular and plural respectively, since the fourteenth century the vast majority of English nouns has formed the plural by affixation of -*(e)s* (Mossé 1952: 50). Though variability has been attested, most recurrently in nouns of weight, measure and monetary denomination, particularly when these are preceded by numerals, this has long been considered "obsolete or vulgar" (Sweet 1891: 316), and associated with regional, folk and/or uneducated dialects (e.g. Hughes and Trudgill 1979; Marckwardt 1958; McDavid and McDavid 1960, 1964; Pederson 1983).

Summarizing, both contemporary English and contemporary AAVE tend to form the plural with -*s*. Early AAE on the other hand, like older forms of English *and* (reports on) English-based creoles, features much zero plural. Which system gave rise to Early AAE plural marking? The property of plural -*s* variability with most repercussions for the origins debate is the fact that its competing realizations – *-s* and zero – surface not only in contemporary AAVE, but also in all the relevant putative source varieties: English-based creoles, non-standard varieties of English, and Early AAE. This led Poplack and Tagliamonte (1989, 1991) to conclude that neither the existence of *-s* nor even its rates of occurrence were sufficient in and of themselves to resolve its prior status; this could only be accomplished by examining its *distribution* in the language, as determined by the hierarchy of constraints conditioning its appearance.

3.5   Data and Methods

The Early AAE data on which our analyses are based were extracted from taped conversations with 21 speakers of Samaná English (SE; Poplack and Sankoff 1987), 15 speakers of African Nova Scotian English (ANSE; Poplack and Tagliamonte 1991) and 10 contributors to the Ex-Slave Recordings (ESR; Bailey et al. 1991). We compare these with materials provided by 12 speakers of Nigerian Pidgin English (NPE; Tagliamonte et al. 1997), a West African creole.[2]

3.5.1   Circumscribing the variable context

We first delimit the context of occurrence of the plural marker *-s*, ensuring that the resulting data set is equally amenable to analysis in all of the comparison varieties (cf. Tagliamonte and Poplack 1993). Observing first that the plural categorically surfaces as zero in the vestigial contexts detailed in section 3.3 and example (2) above, we excluded these from ensuing quantitative analyses of variability, focusing instead on the variable occurrence of *-s* in regular, individuated, semantically plural nouns. These contexts exhaust the possibilities for productive plural marking in English and creoles, and additionally cover contexts where plural need not be overtly marked in the latter. As we shall see, the key difference between English and creoles resides in the category of generic reference. In creoles, generics are construed as non-individuating, and as such remain bare. Although number is also neutralized, strictly speaking, on English nouns with generic reference, these may either surface bare (in the context of definite and morphologically singular indefinite determiners: *the* or *a*) or be inflected with *-s*. Only the latter fall within the scope of this study. Such contexts (i.e. generics and, according to Dijkhoff (1983), disambiguated indefinites), in which the languages display different requirements for plural marking, will constitute the crucial test of the system underlying the distribution of *-s* and zero in Early AAE.

Even within the variable context of regular individuated nouns with plural reference, *-s* usage may be subject to exceptional distributions, phonetic neut-ralization and referential ambiguity, as detailed in Poplack and Tagliamonte (1994) and Tagliamonte et al. (1997). As is standard in variationist studies, we excluded forms for which plural reference could not be unambiguously infer-red, basing our quantitative analysis only on productive participants in the regular process of plural formation. In the remainder of this chapter we use the term *plural marking* to refer only to (actual or potential) morphological marking by affixation of *-s*, as in the italicized portion in (3).

(3)   When I look in like that, and I look in that door, and I look back in the corner, I seen them great big *eyeØ*.   (ANSE/3/884–6)

3.5.2   Coding and analysis

From the tape-recorded conversations constituting our corpora, we extracted every semantically plural individuated count noun eligible for *-s* affixation, totalling 2452 for the quantitative analysis of Early AAE and 1316 for NPE. Each was coded for phonological, morphological, lexical, syntactic and semantic factors selected to reveal the origins of the observed variability by testing hypotheses about plural marking in Caribbean (e.g. Dijkhoff 1983; Mufwene 1986) and West African (Agheyisi 1971; Faraclas 1989) creoles, contemporary AAVE (Kessler 1972; Labov et al. 1968; Schneider 1989; Wolfram 1969) and vernacular and StdE (e.g. Allan 1976, 1980; Fries 1940; McDavid and McDavid 1964), as well as to replicate empirical analyses of Gullah (Rickford 1986) and Liberian English (Singler 1989, 1991). These are described below.

3.5.2.1   Lexical identity of the head noun
Reports on the origins, development and present state of plural marking in English suggest that the occurrence of *-s* is highly dependent on the lexical identity of the noun to which it is affixed. To ascertain whether this also accounts for the observed variability in Early AAE, lexical entries occurring frequently (ten times or more) were distinguished from (the vast majority of) singletons.

3.5.2.2   Semantic classification
Another feature widely acknowledged to condition the variable occurrence of plural *-s* in English is the semantic classification of the noun to which it is affixed. The English language, both modern and early, has at its disposal a process of *collectivization*, expressed by a zero plural. Some noun classes are

purportedly more susceptible to collectivization than others (Baughan 1958; Curme 1977; Ekwall 1912; Wyld 1927). Perhaps most salient are (i) the class of gregarious animals that are wild and/or hunted for food or sport (e.g. *giraffe, lion, bear* etc.) and (ii) nouns of weight (e.g. *bushel, pound, ton*), measure (e.g. *year, mile, day*), and monetary denomination (e.g. *dollar, cent, pound*). Each noun retained in the data was categorized according to its membership in one of these classes.

3.5.2.3 *Phonological conditioning*

The existence of phonological conditioning is associated with the presence of an underlying form. Although the extent to which it can reveal the nature of the underlying system (and hence its origins) is unclear, we re-examine this factor for two reasons. First, two varieties characterized as English-based creoles (Gullah and Liberian Settler English) were reported to exhibit phonological conditioning (Rickford 1986; Singler 1989). Secondly (in contrast with the inconclusive results in contemporary AAVE), phonological effects also contribute significantly to the variable realization of the homophonous verbal -*s* morpheme in Early AAE (Poplack and Tagliamonte 1989; Tagliamonte and Poplack to appear). Analysis of environmental effects in Early AAE will enable us to situate it with respect to these varieties.

3.5.2.4 *Disambiguation*

By virtue of our definition of the variable context given in section 3.5.1, each noun retained for analysis is fully disambiguated with regard to number reference. In what follows, however, the use we make of the term *disambiguation* refers only to the concept of *local* disambiguation, i.e. the existence of (non-inflectional) indicators of plurality within the NP headed by the noun in question. Only local disambiguation is considered to affect plural marking in creoles; in StdE, disambiguation, whether local or global, should have no effect. Accordingly, each noun was also coded according to (i) whether its NP contained a transparent indication of number (e.g. numeral, demonstrative) and (ii) whether it was individuated, insofar as this was indicated by the choice of determiner.

3.5.2.5 *Type of nominal reference*

Type of nominal reference is the factor most widely invoked to explain variation in plural marking in creoles. Creoles do not assign an overt mark to nouns with generic, and by some accounts (Alleyne 1980a; Dijkhoff 1983), other indefinite reference, whereas in English, nouns (falling within the variable context for inflection with -*s*) are not differentiated in this regard. Though not generally acknowledged, categorization and operationalization of referential status is very complex, especially in the case of non-specific nouns, which (depending on scope considerations) sustain readings with varying degrees of indefiniteness. Using a combination of syntactic criteria (Huddleston 1984; Mufwene 1986) and observations of prescriptive and descriptive grammarians (Jespersen 1909/1949; Quirk et al. 1972, 1985), we devised the following protocol, detailed in Poplack and Tagliamonte (1994).

Nouns modified by a possessive, a demonstrative (*them/those/these*), the definite article (when used with definite reference), and/or previously mentioned in the discourse, were coded as *definite*. *Indefinites* included (i) numeric quantifiers (with indefinite reference), (ii) other pluralizing quantifiers (e.g. *a lot*, *some* etc.), (iii) partitive structures of the type *one/some/none/any of*, and (iv) other indefinite expressions. Under *generic* reference, we included only nouns that were unmodified by determiners, quantifiers, articles or pronouns, as in (4) below, i.e. "pure" generics. For a modified noun to qualify as generic, it had to be substitutable with its bare counterpart without changing meaning, as in (4b).

(4)   a.   Interviewer: So what did you used to use *onion* for?

      b.   Informant: ... just used *the onions* for to cook with.   (ANSE/6/
           474–5)

Despite our efforts to capture the nuances of nominal reference, pilot analysis reveals that the independent effect of this factor group on variability in plural marking cannot be assessed once combined in a multivariate analysis with the factors of disambiguation and individuation. This is because these factors overlap (Poplack and Tagliamonte 1994): nouns delimited by demonstratives and possessives have definite reference, those delimited by [+numeric, +individuating] or [−numeric, +individuating] quantifiers fall into the category of indefinites, while those with no determiner tend to be generics.[3]

3.5.2.6   *NP constituency*

To alleviate the problem of statistical interaction, we combined these factors into a single factor group we refer to as "NP constituency," which contains all the distinctions of reference and determination adequately represented in the data. This is an operationalization of Mufwene's (1986) predictions, originally presented in Singler's analyses of plural marking in Liberian Settler English (Singler 1989) and Liberian English (Singler 1991). We replicate it here, first to enhance comparability, and secondly, because poor data distribution (which, as noted above, is not unique to these data, but rather inherent) in fact precludes any other coding scheme. We therefore categorize nouns according to prenominal modification, with the exception of generics, which may occur in bare or determined form. The factors are then regrouped to examine the effects of disambiguation, individuation and nominal reference independently.

3.5.3   Hypothesis

If the Early AAE plural-marking system is a creole heritage, only semantically plural nouns delimited by a possessive pronoun or a definite article, as in the italicized portions in (5), should be marked morphologically. In variable terms, we may predict that such cases will be marked more frequently than those that are not so delimited.

(5)   a.   I went to the door. I said, "put *your hands* on. I'll cut *your fingers* off!"   (ANSE/39/1336–7)

   b.   Yes, many time I've stump *my toes* and blood run out.

(ESR/8/89–90)

   c.   I get along good with *the ones* I know.   (ANSE/7/765–6)

   d.   An' so he shot three *timeØ* and he commence to shoot until *the plateØ* commence to rattle on the table.   (ESR/2/23–4)

Although, as we shall see, the specific creole postnominal pluralizer *dem* is not attested in any of our corpora, note that the system governing its appearance (in those creoles in which it is said to function as a plural marker) may also account for the variable occurrence of other morphological marks in Early AAE. Such a scenario has been proposed (in another connection) by Bickerton (1975), Winford (1985), and Mufwene (1983), and demonstrated by Singler (1989) for plural marking in acrolectal Liberian English. Indeed, plural marking with *-s* has been said to be inversely correlated with position on the creole continuum. Thus, the possibility of inferring the underlying grammar from the organization of variable marking behavior should not hinge on the presence or absence of a particular surface form. Ensuing analyses will help us determine which system best accounts for the observed variability in plural marking in Early AAE.

3.6   Results

Table 3.1 gives the results of three independent variable rule analyses (Rand and Sankoff 1990) of the contribution of phonological and semantic factors to

Source of Early AAE Plural Marking 83

Table 3.1 Variable rule analysis of the contribution of phonological, structural, and semantic factors to the probability of zero plural in Samaná English (SE), the Ex-Slave Recordings (ESR), and African Nova Scotian English (ANSE)[a]

Corrected mean:		SE .22		ESR .24		ANSE .34	
		Factor weight	N	Factor weight	N	Factor weight	N
NP constituency							
[+numeric, +individuating] Q		.60	571	.63	107	.62	245
Partitive quantifier		.54	76	.59	18	.66	65
[−numeric, +individuating] Q		.49	279	.67	26	.55	108
Demonstrative		.46	62	.62	35	.70	125
Definite article		.43	225	.54	36	.37	203
Generic		.42	246	.24	101	.41	308
Possessive		.33	109	.57	43	.40	141
	Range	27		43		33	
Semantic classification							
Non-weight/measure		[.53]	1217	[.52]	334	.52	1108
Weight/measure		[.42]	455	[.43]	93	.40	245
	Range					12	
Preceding phonological segment							
Non-sibilant consonant		.56	951	.60	198	[.51]	780
Sibilant consonant		.56	71	.28	28	[.54]	75
Vowel		.44	650	.41	201	[.48]	498
	Range	12		32			
Following phonological segment							
Consonant		.62	451	.53	91	.71	292
Vowel		.46	436	.37	151	.41	501
Pause		.43	562	.65	122	.45	429
	Range	19		28		30	
Factors not selected:							
Semantic classification		X		X			
Preceding phonological segment						X	

[a] Brackets here and in ensuing tables indicate that the factor in question was not selected as significant by the stepwise multiple regression procedure incorporated in the variable-rule analysis program. Although there are not enough data to rigorously establish statistical significance for these factors, we note the remarkable similarities across varieties in direction of effect.

the probability the plural marker will surface as zero in each of the Early AAE varieties.

We first observe the by now familiar finding that non-sibilant consonants, in both preceding and following environments, favor zero plural, while vowels disfavor. This behavior, identical to that already found for the homophonous 3rd person singular -*s* marker in Early AAE (Poplack and Tagliamonte 1989), is consistent with the phonotactic principles of many varieties of AAVE and English-based creoles, which tend to avoid syllable-final clusters and (to a lesser extent) syllable-final consonants. A much greater effect, as assessed by the range, is contributed by the factor we have referred to as NP constituency. Table 3.1 shows that the contexts predicted (section 3.2) to co-occur with an overt plural mark in creoles, namely the definite article and the possessive, show a marked tendency to retain -*s* (i.e. to disfavor zero) in Early AAE as well. But the fact that nouns with generic reference (the "bare" category par excellence in creoles) cluster among the factors with the lowest probabilities of zero plural in each of the datasets precludes explaining the variability in our materials by those creole predictions. Nor do the results correspond in any obvious way to what would be expected of StdE, as we shall see below. Yet NP constituency contributes the greatest effect to plural marking in each dataset, so we must ascertain how to interpret it. We first review the possible sources of zero plural in English.

3.7   Sources of Zero Plural in English

Although a morphological mark is prescribed for StdE individuated nouns with plural reference, there exist at least five sources of zero plural, which if not specifically predicted by the English number system, are not inconsistent with it. We now review their effect on the morphological expression of plural in Early AAE.

3.7.1   The definite/indefinite effect

The English requirement that the countability of the NP reference be known affects NP constituency through application of a disambiguation rule, formulated by Allan (1976) as in (6).

(6)   "If his listeners do not already know the countability of the NP reference, the speaker must make it known to them."   (Allan 1976)

Where the speaker judges that the NP reference is already known, s/he chooses a definite NP; otherwise the NP will be indefinite. Since awareness of NP reference entails awareness of its countability, plural indefinites are typically morphologically marked as countable. Translating this observation into variable terms, we may predict that in an English system, indefinites would be marked more frequently than definites. Poplack and Tagliamonte (1994) tested this prediction, by replacing the factor of "NP Constituency" with "Type of Nominal reference". But in none of the corpora could definite be distinguished from indefinite reference in terms of overt plural-marking probabilities.

3.7.2   The individuation/ saliency effect

We noted in section 3.2 that nouns are said to alternate between individuated and non-individuated uses in creoles. The same is also true of English. Whether or not the referent is individuated is basically revealed through quantifier selection, such that numerals and individuating quantifiers co-occur, almost without exception, with individuated nouns. This observation, in conjunction with the principle of saliency (Lemle and Naro 1977), would lead us to expect more overt marking in individuated contexts, i.e. those including [+numeric, +individuating] quantifiers, [−numeric, +individuating] quantifiers (*many, several*) and pluralizing demonstratives (*them/ these/ those*). Contrary to the expectation just enunciated, however, the probabilities of zero plural for individuating determiners (figures in bold in table 3.1) are highest.

3.7.3   The collectivization effect

Another exception to the requirement that pluralizing individuating determiners must co-occur with marked count nouns in English involves the process of collectivization (Sweet 1891: 315; 1898: 46; Wyld 1927: 245). A collective reading may apply to nouns with "regular" (i.e. inflected) plurals which are used in the "singular" (zero) form (7a), and with plural concord (7b) (Allan 1976: 99).[4] This reading is said to be strictly limited to the class of nouns referring to birds and animals that are hunted for food or sport, but not as vermin, in the specific contexts of hunting or conservation (Allan 1976: 99; Hansen and Nielsen 1986), also exemplified in (7).

(7) a. We bagged three *elephantØ* that day.   (Allan 1976: 102)

     b. The *herdØ were* grazing peacefully when a lion disturbed them.   (Allan 1976: 550)

As indicated in section 3.4, use of the singular (zero) variant for plural reference dates back to the Old English neuter inflection, whose form is said to have spread to these contexts by analogy with a new meaning of collectivity (Brunner 1963: 50; Curme 1977: 117). Has this process been extended, in Early AAE, to still other contexts, such as those in (1)? If so, zero plural should be favored in at least one of the source contexts. Poplack and Tagliamonte (1994) examined the distribution of zero plural in Early AAE nouns coded according to their membership in classes like weight/measure, hunted animals, and plants. They found such contexts to be exceedingly rare in the data, but zero plurals were also very sparse within them, leading them to conclude that the process of collectivization is not the source of the zero plurals in Early AAE.

3.7.4   The lexical effect

Different countability preferences of English nouns result in certain lexical items occurring in unmarked form in vernacular varieties. Zero plural is best documented in nouns of weight, measure and monetary denomination, especially after numerals, as in (8a), taken from Nova Scotian Vernacular English (NSVE; Poplack and Tagliamonte 1991). Zero plural in such contexts has been attested for general American (e.g. Fries 1940; Marckwardt 1958; McDavid and McDavid 1960, 1964; Mencken 1971), and British English (e.g. Hughes and Trudgill 1979; Wakelin 1977), as well as in specific dialects like Appalachian (Wolfram and Christian 1976), East Tennessee Folk Speech (Pederson 1983), and Cockney (Wright 1981: 115). To judge by these sources, zero plural is limited almost exclusively to the lexical items *foot, mile, year, gallon, pound, bushel* and *month. Inch, ton, hour, week, dollar* and *cent* are cited sporadically.

(8) a. I had to go about twenty *mileØ* into Swift Current.   (NSVE/JG/1A)

     b. I . . . paid twenty five *dollarØ* for the dress and ten *dollarØ* for the ring.   (ANSE/8/87–9)

     c. I'm a hundred *years* old and I don't owe nobody five *cents* . . .
                                                              (ESR/8/25–6)

Although the "weight and measure" effect is not characteristic of Early AAE (table 3.1), where such nouns feature more *overt* marks, this does not mean that there are no individual lexical preferences for zero plural. Indeed, a number of frequently-occurring Early AAE nouns show a propensity either for zero plural (e.g. *time*, *day*) or for *-s* (e.g. *year*), and these marking patterns are shared across varieties (Poplack and Tagliamonte 1994: 246). We return to this observation below.

Summarizing, none of the above-mentioned sources of zero plural in English offers a straightforward explanation of the observed variability in the Early AAE, with the possible exception of the countability preferences of particular lexical items. What then is the explanation for the robust effect of NP constituency?

3.7.5   A functional effect

Table 3.2 reproduces from table 3.1 the probabilities of zero plural associated with the factors making up the NP constituency group, this time organized according to the factor of (local) disambiguation. The table shows that nouns least likely to surface with a zero plural are those appearing in number-neutral syntactic contexts, i.e. those that co-occur freely with singular or plural inflections and thus cannot themselves disambiguate number reference. These include nouns modified by a definite article or possessive as well as undetermined nouns, like most generics. On the other hand, in contexts in which number

Table 3.2   Variable rule analysis of the contribution of NP constituency factors, grouped according to disambiguation, in Samaná English (SE), the Ex-Slave Recordings (ESR), and African Nova Scotian English (ANSE) to the probability of zero plural (reproduced from table 3.1)

		+/− Disambiguation		
NP constituency		SE	ESR	ANSE
[+numeric, +individuating] Q	+dis	.60	.63	.62
Partitive Q	+dis	.54	.59	.66
[−numeric, +individuating] Q	+dis	.49	.67	.55
Demonstrative	+dis	.46	.62	.70
Definite article	−dis	.43	.54	.37
Generic	−dis	.42	.24	.41
Possessive	−dis	.33	.57	.40

delimitation is expressed independently of the plural affix (those including numerals or [–numeric, +individuating] quantifiers), zero plural is preferred. Note that although the individual factor weights may vary from dialect to dialect, a comparison of factor weights relative to each other *within* each variety reveals a distinction (clearest in ANSE and SE) between nouns that are disambiguated and nouns that are not: the former favor zero plural. Nowhere is the creole pattern of high zero in generics in evidence. A major pattern of the observed variability, then, is functional: the plural marker is affixed to a noun when plurality has not been otherwise overtly expressed within the clause containing it.

3.7.6   Functionalism and the creole hypothesis

Now, we have seen that the factor of disambiguation – specifically, *local* disambiguation – plays an important role in plural-marking predictions (Bickerton 1975; Dijkhoff 1983; Mufwene 1986; Rickford 1986) for creoles. To what extent does the Early AAE pattern depicted in table 3.2 mirror those predictions? There is at least one critical difference. Under a strict local disambiguation system, generics (which tend to surface undetermined) should show high rates of morphological marking, as in fact they do in these materials. But in creoles, the opposite is predicted. Indeed, the only way to distinguish between a garden-variety disambiguation system and the creole *local* disambiguation system is through the behavior of generics. Interestingly, when Singler (1989) first operationalized and tested Mufwene's predictions (section 3.2) on the Liberian English creole continuum, as well as on the diaspora variety, Liberian Settler English, he found that they basically did not hold. But it was the behavior of generics, throughout the Liberian continuum as well as with the three Settlers Singler studied, that led him to observe that "in retaining a tendency to avoid marking generic nouns as plural, Liberian Settler English displays a creole characteristic" (1989: 58).

3.8   Plural Marking in Nigerian Pidgin English

In this context it will be instructive to confront our findings for plural marking in Early AAE with reports and findings for plural marking in creoles, and to compare these in turn with observed plural marking behavior in such a system. In this section we examine NPE, spoken since the eighteenth century in Nigeria (e.g. Fayer 1982, 1990: 185), where it now qualifies as a lingua franca (Agheyisi 1988; Faraclas 1989; Fayer 1990; Mafeni 1971; Shnukal and Marchese 1983).

Although technically an "extended pidgin" (Alleyne 1980b; Todd 1974), since for much of the population it does not enjoy mother-tongue status, on linguistic grounds such varieties are indistinguishable from creoles (Singler 1988). Indeed, NPE has figured prominently in a recent effort to assess West African substrate influence on the tense-mood-aspect and copula systems of AAVE (DeBose and Faraclas 1993). The authors stress the considerable morphosyntactic correspondences between this and the other languages of Southern Nigeria, observing further that the structures which typify these languages are in turn "almost identical to those which characterize the great majority of Afro-American language varieties, and that the forms used in Nigerian Pidgin are strikingly similar to those used in the English lexifier creoles of the Caribbean" (1993: 375).

3.8.1   Number marking in NPE

Little has been published about number marking in NPE, beyond the widespread assumption that it is optional now (Agheyisi 1971: 131; Faraclas 1989: 353), and apparently has been since at least the eighteenth century (Fayer 1982: 102). According to Faraclas (1989), most nouns are assumed to be singular in NPE unless otherwise indicated morphosyntactically or pragmatically. In addition, a generic reading is said to be available for bare nouns. Among the morphosyntactic means reported to signal plurality are the following, illustrated with data from our corpus of relatively acrolectal NPE: prenominal determiners, such as numerals and number-transparent indefinite quantifiers, as in (9), and postnominal *dem*, as in (10), which is claimed to be the most common (Faraclas 1989: 353), if not the only (Mafeni 1971: 110) plural marker in NPE. Not specifically listed among plural markers in the sources we consulted (though it is cited in Faraclas's (1989) example 768 as a "borrowing") is the (StdE) affix *-s*. This is exemplified in (9) and (11). Other ways of signaling plurality in the absence of a mark are said to be contextual, relying on prior information to disambiguate the number of the noun in question.

(9) a. a dɔn taya kɔs a bIn put *fIftin awas* tude.   (01/538)
         "I'm tired because I put in fifteen hours (at work) today."

     b. *mɛni giels* wan mek a bi dea bɔifrɛn.   (09/2261)
         "Many girls wanted me to be their boyfriend."

(10) bifɔ na *dɔg*, dey de sɛn . . . nao *yumən bi:n dɛm* de go . . .   (07/293)
     "Before, it was dogs that they were sending [to the moon] . . . now human beings are going."

Table 3.3 Overall distribution of plural markers in
Nigerian Pidgin English

	% of data	N
-s	59	783
zero	39	519
post-nominal *dem*	.7	9
-s + dem	.4	5
Total N		**1316**

(11) a. If yu go daun Walkley, at *taim* na brɛd, ɔdinɛri brɛd, at *taims* na
kek. (06/257)
"If you go down to Walkley, at times it's ordinary bread; at times it's
cake."

b. awa pipl se wɛn mɔni no kil man, *frɛns* an ɔda *rilešn* no kil am,
wuman no kil am, se im go las lɔng.   (09/1744)
"Our people say that when money doesn't kill a man, friends and
other relations don't kill him, women don't kill him, he'll last a long
time."

These observations correspond in essence to the characterizations of plural
marking in Caribbean English-based creoles in section 3.2 above. There are
also clear parallels with the number systems of the various West African languages spoken by our informants, which tend not to distinguish singular and
plural morphologically (Carnochan 1962; Lawal 1986; Welmers 1973). Rather,
in both Igbo and Yoruba, for example, bare nouns receive generic reading, and
individuation (singular or plural) is expressed through the addition of specific
modifiers. In Igbo, the first language of most of the NPE speakers in our
sample, animate and inanimate nouns must be further distinguished. Bare inanimate nouns have generic reference, while bare human nouns receive a singular interpretation, unless plurality is otherwise specified (Welmers 1973: 220).
A similar contrast between [±human] and [±animate] is found in a number of
other West African languages.

NPE has an additional interesting property: like the Early AAE varieties, it
features robust use of *-s* and zero in plural marking contexts, making it ideal for
our comparative purposes. This may be seen in table 3.3, which gives the
overall distribution of plural markers in our NPE data.

We first note that postnominal *dem*, as in (10) and (12), claimed to be the most commonly utilized means of signaling plurality in NPE nouns, is vanishingly rare, not even accounting for 1 percent of the data.

(12) a.   an ɔl doz *tiŋz dɛm*, a no de si.   (02/887)
           "And all those things, I don't see them."

The English affix *-s*, on the other hand, though not cited in treatments of NPE number marking, represents the most frequent variant, at 59 percent. Has it been "borrowed" into NPE, as suggested by Faraclas (1989: 358)? The response to this question lies, once again, in the conditioning of its variable occurrence. If the factors determining the appearance of *-s* in the data are consistent with those relevant to an English system of plural marking (as established in section 3.7 above), we may conclude in the affirmative.

Accordingly, we begin by replicating on NPE our analyses of plural marking in Early AAE. Subsequently, we incorporate the factor of animacy, to assess whether this key determinant of number marking in the West African languages these informants speak natively (Tagliamonte et al. 1997) also plays a role in their NPE.

3.9   Results

The results of the variable rule analysis of the contribution of these factors to plural marking in NPE are as in table 3.4. As a first observation, neither preceding nor following phonological segment was selected as significant to the morphological expression of plural. Unlike Early AAE, where phonological factors exercise a robust and statistically significant effect, a null plural in NPE cannot be construed as resulting from the application of a phonological rule, and should rather be viewed as the output of a grammatical process. What is this process? The same table shows that two non-phonological factors were selected as significant – semantic classification of the noun and NP constituency. But the specific noun–class effect associated with zero plural in English is not characteristic of NPE. If anything, as in Early AAE, nouns of weight and measure appear to favor an *s*-marked plural. This is exemplified in (13).

(13) a.   a dey sIks *mɔns* wIt am fɔ Englan.   (01/13)
           "I was with them for six months in England."

Table 3.4   Variable rule analysis of the contribution of phonological, structural, and semantic factors to the probability of zero plural in Nigerian Pidgin English

Corrected mean	.397	Factor weight	N
NP constituency			
Generic		.57	511
Partitive quantifier		.57	23
Possessive		.51	86
[–numeric, +individuating] Q		.49	227
Definite article		.46	160
[+numeric, +individuating] Q		.42	235
Demonstrative		.39	74
	Range	*18*	
Semantic classification			
Non-weight/measure		.54	1141
Weight/measure		.29	175
	Range	*25*	
Preceding phonological segment			
Non-sibilant consonant		[ ]	604
Vowel		[ ]	361
Following phonological segment			
Consonant		[ ]	552
Vowel		[ ]	165

Factors not selected:
Preceding phonological segment; following phonological segment

b.   i gIv mi wɔn hɔndrɛd *pounds*; a valyu dat wɔn hɔndrɛd *pounds*.   (09/ 994–5)

"He gave me one hundred pounds; I valued that one hundred pounds."

More revealing is the effect of "NP constituency," the factor group operationalizing Mufwene's (1986) and other predictions for creoles. Recall that empirical tests of these predictions (Singler 1989, 1991) on Liberian varieties revealed that only one important effect could be confirmed: NPs with generic reference, as in (14), showed a greater propensity to surface bare than any other NP type, the tendency Singler (1989: 58) referred to as a "creole characteristic."

(14)   a.   na de wey *got* de slip.   (09/955)
            "That's where goats sleep."

       b.   wi gɛt *frɛns* wey wi de cɔmɔt ɔl di taim.   (01/647)
            "We have friends that we go out with all the time."

NPE resembles Liberian Settler English in showing a high generic effect with regard to the other factors in the NP constituency group. This result supports both the predictions for creoles and Singler's empirical findings, at least insofar as the behavior of generics is concerned. But the effect in table 3.4 is not as clear as that found by Singler: in NPE the distinction between the effect of generic reference and that of the other factors is gradient, rather than sharp. In particular, generics appear to contribute the same effect as partitives, a finding that does not correspond to any predictions.

In seeking to explain this result, we now consider the possibility that the analysis we have imposed in table 3.4 (via factors selected to replicate our analyses of Early AAE) does not fit well with the facts of NPE. We noted earlier that animacy is a key determinant of morphological structure in many West African, as well as other languages of the world. One opposition that correlates closely with animacy (or with its common linguistic reflection, the distinction between human and non-human) is the existence of number. NPs ranking higher on the animacy hierarchy (e.g. those referring to humans) generally feature a number distinction, while those ranking lower do not (Comrie 1981: 181). This is exemplified in (15a–b).

(15)   a.   di *bɔiz* de lisin tu am.   (01/639)
            "The boys were listening to him."

       b.   a kɔm ɛnta bigIn wash *plet.*   (01/098)
            "I came in and started washing plates."

Translated into variable terms, if NPE plural-marking patterns are the grammatical legacy of a typical West African language, the factor of animacy should exercise a statistically significant effect on the choice of overt plural marks. Table 3.5 incorporates the factor of animacy into an analysis also testing the effects of phonological environment and type of determiner.

Table 3.5   Variable rule analysis of the contribution of phonological, structural, and semantic factors to the probability of zero plural in Nigerian Pidgin English, incorporating the factor of animacy

Corrected mean	.397	Factor weight	N
Animacy of the noun			
[−animate, −human]		.55	992
[+animate, +human]		.35	324
	Range	*20*	
Type of determiner			
Undetermined		.59	515
Possessive		.57	86
Definite Article		.53	192
Demonstrative		.50	162
Non-numeric Quantifier		.44	122
Numeric Quantifier		.29	237
	Range	*30*	
Preceding phonological segment			
Non-sibilant consonant		[ ]	604
Vowel		[ ]	361
Following phonological segment			
Consonant		[ ]	552
Vowel		[ ]	165

Factors not selected:
Preceding phonological segment; following phonological segment

Both determiner type and animacy are selected as significant. Number-neutral determination structures, including possessives, definite articles and bare nouns (figures in bold in table 3.5), favor a null mark. This runs counter to the received wisdom about plural marking in creoles, according to which a mark should be favored in contexts where plurality has *not* been otherwise disambiguated in the NP headed by the noun in question. In NPE, in contrast, these contexts show the *greatest* probability of zero plural, even possessives and definites, the determiners predicted in the creole literature to receive an *overt* mark. What seems to be operating here is not a "functional" effect, as has been

invoked for other English-based creoles, but a counter-functional one, akin to
the principle of saliency proposed by Lemle and Naro (1977) with regard to
subject–verb agreement. As in the Brazilian Portuguese case they describe, the
NPE plural also tends to be marked overtly in contexts in which its absence
would be most noticeable. This is illustrated in the examples in (16a) and (16b),
where the nouns follow number-transparent determiners.

(16) a. a kɔm du sociology fo *tri yias* a kɔm kɔm aut.   (013/217)
          "I did sociology for three years. I came out."

      b. ɔl *doz* dɛti *jɔbs* wey ɔl *doz* yeye *bɔis* wey dey fo strit de du yu no.
          (01/479)

          "All those dirty jobs that all those worthless boys in the street do,
          you know."

The greatest probability of zero marking is contributed by the undetermined
nouns, which we know to consist mainly of generics. This effect was confirmed
in Poplack and Tagliamonte (1994), who re-analyzed the data according to
referential status of the NP. Recall that the behavior of generics, though characterized as the "creole" effect in discussions on plural marking, is in the first
instance, an African-language effect. For example, Igbo, the first language of
most of our informants, is basically devoid of nominal inflectional morphology,
and bare nouns normally receive generic reading. As mentioned above, because
animacy crosscuts nominal reference and determination in Igbo, if a system
analogous to it were operating in NPE, we should expect to find most zero
plural on [–animate] nouns and most overt marking on [+human] nouns, with
[+animate, –human] nouns showing an intermediate effect. And indeed, the
factor of animacy favors morphological marking in the direction posited, regardless of the configuration of other factors.

Summarizing, variability in plural marking in NPE is conditioned by two
factors. One is animacy: nouns with human referents favor overt marking. The
other is some combination of the syntactic structure of the noun phrase and the
referential status of its head, particularly insofar as this is manifested in the
behavior of undetermined nouns, which in turn tend to have generic reference.
Such nouns display the highest probabilities of null marking.[5]

How do these findings hold up against the predictions for creole systems
more generally? First, overt marking is predicted to occur least in otherwise
disambiguated contexts; the opposite is the case in NPE. Second, more overt
marking is predicted in definite contexts, yet these feature most zero in our

data. Third, and perhaps foremost, is the prediction that nouns with generic reference will surface with no overt mark. This effect does obtain in NPE. But our analyses show that it cannot be unambiguously disentangled from the undetermined status of most generic nouns in the plural, nor, as it turns out, from the factor of animacy. We conclude that the results, while not inconsistent with all the predictions for creoles, at least as enunciated by Mufwene (1986) and others, do not support them in detail. A similar finding was reported by Singler (1989) for Liberian Settler English. On the other hand, the factors contributing significant effects to plural marking in NPE are entirely consistent with a scenario involving substratum influence from Igbo, a hypothesis which was confirmed by Tagliamonte et al. (1997).

More important to our comparative endeavor in this chapter, no factors relevant to, or even consistent with, an English system of plural marking were revealed to be significant in any of the analyses of NPE, regardless of configuration of data. This despite the extensive contact experienced by the speakers in our sample with that language. Rather, the factors selected as significant may only be construed as relevant to the substrate or to NPE itself.

3.10   Situating Early AAE vis-à-vis Other Comparison Varieties

What are the implications of these results for assessing the origins of contemporary AAVE? We have stressed that inferences in this regard should be based on systematic comparison of plural marking in its precursor(s) as well as in English-based creoles, as made in preceding sections. But we must also rule out the possibility that the Early AAE data were coded in ways that obscured the relevant distinctions, as we have seen to be the case for the analysis of NPE in table 3.4, an issue first raised by Bickerton (1975: 131) with regard to Labov et al.'s (1968) and other early analyses (Fasold 1972; Labov 1969; Wolfram 1969) of past-tense marking in AAVE. Accordingly, table 3.6 compares the NPE patterns with those for Early AAE, now recoded for the factors of animacy and nominal reference to enhance comparability, as well as with results for several English-based creoles.

The factors conditioning plural marking in Early AAE could hardly differ more from those operative in NPE. Early AAE shows a robust phonological effect, NPE has none. Early AAE shows a local disambiguation effect, with more morphological marking in contexts that are number-neutral, while NPE shows the opposite, with more plural marking in contexts that are number-transparent

Table 3.6 Variable rule analysis of the contribution of recoded factors to the probability of zero plural in Samaná English (SE), the Ex-Slave Recordings (ESR), and African Nova Scotian English (ANSE), compared with Gullah (Rickford 1986: table 3), Nigerian Pidgin English (NPE), Liberian Settler English (LSE) (Singler 1989: table 9), and Liberian English (LE) (Singler 1991: table 36.2)

	Early AAE			Pidgin/creole/varieties			
	ANSE	ESR	SE	Gullah	NPE	LSE	LE
Corrected mean	.34	.25	.23	.22	.40	.35	
Total N	1353	427	1672	128	1316	574	571
Animacy of the noun							
[−animate, −human]	[ ]	[ ]	[ ]	−	.54	[ ]	.67
[+animate, +human]	[ ]	[ ]	[ ]	−	.38	[ ]	.33
Type of nominal reference							
Generic	.44	.27	[ ]	[ ]	.57	.59	.65
Definite and indefinite	.52	.58	[ ]	[ ]	.47	.41	lower
Preceding phonological segment							
Non-sibilant consonant	[ ]	.58	.55	.65	[ ]	.64	.72
Sibilant consonant	[ ]	.27	.56	.59	[ ]	.37	.21
Vowel	[ ]	.45	.42	.26	[ ]	.49	.63
Following phonological segment							
Consonant	.71	.53	.62	.61	[ ]	[ ]	−
Vowel	.41	.37	.46	.23	[ ]	[ ]	−
Pause	.46	.65	.43	.60	[ ]	[ ]	−

(cf. tables 3.1 and 3.5). Generic reference, or zero determiner, contributes the lowest probability of zero marking in the Early AAE varieties in which it was selected as significant, the highest in NPE. Animacy is not significant in Early AAE; it contributes the strongest effect in NPE. We interpret the latter two effects as being related to substratum influence in the NPE case, and lack thereof in Early AAE.

How do the NPE results compare with those of the other pidgin/creole varieties? The accountable empirical methodology afforded by the variationist paradigm is beginning to yield results suitable for cross-linguistic comparison of the contributions to plural marking in the English-based creoles.[6] Table 3.6

reveals that these are: (i) the generic reference effect, which shows up in each of NPE, Liberian Settler English and Liberian English, and (ii) the animacy effect, which shows up in NPE and Liberian English. Preceding phonological segment is selected as significant in most varieties; these share a variable process of consonant cluster simplification, though they handle epenthetic vowel insertion after sibilants differently. Where the Early AAE varieties differ from English-based creoles is with regard to *following* phonological segment.[7] In each of the former (but none of the latter), we observe the by now familiar effect: consonants favor zero realization. We conclude that though Early AAE and English-based creoles mark the plural by means of the same two variants (-*s* and zero), their selection is constrained by different configurations of constraints.

3.11   Discussion

Summarizing, in the three varieties of Early AAE studied here, plural marking via -*s* was far more variable than in contemporary AAVE. We have attempted in this chapter to uncover the source of that variability. Our findings indicate that despite rates of zero plural far in excess of what is reported today, a robust system of variable plural marking was already in place. Motivating that system was the rule in (17).

(17)   Mark semantically plural regular individuated count nouns with -*s*.

Competing with this rule was the well-documented African American English phonological tendency to remove the -*s* where its presence would result in a syllable-final cluster, or, to a lesser extent, consonant. And cross-cutting these was the functional rule in (18).

(18)   Make the number reference of the NP known when not otherwise overtly expressed clause-internally.

This type of interplay between (morpho-)phonological reduction and function is a well-documented process in language and is not unique to either English or creoles.

   What then is the origin of these plural-marking patterns in Early AAE? To the extent that they can be characterized as language-specific, they are consistent with those attested in the development of contemporary English. The historical record leaves no doubt that the zero plural was once a fully viable entity in English in its capacity as neuter inflection, as detailed in section 3.2. Though this plural type is reported to have merged with its more productive counterpart in -*s* by the Middle English period, it is equally clear that an important residue of forms remained recalcitrant, constituting a (continuing) source of embarrassment for the grammarian. Indeed, perusal of grammars of English, whether early or modern, confirms that the zero variant has always featured in treatments of plural marking. Three explanations are traditionally offered for its persistence, one invoking word-class membership, a second attributing it to determiner type, and the third endowing it with a "new" meaning, namely collectivization. The first two of course recall those more recently invoked to explain plural marking variability in AAVE (section 3.3).

Though these may well be different labels for a single effect (Poplack and Tagliamonte 1994), we stress here that they include a robust precedent for the variability observed in many descendant varieties. Our findings suggest that this variability is what Early AAE inherited: the phonological effect may be viewed as a reflection of the preference (also observed in contemporary Nova Scotian Vernacular English) for deleting plural -*s* where this results in cluster simplification. The English tendency for zero plurals to cluster in certain word classes is evidenced, if not by a propensity towards zero-marking specifically in nouns of weight and measure (which in turn rarely occur without numeric determiners), then by a shared preference for zero forms in other lexical items (section 3.6). Perhaps the most compelling evidence in favor of the suggestion that the plural-marking patterns observed in our materials were acquired from English, however, comes from the behavior of the (functional) factor of disambiguation. We noted earlier that the oft-cited English "numeric determiner effect" could itself be construed as functional, a suggestion supported by the fact that as far back as Old English, prenominal adjectives were already doing double duty as number markers in at least two nominal declensions. Indeed, such disambiguated contexts were found to contain proportionally more zero plurals in a neighboring Nova Scotian Vernacular English variety than in Early AAE (Poplack and Tagliamonte 1994). We may interpret this as further evidence that disambiguation constraints interact with morphological marking in varieties of English permitting plural-marker deletion.

Our conclusions with regard to the source of the plural-marking patterns in Early AAE are bolstered by a (methodologically consistent) comparison with NPE. Although Early AAE and NPE share the same plural markers, their variable selection is conditioned by factors of a different order. Those identified for Early AAE are remnants of those operating at an earlier stage of the English language (and still visible in the variability featured by other contemporary vernacular varieties of English). Those relevant to NPE are arguably substratal features, since they are precisely the ones attested in Igbo, the first language of most of our informants, as well as in other African languages. Such influence is to be expected of an extended pidgin like NPE, among whose characteristics are continued contact with the substrate(s). The quintessentially creole "generic effect" is also apparent in both the West African creoles studied by Singler, while neither nominal reference nor animacy affect Early AAE in the directions predicted by creole or African substrate influences.

In this chapter we have complied with Bickerton's (1975: 25) observation that similarity between languages cannot be proven "by simply producing super- ficially similar surface structures in those languages, [but rather] by producing grammars which [are] substantially identical." This caveat is particularly germane to the study of plural marking, since in each of the comparison varieties, the same variants – the English affix -*s* and phonetic zero – account disproportion- ately for the available options. In none of them do the overt creole (or relevant African-language) plural *form(s)* figure in the productive inventory. Yet making use of systematic variationist methodology, and a broadly comparative base, we have succeeded in demonstrating that the factors responsible for their variable organization in Early AAE and NPE discourse are different. This provides strong empirical confirmation, *contra* Patrick et al. (1993), of our earlier demon- strations (following Bickerton 1975, and Singler 1990; cf. also Mufwene 1984; Rickford 1977; Winford 1985) that the grammar underlying variable linguistic elements may be inferred from their distribution and conditioning in discourse. Moreover, this is the case even when none of the surface forms originate from that grammar.

We have also documented substantial similarities among the three varieties studied here, despite their having evolved in widely separated parts of the world for nearly two centuries. This, along with a growing body of other evidence (Poplack and Tagliamonte 1991, and forthcoming), militates in favor of a genetic relationship among them. Notably, none of the effects reported (or documented by us) for NPE, or for the other English-based creoles, are operat- ive in Early AAE. This is particularly evident in the behavior of generics. An explanation of Early AAE number marking based on decreolization thus cannot be substantiated.

The existence of robust variability and the constraints operating upon it has heretofore been obscured by the (parallel?) development in both StdE *and* contemporary AAVE of a plural-marking system in which -*s* is the norm. This points up the problems involved in exclusive reliance on contemporary StdE as a comparison point, without also considering the details of its development. We are now in a position to explain the anomalous finding that Early AAE features more zero marking than contemporary AAVE, when the opposite is true in most other cases of morphological variability we have examined: both the zero marks and the variable grammar giving rise to them were present in contemporaneous varieties of English which formed the models for Early AAE speakers.

Notes

* We gratefully acknowledge the support of the Social Science and Research Council of Canada for the project of which this research forms part. This chapter is an abridged and synthesized version of Poplack and Tagliamonte (1994) and Tagliamonte et al. (1997).

1 Codes in parentheses identify speaker and line number in the following corpora: Samaná English (SE), the Ex-Slave Recordings (ESR), African Nova Scotian English (ANSE), Nova Scotian Vernacular English (NSVE), and Nigerian Pidgin English (NPE).

2 Full details of data collection, coding and analytical procedures may be found in Poplack and Tagliamonte (1991, 1994) and Tagliamonte et al. (1997).

3 This dependence explains the erratic behavior (not shown here) of the factor of nominal reference in variable rule analyses also containing the factors of disambiguation and individuation, as inferred from type of determiner. It may well also be responsible for the fact that neither (what we have called) nominal reference nor type of determiner was selected as significant in Rickford's (1986) variable rule analysis of plural marking in Mrs Queen's speech (section 3.2).

4 Variability in the treatment of collective nouns as singular or plural persists to this day (cf. British and American English).

5 We noted in section 3.5.2.5 that the factors of nominal reference and NP constituency could not be combined in a multivariate analysis because of the overlap between them. However, independent analysis of their contributions to plural marking (Tagliamonte et al. 1997) reveals that these are basically just different labels for the same phenomenon.

6 In fact, the quantitative results in table 3.6, though all derived from variable rule analyses, are not entirely analogous, for the usual reasons relating to coding practices, factor-group configurations and factors considered. We therefore reproduce only factors directly comparable to the ones discussed here. Some figures were recalculated for purposes of clarity. For example, factor weights for Liberian English, Liberian Settler English, and Jamaican Creole were given for -*s* presence; we converted them to probabilities for zero. Because no totals were given in the analysis of Liberian English, we reproduce the probability for the generic category only, and indicate that the other factors in its factor group contributed a lesser effect to the probability of zero plural. Similarly, although Patrick et al. did not code the factor of "Type of Nominal reference" identically to the way we did, we were able to convert the percentages and totals they provided into figures comparable to those reported here. The results reproduced in table 3.6 all come from runs including several other

factor groups. These may have affected their relative importance (as assessed by the range), and even whether or not they were selected as significant. The comparisons we make in section 3.10 therefore involve only the constraint hierarchies. We follow convention in referring to the speech of "Mrs Queen" as Gullah, and that of Singler's three informants as Liberian Settler English. As previously, factor groups indicated by square brackets were included, but not selected as significant in the analysis. Factor groups indicated by a dash were not considered.

7   With the exception of Gullah (on whose status we take no stand), which patterns like the Early AAE varieties. Rickford himself observed that the absence of the plural marker in Mrs Queen's speech was best described as a deletion rule with phonological constraints (Rickford 1986, 1990).

References

Agheyisi, R. N. (1971) West African Pidgin English: Simplification and simplicity. Ph.D. dissertation, Stanford University.

Agheyisi, R. N. (1988) The standardization of Nigerian Pidgin English. *English World-Wide*, 9 (2): 227–41.

Allan, K. (1976) Collectivizing. *Archivum Linguisticum*, 7 (2): 99–117.

Allan, K. (1980) Nouns and countability. *Language*, 56 (3): 541–67.

Alleyne, M. C. (1980a) *Comparative Afro-American: An Historical-Comparative Study of English-Based Afro-American Dialects of the New World*. Ann Arbor: Karoma.

Alleyne, M. C. (1980b) Introduction: Theoretical orientations in creole studies. In A. Valdman and A. Highfield (eds), *Theoretical Orientations in Creole Studies*. New York: Academic Press, 1–17.

Bailey, G., Maynor, N., and Cukor-Avila, P. (1991) *The Emergence of Black English: Texts and Commentary*. Amsterdam and Philadelphia: John Benjamins.

Baughan, D. E. (1958) Pluralization of flower names. *Word Study*, 34 (1): 3–4.

Bickerton, D. (1975) *Dynamics of a Creole System*. New York: Cambridge University Press.

Bickerton, D. (1979) The status of *bin* in the Atlantic creoles. In I. Hancock (ed.), *Readings in Creole Studies*, Ghent: E. Story-Scientia, 309–14.

Brunner, K. (1963) *An Outline of Middle English Grammar*. Oxford: Blackwell.

Carnochan, J. (1962) The category of number in Igbo grammar. *African Language Studies*, 3: 110–15.

Comrie, B. (1981) *Language Universals and Linguistic Typology*. Oxford: Blackwell.

Curme, G. O. (1977) *A Grammar of the English Language*. Essex, CT: Verbatim.

DeBose, C. E., and Faraclas, N. (1993) An Africanist approach to the linguistic study of Black English: Getting to the roots of the tense-aspect-modality and copula systems in Afro-American. In S. S. Mufwene (ed.), *Africanisms in Afro-American Language Varieties*, Athens, GA: University of Georgia Press, 364–87.

Dijkhoff, M. B. (1983) The process of pluralization in Papiamentu. In L. D. Carrington (ed.), *Studies in Caribbean Language*, St Augustine, Trinidad: Society for Caribbean Linguistics, 217–29.

Dillard, J. L. (1972) *Black English: Its History and Usage in the United States*. New York: Random House.

Ekwall, E. (1912) *On the Origins and History of the Unchanged Plural in English*. Gleerup: Lund.

Ekwall, E. (1975) *A History of Modern English Sounds and Morphology*. Oxford: Blackwell.

Faraclas, N. G. (1989) A grammar of Nigerian Pidgin. Ph.D. dissertation, University of California at Berkeley.

Fasold, R. (1972) *Tense Marking in Black English: A Linguistic and Social Analysis*. Washington, DC: Center for Applied Linguistics.

Fayer, J. M. (1982) Written Pidgin English in Old Calabar in the eighteenth and nineteenth centuries. Ph.D. dissertation, University of Pennsylvania.

Fayer, J. M. (1990) Nigerian Pidgin English in Old Calabar in the eighteenth and nineteenth centuries. In J. V. Singler (ed.), *Pidgin and Creole Tense-Mood-Aspect Systems*, Amsterdam and Philadelphia: John Benjamins, 185–202.

Fries, C. C. (1940) *American English Grammar*. New York: Appleton, Century, Crofts.

Hansen, E., and Nielsen, H. F. (1986) *Irregularities in Modern English*. Gylling, Denmark: Odense University Press.

Harrison, J. A. (1884) Negro English. *Anglia*, 7: 232–79.

Huddleston, R. (1984) *Introduction to the Grammar of English*. Cambridge: Cambridge University Press.

Hughes, A., and Trudgill, P. (1979) *English Accents and Dialects: An Introduction to Social and Regional Varieties of British English*. London: Edward Arnold.

Jespersen, O. H. (1909/1949) *A Modern English Grammar, Part VI: Morphology*. London: George Allen & Unwin.

Kessler, C. (1972) Noun plural absence. In *Tense Marking in Black English: A Linguistic and Social Analysis*, Washington, DC: Center for Applied Linguistics, 223–37.

Labov, W. (1969) Contraction, deletion, and inherent variability of the English copula. *Language*, 45 (4): 715–62.

Labov, W., et al. (1968) *A Study of the Non-Standard English of Negro and Puerto Rican Speakers in New York City*, Co-operative Research Report 3288, Vol. I. Philadelphia: US Regional Survey.

Lawal, N. S. (1986) Some Yoruba quantifier words and semantic interpretation. *Studies in African Linguistics*, 17 (1): 95–105.

Lemle, M., and Naro, A. (1977) *Competências Básicas do Português*. Rio de Janeiro: MOBRAL.

Mafeni, B. (1971) Nigerian Pidgin. In J. Spencer (ed.), *The English Language in West Africa*, London: Longman, 95–112.

Marckwardt, A. H. (1958) *American English*. New York: Oxford University Press.

McDavid, R. I., Jr, and McDavid, V. G. (1960) Grammatical differences in the North Central States. *American Speech*, 35 (1): 5–19.

McDavid, R. I., Jr, and McDavid, V. G. (1964) Plurals of nouns of measure in the United States. In A. H. Marckwardt (ed.), *Studies in Linguistics in Honor of Charles C. Fries*, Ann Arbor: English Language Institute, University of Michigan, 271–301.

Mencken, H. L. (1971) *The American Language*. New York: Alfred A. Knopf.

Mossé, F. (1952) *A Handbook of Middle English*. Baltimore: Johns Hopkins University Press.

Mufwene, S. S. (1983) Some observations on the verb in Black English Vernacular. *African and Afro-American Studies and Research Center Papers*, 5 (2): 1–46.

Mufwene, S. S. (1984) The count/mass distinction and the English lexicon. In D. Testen, V. Mishra, and J. Drogo (eds), *Papers from the Parasession on Lexical Semantics*, Chicago: Chicago Linguistic Society, 200–21.

Mufwene, S. S. (1986) Number delimitation in Gullah. *American Speech*, 61 (1): 33–60.

Patrick, P., et al. (1993) Number marking in the speech of Jamaican women. Paper presented at NWAVE 22, Ottawa, Canada.

Pederson, L. (1983) *East Tennessee Folk Speech*. Frankfurt am Main: Verlag Peter Lang.

Poplack, S., and Sankoff, D. (1987) The Philadelphia story in the Spanish Caribbean. *American Speech*, 62 (4): 291–314.

Poplack, S., and Tagliamonte, S. (1989) There's no tense like the present: Verbal -*s* inflection in Early Black English. *Language Variation and Change*, 1 (1): 47–84.

Poplack, S., and Tagliamonte, S. (1991) African American English in the diaspora: The case of old-line Nova Scotians. *Language Variation and Change*, 3 (3): 301–39.

Poplack, S., and Tagliamonte, S. (1994) -*S* or nothing: Marking the plural in the African American diaspora. *American Speech*, 69 (3): 227–59.

Poplack, S., and Tagliamonte, S. (forthcoming) *African American English in the Diaspora*. Oxford: Blackwell.

Quirk, R., et al. (1972) *A Grammar of Contemporary English*. New York: Harcourt Brace Javanovich.

Quirk, R., et al. (1985) *A Comprehensive Grammar of the English Language*. New York: Longman.

Rand, D., and Sankoff, D. (1990) *GoldVarb. A Variable Rule Application for the Macintosh*, Version 2. Montreal, Canada: Centre de recherches mathématiques, Université de Montréal.

Rickford, J. (1977) The question of prior creolization of Black English. In A. Valdman (ed.), *Pidgin and Creole Linguistics*, Bloomington: Indiana University Press, 190–221.

Rickford, J. (1986) Some principles for the study of Black and White speech in the South. In M. B. Montgomery and G. Bailey (eds), *Language Variety in the South*, Tuscaloosa, AL: University of Alabama Press, 38–62.

Rickford, J. R. (1990) Number delimitation in Gullah: A response to Mufwene. *American Speech*, 65 (2): 148–63.

Schneider, E. W. (1989) *American Earlier Black English*. Tuscaloosa, AL: University of Alabama Press.

Shnukal, A., and Marchese, L. (1983) Creolization of Nigerian Pidgin English: A progress report. *English World-Wide*, 4 (1): 17–26.

Singler, J. V. (1988) The homogeneity of the substrate as a factor in pidgin/creole genesis. *Language*, 64 (1): 27–51.

Singler, J. V. (1989) Plural marking in Liberian Settler English. *American Speech*, 64 (1): 40–64.

Singler, J. V. (ed.) (1990) *Pidgin and Creole Tense-Mood-Aspect Systems.* Amsterdam and Philadelphia: John Benjamins.

Singler, J. V. (1991) Social and linguistic constraints on plural marking in Liberian English. In J. Cheshire (ed.), *English Around the World: Sociolinguistic Perspectives,* Cambridge: Cambridge University Press, 545–61.

Stewart, W. A. (1966) Nonstandard speech patterns. *Baltimore Bulletin of Education,* 43: 52–65.

Sweet, H. (1891) *A New English Grammar, Part I: Introduction, Phonology, and Accidence.* Oxford: Clarendon.

Sweet, H. (1898) *A New English Grammar: Logical and Historical, Part II: Syntax.* Oxford: Clarendon Press.

Tagliamonte, S., and Poplack, S. (1993) The zero-marked verb: Testing the creole hypothesis. *Journal of Pidgin and Creole Languages,* 8 (2): 171–206.

Tagliamonte, S., and Poplack, S. (to appear) Back to the present: Verbal -*s* in the (African American) English Diaspora. In J. Lipski (ed.), *African American English and its Congeners,* Amsterdam and Philadelphia: John Benjamins.

Tagliamonte, S., et al. (1997) Pluralization patterns in Nigerian Pidgin English. *Journal of Pidgin and Creole Languages,* 12 (1): 103–29.

Todd, L. (1974) *Pidgins and Creoles.* London: Routledge & Kegan Paul.

Wakelin, M. F. (1977) *English Dialects: An Introduction.* London: Athlone Press.

Wardale, E. E. (1937) *An Introduction to Middle English.* London: Routledge & Kegan Paul.

Welmers, W. E. (1973) *African Language Structures.* Berkeley: University of California Press.

Winford, D. (1985) The concept of "diglossia" in Caribbean creole situations. *Language in Society,* 14 (3): 345–56.

Wolfram, W. (1969) *A Sociolinguistic Description of Detroit Negro Speech.* Washington DC: Center for Applied Linguistics.

Wolfram, W., and Christian, D. (1976) *Appalachian Speech.* Arlington, VA: Center for Applied Linguistics.

Wright, P. (1981) *Cockney Dialect and Slang.* London: B.T. Batsford.

Wyld, H. C. (1927) *A Short History of English.* London: John Murray.

Part II
Morphosyntactic Variables

4

Negation and the Creole-Origins Hypothesis: Evidence from Early African American English*

Darin M. Howe and James A. Walker

4.1 Introduction

Negation has recently begun to occupy a place at the forefront of the debate over the origins of African American Vernacular English (AAVE). Following on Labov's (1972a, 1972c) seminal work, which drew attention to the properties of negation that distinguish AAVE from Standard English (StdE), others have subsequently drawn parallels between these properties and those of English-based creoles (EBCs). In fact, Winford (1992: 350) characterizes negation as one of "the chief areas in which it [AAVE] shows traces of its creole origin".[1] Certain features of the negation system have thus assumed the role of a creole *diagnostic*, in that their mere presence is taken as evidence of a creole origin. Since such features do not exist in StdE and bear similarities to features of EBCs, the argument goes, they cannot have an English origin. As we will show, closer inspection of the putative creole diagnostic of negation in AAVE reveals that they can also be found in other varieties of English, whether standard, nonstandard, regional or historical. Can such features simultaneously exist in other English varieties *and* be creole diagnostics? Or are they better characterized as either superficial, perhaps coincidental, similarities between different languages or a common legacy of English in both AAVE and EBCs? Answering these questions requires recourse to a method which allows us to discover the linguistic factors conditioning the occurrence of each feature and to systematically compare this conditioning across varieties. In this chapter, we make use of such a method to determine whether features of AAVE's negation system are in fact creole diagnostics.

Here we consider four types of negation, listed with examples from Early African American English (AAE) in (1) to (4), all of which have been reported in contemporary AAVE and variously claimed as creole diagnostics.

Table 4.1   "Diagnosticity" of negative constructions

	AAVE	Creoles	English Nonstandard	English Standard
ain't	✔	✔	✔	✘
Concord (clause-internal)	✔	✔	✔	✘
Concord (clause-external)	✔	✘	✔	✘
Inversion	✔	✘	✔	✘
Postposing	✔	✘	✔	✔

(1)   *ain't*
  . . . *an' I **ain't** been to the courthouse but twice.*   (ESR/001/90)[2]

(2)   **negative concord**
  a.   to indefinites in the same clause:
    *I **ain't** got **no** money.*   (ESR/008/45)

  b.   to verbs in the same clause:
    *No stranger **ain't** got to come.*   (SE/002/476)

  c.   to verbs outside the clause
    *But **don't** you think that I'm **not** gon' take it.*   (SE/007/1291)

(3)   **negative inversion**
  ***Didn't** nobody say **nothing** about it.*   (ANSE/038/523)

(4)   **negative postposing**
  *That one had time to take out **nothing**.*   (SE/002/228)

For some of these constructions, we shall see that *synchronic* evidence from contemporary varieties of AAVE is in fact consistent with such an origin (e.g. sections 4.3.4.2 and 4.4.2). But not all of these forms are equally diagnostic in the sense discussed above. Table 4.1 shows which of these features occur in EBCs and which in (standard and nonstandard) English.

As it happens, *ain't* and clause-internal negative concord, the two features most commonly claimed to be creole, are found not only in EBCs but also in nonstandard English, while clause-external concord and inversion are found only in nonstandard English, and postposing is also found in StdE. Since the first two features are shared by both comparison varieties, their mere presence, or even their overall rate of occurrence, reveals little about the underlying grammar giving rise to them. Instead, we look to their *patterns* of occurrence: is the variability *conditioned* by factors relevant to creole grammar or to English grammar?

An additional consideration is that prior creolization presupposes linguistic *change* (see Poplack, this volume), and we cannot study change without knowing about an earlier stage of the language. Using a distribution in contemporary AAVE distinct from that of English as evidence for a creole origin (as suggested by, e.g., DeBose 1994 and Winford 1992) requires determining whether these properties derive from an earlier stage of AAE. To this end, we deal with each of the four types of negation discussed above by examining data from three varieties of Early AAE. Where possible, we compare the distribution and conditioning of each feature in Early AAE with analogous features in EBCs and in different varieties of English. Because the variable context for each of these features is different, we define each context separately in the relevant section.

Our prediction is that if the underlying grammar of negation in AAVE derives from a prior creole, features such as *ain't* and clause-internal negative concord, which exist in both EBCs and nonstandard English, should pattern in ways consistent with the former but not with the latter, while features such as clause-external negative concord and negative inversion and postposing, nonexistent in EBCs but characteristic of (nonstandard and Standard) English, should either be absent from Early AAE or used differently than in English.

4.2 Data

The data on which this study is based were extracted from three corpora of Early AAE housed at the Sociolinguistics Laboratory at the University of Ottawa (see Poplack, this volume, for an overview of the historical, geographic, and social background of these varieties):

1. African Nova Scotian English (ANSE; Poplack and Tagliamonte 1991)
2. Samaná English (SE; Poplack and Sankoff 1987)
3 The Ex-Slave Recordings (ESR; Bailey et al. 1991)

From the ANSE corpus, six speakers were selected for the study of *ain't* and seven for the study of negative concord. From the SE corpus, the six most vernacular speakers were selected (see Howe (1995: 12–19) for a more detailed description of the selection protocols). Because the ESR constitutes a relatively small corpus, all 11 speakers were included.

4.3   *Ain't*

In contemporary AAVE, *ain't* has been argued (DeBose 1992, 1994; DeBose and Faraclas 1993) to be a universal negator, equivalent to the creole preverbal negator, an example of which is given in (5).

(5)   *Jan no waan go.*
      "John *does not* want to go."   (Jamaican Creole English, Holm 1988: 171)

Creole negators are tense-neutral, neither depending on nor indicating temporal reference. DeBose and Faraclas argue that *ain't* in AAVE is not only tense-neutral, but also aspect-neutral – that is, monomorphemic, standing for negation and nothing else. It follows that *ain't* should be used in all configurations of tense and aspect.

There is evidence that *ain't* in contemporary AAVE varies with *isn't*, *don't*, and *didn't*, just like *eh* in Trinidadian Creole (TC; Winford 1983: 203), as shown in (6).

(6)   a.   *The man eh a thief.*   "The man isn't a thief."

      b.   *The girl eh crying.*   "The girl isn't crying."

      c.   *The girl eh know.*   "The girl doesn't know."

      d.   *The girl eh lie.*   "The girl didn't lie."   (TC; Winford 1983: 203)

In contrast, *ain't* is used in nonstandard English only in the present, and only to negate *be* and *have* (Cheshire 1982; Christian et al. 1988; Feagin 1979). Given these differences between EBCs and nonstandard English, the creole-origin hypothesis predicts that Early AAE should employ *ain't* indifferently with past and non-past reference (see Bickerton 1975: 99), and as a negator of all auxiliaries, *be*, *have* and *do*. In the following sections, we first describe the variable contexts of *ain't*, before dealing with each of the three auxiliary contexts (*have + not*, *be + not*, *do + not*) in turn.

4.3.1   *The variable context(s)*

All negated sentences in which *ain't* occurred or could have occurred were examined, including both copula (present-tense *be*/Ø (Neg) + Predicate, as in

(7)) and auxiliary environments (present-tense *be*/Ø (Neg) + Verb-*ing*, as in (8); present-tense *have*/Ø (Neg) + Participle; or past-tense *do* (Neg) + Verb), as in (9)).

(7) a. *That's not the finish part.* (ANSE/032/836)

   b. *That ain't no cattle.* (ANSE/032/271)

(8) a. *He's not worrying about me.* (SE/003/75)

   b. *He ain't worrying with me.* (SE/003/74)

(9) a. *He didn't give the man nothing.* (SE/001/989)

   b. *He ain't give the man nothing.* (SE/001/987)

Because *ain't* also varies with *wasn't/weren't* in Early AAE, past tense *be* was also included. We did not include environments in which *ain't* never occurred, such as present-tense *do* and modals, sentences in which negation is carried exclusively by an adverb (e.g. *never*, *hardly*) or in which negative postposing (see section 4.5) occurred, and zero predication. Some sentences, such as (10), were difficult to classify.

(10) *I say, you ain't told me to take that.* (SE/007/1277)

Although the past participle suggests that *ain't* here varies with *haven't* (i.e. the perfect), the variability of participles in Early AAE makes *ain't* ambiguous between the perfect (*haven't*) and the preterit (*didn't*). Unless the larger discourse context could resolve this ambiguity, such sentences were not considered. The total number of tokens was 626 for ANSE, 482 for SE, and 215 for the ESR.

4.3.2 Ain't *versus* have + not

Variation between *ain't* and *have + not* has been attested in older varieties of English throughout Great Britain (Yorkshire, Nottingham, Warwick, Hereford, Suffolk, Kent, Surrey, Sussex, and Hampshire) (Wright 1902: III, 88), and remains robust in nonstandard English, as exemplified in (11).

(11) a. *What do you expect, you ain't been round here, have you?* (Nonstandard British English; Cheshire 1982: 51)

Table 4.2 Distribution of *ain't* in *have + not* contexts in SWNE (Feagin 1979: 226), AAVE (Weldon 1994), and Early AAE (in bold)

			Early AAE		
	SWNE	AAVE	ANSE	SE	ESR
N	127	32	4	15	10
ain't	31%	62%	100%	80%	90%

Table 4.3 Distribution of *ain't* in *be + not* contexts in SWNE (Feagin 1979: 214), AAVE (Weldon 1994), and Early AAE (in bold)

			Early AAE		
	SWNE	AAVE	ANSE	SE	ESR
N	421	251	144	159	26
ain't	46%	62%	92%	72%	85%

  b. *I **ain't** been 'ere.*   (Appalachian English; Christian et al. 1988: 169)

  c. *I sent her a wedding present twice and I **ain't** never heard from it.*
      (Southern White Nonstandard English; Feagin 1979: 217)

Table 4.2 displays frequencies for *ain't* versus *have + not* in Early AAE and compares them with those for nonstandard English and AAVE.

Ain't is favoured over *have + not* in all varieties of AAE, Early and contemporary, but not in Southern White Nonstandard English (SWNE). Although this preference for *ain't* appears to be more accentuated in Early AAE than in AAVE, the small number of tokens prevents conclusive interpretation. Since creoles, nonstandard English, Early AAE and AAVE all use *ain't* for *have + not*, these findings are silent with respect to the creole-origins hypothesis.

4.3.3 Ain't *versus* be + not

Table 4.3 shows the distribution of *ain't* in the *be* environment (both copular and auxiliary) for Early AAE, comparing it with those for SWNE and AAVE. While *ain't* is extremely frequent in SWNE, occurring almost half the time, it is

Table 4.4 Distribution of *ain't* in *be + not* contexts in WNBE, SWNE (Feagin 1979: 222), AAVE (Weldon 1994), and Early AAE, by function

			Copula			
				Early AAE		
	WNBE	SWNE	AAVE	ANSE	SE	ESR
N	?	222	132	77	101	16
ain't	61–95%	50%	55%	90%	70%	81%

			Auxiliary			
				Early AAE		
	WNBE	SWNE	AAVE	ANSE	SE	ESR
N	?	54	119	67	101	10
ain't	42–79%	55%	71%	94%	74%	90%

particularly frequent in the AAE varieties. Once again, Early AAE is distinguished by the highest rates, with ANSE displaying near-categorical use of *ain't* in this environment.

In table 4.4, we separate the copular and auxiliary uses of *be*. Contemporary AAVE prefers *ain't* in its auxiliary as opposed to its copular function. Weldon (1993) interprets the high frequency of *ain't* (71%) in the auxiliary environment as evidence that there is no underlying *be* here. If her interpretation is correct, the Early AAE results suggest that there is no underlying *be* at all in the entire *be* environment, especially in ANSE, where the lowest frequency of *ain't* usage is 90%.

If we assume, on the basis of results such as those in table 4.4, that there is no underlying *be*, we must analyze the variation as "bisystemic" (as DeBose 1992, 1994 does). Under such an analysis, *be + not* appears according to the StdE negation system (*not* negates *be*) and *ain't* appears according to the creole negation system (no underlying copula).[3] We must also assume (as Weldon 1993 does, though not Weldon 1994) code-switching between the two systems. Weldon (1993) argues that the bisystemic analysis is supported by the high frequency of *ain't* in precisely those linguistic environments where Labov (1972c: 87) found the fewest surface copulas (i.e. the auxiliary environment).

Although Weldon's observation is plausible, small percentages of a feature do not indicate the underlying absence of that feature: although *be + not* is used much less frequently than *ain't*, it is still an established variant. Furthermore, a convincing analysis of code-switching between two systems should rely not on the overall distribution of the forms but rather on a *systematic* investigation showing that the linguistic factors conditioning the occurrence of the two variants are different. Since the relevant linguistic factors (tense and aspect) are areas of grammar in which English and creole systems are known to differ substantially, differential behavior with respect to these factors could be taken as evidence that there are indeed two distinct systems in AAE.

We test this hypothesis with respect to two tense/aspect distinctions: temporal reference and stativity. Table 4.5 reveals that *ain't* is basically restricted to present temporal reference and, with respect to aspect, has essentially the same distribution as *be + not*.

Although we cannot compare our data with other varieties, because their data were not configured according to these distinctions, we note that the use of *ain't* in the past-copula environment is not a feature of any dialect of English. On the other hand, *ain't* is tense-neutral in EBCs (Bickerton 1975: 99; Winford 1983: 203). Indeed, we would not expect to find negation interacting with tense in such tense-deficient languages. Table 4.5, which shows crucially that tense distinctions strongly condition *ain't* in Early AAE, lends no support to the analysis of *ain't* variation as code-switching to a creole grammar (e.g. DeBose 1994), at least in the *be* environment.

Note, though, that table 4.5 also reports 13 tokens, mainly from ANSE, in which *ain't* does indeed occur in the past, as illustrated in (12).

(12) a. *But the boys **ain't** like the boys is now.*   (ANSE/016/74)

    b. ***Ain't** one of them as strong as they is now.*   (ANSE/009/581)

This past-tense use of *ain't* is restricted to a single contrastive construction, illustrated in (13).

(13) (X) *ain't* (Y) *like* (Z) . . . present tense verb . . . *now*

Accounting for these instances in an English grammatical system would require phonological alternation between *wasn't* and *ain't* (*weren't* is rare in the data). The phonetic basis of this alternation is difficult to explain, since we would have to explain why the use of *ain't* for *wasn't* is not reported in the historical literature, and why its development is restricted to the context in (13).

Table 4.5 Distribution of *ain't* in *be + not* contexts in Early AAE, by function, temporal reference, and stativity. Temporally ambiguous tokens were excluded from the comparison of past with present

	Copula					
	SE		**ANSE**		**ESR**	
	be+not	*ain't*	*be+not*	*ain't*	*be+not*	*ain't*
Past	62%	1%	95%	14%	94%	1%
	(48)	(1)	(154)	(11)	(51)	(1)
Present	38%	99%	5%	89%	6%	99%
	(30)	(71)	(8)	(69)	(3)	(13)
+Stative	100%	100%	100%	100%	100%	100%
	(78)	(73)	(162)	(83)	(54)	(14)
−Stative	0	0	0	0	0	0

	Auxiliary					
	SE		**ANSE**		**ESR**	
	be+not	*ain't*	*be+not*	*ain't*	*be+not*	*ain't*
Past	32%	0	85%	0	N=4	0
	(7)		(23)			
Present	68%	100%	15%	100%	N=1	100%
	(15)	(43)	(4)	(63)		(9)
+Stative	48%	25%	15%	11%	N=0	N=2
	(11)	(11)	(4)	(7)		
−Stative	52%	75%	85%	89%	N=5	N=9
	(12)	(33)	(23)	(57)		

An alternative explanation is that this use of *ain't* is evidence of an earlier stage in AAE when it functioned as a universal tense/aspect-neutral negator (DeBose 1994: 128). This explanation would be plausible if the general loss of *ain't* with past temporal reference could be linked to a general process of decreolization in AAE. Specifically, we could argue that the earliest African slaves spoke a creole in which *ain't* was monomorphemic and tense-neutral; by the nineteenth century, with increasing contact with English, decreolization restricted *ain't* to present temporal reference in all environments *except* the one in (13). Support for this scenario comes from another example where *ain't* is used in the past in the same construction but is not used for *wasn't*:

(14)   *Ain't – they ain't got like big ones they got now but they had them I guess.* (ANSE/009/307)

Such a proposal raises a number of difficult questions. First, according to Winford (p.c.), there is no correlate of this phenomenon in any EBC: for instance, Trinidadian Creole uses invariant *wasn* in such constructions. How then could the use of *ain't* in this context be a reflex of a prior creole? Secondly, this phenomenon has never been reported in any other variety of AAE, including SE and the ESR. Since it is found only in ANSE, it cannot have pre-dated the historical split between the three Early AAE varieties. Thirdly, despite the few uses of *ain't*, the use of *ain't* for *be + not* is essentially restricted to the present tense, where it is the preferred form. This temporal restriction cannot be linked to a process of *decreolization* in ANSE, because there is no *a priori* reason for *ain't* (taken as a tense-neutral negator) to persist so strongly in present temporal reference. It follows that *ain't* is not a tense-neutral negator in the *be* environment, but rather a *bona fide* English variant of *be + not* which in ANSE has begun spreading to a single contrastive past-tense construction in (13). Finally, only one case of *ain't* with past-tense reference has ever been reported for English (Feagin 1979: 215):

(15)   *They ain't like they is now.*   (Melvin H. 72W: 32.I.357)

The fact that it occurs in exactly the same contrastive construction as in (13) suggests a relationship between SWNE and Early AAE. In fact, exactly the same sentence is found in our data:

(16)   *They ain't like they is now.*   (ANSE/030/76)

Note also in table 4.5 that, aspectually, *ain't* behaves like *be + not* in the same linguistic environment. In this case, there are two reasons why this finding cannot be adduced as evidence of either a creole or an English underlying system:

(i)   *Copulas* are by definition aspect-neutral: they are always stative. The proposal that *ain't* is creole-like in being aspect-neutral (e.g. DeBose 1994) is not very convincing in this context.

(ii)   *Auxiliaries* take on the stativity of their lexical verb: in this sense, they too are aspect-neutral. In other words, English auxiliaries follow precisely what DeBose and Faraclas (1993) say about *ain't* in all sentences in AAVE. Consequently, no distinct creole behavior of *ain't* is identifiable in this context either.

The fact that *ain't* is generally restricted to present temporal reference militates against its putative tense-neutrality and therefore also against a creole origin. We conclude that *ain't* in the *be* environment is best analyzed as a variant of *be + not* in Early AAE (see Labov 1972c: 70; and Blake 1997, for AAVE).

4.3.4   Ain't *versus* do + not

4.3.4.1   Ain't *versus* didn't

Variation between *ain't* and *didn't*, as shown in (17), is a widely-attested feature of AAVE (Fasold and Wolfram 1975: 69).

(17)   a.   *I said, "I ain't run the stop sign," and he said, "you ran it!"*   (Baugh 1988: 71)

     b.   *I ain't believe you that day, man.*   (Weldon 1994: 384)

     c.   *Well, he didn't do nothin' much, and I ain't neither.*   (Labov et al. 1968: 255)

This use appears especially diagnostic of a creole origin, both because *ain't/didn't* variation has only been found in AAVE (Wolfram 1991: 293) and because the creole negator can appear in contexts of English *didn't*, as illustrated in (6d). If the creole-origin hypothesis is correct, we would expect to find greater use of *ain't* in the context of *didn't* in Early AAE.

Table 4.6 compares *ain't/didn't* variation in Early AAE and contemporary AAVE. The near-categorical preference for *didn't* in Early AAE is damaging to the creole-origin hypothesis. If we assume that *ain't* is tense-neutral, there is no *a priori* reason for it not to occur in the environment of *didn't*, since this environment is generally [–habitual] and [+punctual] and is therefore consistent with the aspectual requirements of *ain't* that have been suggested (e.g. DeBose and Faraclas 1993: 370). The lack of *ain't* (or any other universal negator) (DeBose 1994) in this overall linguistic environment thus remains unexplained.

Given that Early AAE represents varieties that are at least a century older than that of Weldon's (1993) young informants, her suggestion that there is a

Table 4.6   Distribution of *ain't* in contexts of *didn't* in AAVE
(Weldon 1993) and varieties of Early AAE

		Early AAE	
	AAVE	ANSE	SE	ESR
N	161	258	189	144
ain't	40%	2%	6%	3%
didn't	60%	98%	94%	97%

process of decreolization at work finds no support. On the contrary, table 4.6
shows that the relative prominence of *ain't* for *didn't* in modern AAVE is a
recent and spectacular development. This conclusion is supported by Labov's
(1972c: 284) report that "[a]dults . . . rarely use *ain't* for *didn't*" whereas youth
do in South Harlem. In this respect, these findings lend more support to
the divergence hypothesis (Bailey and Maynor 1989) than to the creole–origin
hypothesis.

Fasold and Wolfram (1975: 69) suggest that *ain't/didn't* variation "probably
developed from rather recent phonetic changes." While the divergence in table
4.6 between AAVE and Early AAE appears to support this view, invoking *recent*
phonetic changes is problematic, since table 4.6 also shows that *ain't/didn't*
variation was in fact incipient in Early AAE. Moreover, they are not very
specific in their explanation of exactly how *ain't* derives phonetically from
didn't. In fact, the only specific phonetic explanation that has been offered is
Rickford's (1977: 203). According to him, the loss of the initial [d] reflects a
process of morphophonological simplification affecting auxiliaries in AAE. To
the extent that phonological simplification is a feature of EBCs, he considers the
reduction of *didn't* to *ain't* as evidence of prior creolization (1977: 195–6).
There are two serious problems with this account. First, the loss of initial [d]
represents the loss of a syllable onset, which is a universally marked process in
phonology (see, e.g., Prince and Smolensky 1993) and cannot be considered
simplification. Secondly, Rickford's (1977: 203) contention that "morphophonemic
condensation of certain auxiliaries [in AAE] is [. . .] unparalleled in [. . .]
white nonstandard dialects" is contradicted by Feagin's (1979: 212) finding that
initial [d] is also lost in SWNE.

Winford believes that *ain't/didn't* variation was probably present from
the earliest stages of AAE, when a process of approximation to standard English similar to decreolization was taking place (p.c.). Although this belief is

plausible, Feagin (1979: 215) did find three examples of *ain't* functioning as *didn't* in SWNE:

(18) a. *I ain't notice that.*

  b. *I ain't go huntin but four or five times.*

  c. *That knock you down, ain't it!* (SWNE; Feagin 1979: 215)

Weldon (1993: 17) dismisses these occurrences as "idiosyncratic" and "non-productive" in Alabama English (compared with their productive use in her data on modern AAVE). But as table 4.6 shows, the use of *ain't* for *didn't* was also rare in Early AAE. The most plausible explanation is that early African Americans acquired the possibility of *ain't*/*didn't* variation from the speech of Southern whites, but later exploited this variation in ways that Southern whites never did.

4.3.4.2 Ain't *versus* don't

Despite the fact that the creole preverbal negator can appear in the context of English *don't*, as shown in (6c), there are no reports of *ain't* as a negator of *don't* in any variety of contemporary AAVE. SE and the ESR do occasionally use *ain't* for *don't*, as in (19) (as do the Ex-Slave Narratives; Schneider 1989: 201).

(19) a. *I ain't know nothing 'bout that. These the only thing what I know about.* (SE/007/1674)

  b. *If they whip you half a day, you ain't want to eat.* (ESR/013/181)

This variation has no correlate in any other variety of English, whether modern, regional, or historical: it is unique to Early AAE. While this fact, in isolation, could be taken as evidence that AAVE evolved from a variety that was different from colonial English, the phenomenon is too rare to draw such a conclusion. There are hundreds of instances in our Early AAE data in which *ain't* fails to replace *don't*. For instance, in the ANSE data, *ain't* is never used for *don't*, despite 347 potential environments. If *ain't* were truly universal, there would be no reason for *don't* to be so strongly preferred over *ain't*.

   Weldon (1993, 1994) reports apparently productive variation between *ain't* and *don't* in one specific environment: before the verb *got*, as in (20):

(20) a. *He **ain't** even got a crease in his face.*

  b. *He **don't** got one crease.* (Ohio AAVE; Weldon 1994)

Table 4.7   Distribution of *ain't* versus *have + not* or *don't* in environment before *got* in SWNE, AAVE (Weldon 1994), and varieties of Early AAE

	ain't/ have+not	*ain't/ don't*	*ain't/?* **Early AAE**		
	SWNE	AAVE	ANSE	SE	ESR
N	29	63	24	45	10
ain't	72%	65%	**100%**	**100%**	**100%**

This variation appears to be a creole diagnostic, since in other nonstandard varieties of English, whether historical or regional, *ain't* only alternates with *have + not* before *got* (Cheshire 1982: 51; Christian et al. 1988: 169–70; Feagin 1979: 226–7). Thus, compare (21a) with (21b) in SWNE:

(21)   a.   *Now you've told me four times, and I* **ain't** *got any idea of doin' it, so hush!*

      b.   *You* **hadn't** *[hasn't] got that turned on, have you?*   (SWNE; Feagin 1979: 217, 213)

We now consider whether, in Early AAE, *ain't* varies with *don't* (before *got*) as in modern AAVE or with *have + not* as in nonstandard English. As it happens, *ain't* is used categorically before *got* in Early AAE, as shown in table 4.7. Thus, there is no way of telling whether *ain't* corresponds to *don't* or to *have + not*.

The most reasonable explanation for the distribution in table 4.7 is that *ain't* was originally used for *have + not* and was particularly favored before *got*, becoming categorical in Early AAE. To explain the use of *don't* before *got* in modern AAVE, we can consider two possibilities: *got* could have first been relexicalized as a stative verb (since it has the same denotational meaning as lexical *have*) and then *don't* could have come into use because the new stativity of *got* was inconsistent with the non–habitual/punctual requirements of *ain't* (as postulated by DeBose and Faraclas 1993, and Bolton 1982). Alternatively, *don't* could have begun to replace *ain't* by simple analogy of *got* with *have* (again, because they share denotational meaning). Neither of these accounts is defensible from general principles of linguistic change. As Christian et al. (1988: 7) point out:

If nothing else, the past two decades of variation studies have demonstrated that language change implies language variation of some type. Speakers undergoing change do not simply go to bed one evening with an old form intact and wake up the [next] morning with a new form firmly in place. On this point, there is apparent agreement among linguists with quite different orientations concerning language change (Weinreich, Labov and Herzog 1968; Bailey 1973; Wang 1977; Labov 1981; Romaine 1983).

The problem that table 4.7 poses for the above two accounts is that modern AAVE would have to have developed the use of *don't* before *got* without variation, since this use is invariably absent from both Early AAE and SWNE.

Here we consider a third possibility, that of prior variation, not between the auxiliaries *ain't* and *don't*, but rather between the main verbs *have* and *got*. This possibility is supported by the presence of such variation in Early AAE, as shown in (22–3):

(22)   a.   *I never had a strapping.*   (ANSE/039/350)

       b.   *I never got a strapping.*   (ANSE/039/350)

(23)   a.   *They got things what you ain't got to operate.*   (SE/002/1250)

       b.   *They gots many a things they ain't have to operate.*   (SE/002/1250)

Accordingly, we suggest that the apparent *ain't/don't* variation before *got* reported by Weldon (1993, 1994) originates from prior variation between *have* and *got*. That is, the use of *ain't* for *don't* in this specific environment is yet another innovation of contemporary AAVE, rather than a result of decreolization.

4.3.5   Summary

Since *ain't* is one of the few variables that remains robust in all comparison varieties, the comparative endeavor has proven particularly fruitful, especially diachronically, enabling us to determine which features are innovations and which were inherited. The linguistic conditioning of *ain't* in Early AAE argues against its status as the relic of a creole-like universal negator. If it were such, we would expect it to occur indifferently across all tense/aspect environments. Yet *ain't* behaves much like *be + not* with respect to aspectual distinctions, and is essentially restricted to present temporal reference in the *be + not* environment and to past temporal reference in the *do + not* environment. Similarly, our comparison of the distribution of *ain't* in Early AAE with its distribution in

AAVE and in nonstandard English reveals differences more of degree than of kind. While the AAE varieties (early and modern) prefer *ain't* in the *have + not* environment, *ain't/ have + not* variation is a feature of all varieties. Although *ain't/ didn't* variation is restricted to AAE varieties, Early AAE almost categorically prefers *didn't*, while modern AAVE prefers *ain't*. These findings suggest that contemporary AAVE's preference for *ain't* in all environments is a recent innovation rather than a creole legacy. In short, we conclude that the use of *ain't* is an English legacy, and that apparent differences between AAE and other varieties of English, standard or nonstandard, result from relatively recent innovations made by African Americans to the system they originally acquired.

4.4   Negative Concord

The term "negative concord"[4] (Labov 1972a) describes constructions in which "the negative feature is spread . . . over all elements in the sentence (or the clause) that can bear it" (van der Wouden 1994: 93). Following Labov (1972a), we distinguish three types of negative concord: to indefinites within the same clause, as in (24); to verbs within the same clause, as in (25); and to verbs outside the clause, as in (26).

(24)   *I didn't had no chance to go to no school.*   (SE/001/214)

(25)   *No stranger ain't got to come.*   (SE/002/476)

(26)   *Well isn't nobody wouldn't go out.*   (ANSE/030/812)

We treat these phenomena separately in sections section 4.4.2, section 4.4.3 and section 4.4.4, respectively.

According to Bickerton (1981: 65), negative concord is a prototypical feature of creole languages, as illustrated in (27).

(27)   a.   *Non dag na bait non kyat.*
            "No dog bit any cat."   (Guyanese Creole; Bickerton 1981: 66)

       b.   *Nonbadi na sii am.*
            "Nobody saw him."   (Guyanese Creole; Bickerton 1984: 185)

The creole negator is obligatory even when another negative word appears in the verb phrase (Bickerton 1981: 65), as shown in (28), and negative concord to indefinites in the same clause is obligatory.

(28)   *He ain' answer nothin'.*
       "He didn't answer anything."   (Bahamian Creole English; Holm 1988:
       172)

Negative concord also has a long history in other varieties of English: it was
the norm in Old English (OE; Traugott 1992: 170) and persisted throughout
Middle (ME) and Early Modern English (Early ModE), as shown in (29).

(29)   a.   *& ne bid dær nænig ealo gebrowen mid Estum.*
            "and no ale is brewed among the Ests"   (OE; *Orosius* 1 1.20.18;
            Traugott 1992: 268)

       b.   *But nevere gronte he at no strook but oon.*
            "But he never groaned at any of the blows but one."   (ME; *Canterbury
            Tales*; Fischer 1992: 284)

       c.   *I cannot goe no further.*
            (Early ModE; *As You Like It*; Barber 1997: 198)

Despite the valiant efforts of prescriptivists, negative concord has never completely disappeared, though nowadays it is considered a shibboleth of nonstandard speech throughout the English-speaking world (Gramley and Pätzold 1992:
309, 377). Examples from SWNE (Feagin 1979: 241, 229) are shown in (30).

(30)   a.   *. . . and nobody didn' do nothin' about it.*

       b.   *Nobody don't believe it now.*   (Feagin 1979: 241, 229)

Since negative concord is characteristic of many varieties of English as well
as of EBCs, we must establish whether Early AAE inherited its use directly
from colonial English or via creolization. As we did with *ain't*, we compare the
system of negative concord in Early AAE with the systems of negative concord
in historical and regional varieties of English and in EBCs.

4.4.1   The variable context

Because the variable context for negative concord is controversial, we first
provide empirical and semantic justification for our assumptions. First, we
assume that the presence or absence of negative concord does not affect the
meaning of the sentence: that is, we consider analogous negative sentences with

and without negative concord to be variants of the same logical negation. Consider the following pairs of sentences:

(31) a. *I wouldn't take **anything** from him.* (ESR/002/83)

    b. *I wouldn't take **nothing** from him.* (ESR/002/88)

(32) a. *He **never** saw them **any** more.* (SE/011/1181)

    b. *And **never** saw them **no** more.* (SE/006/458)

Since negative polarity items are indefinite (Heim 1984), *anything* is interpreted as *thing* in (31a) and *any more* is interpreted as *more* in (32a). Similarly, despite their negative morphology, *nothing* and *no more* fail to contribute any negative force to (31b) and (32b): they are also interpreted as *thing* and *more*, respectively. Therefore, each pair of sentences is completely equivalent in terms of truth-conditional semantics. Since the sentences in (31) had the same referents and were uttered only seconds from each other in the same context by the same speaker, we can assume that the referential meaning has not changed in any way.

The interpretation of sentences with indefinites, as in (33), is more controversial.

(33) a. *I don't sass old people.* (ANSE/019/452)

    b. *I don't sass **no** old people.* (ANSE/019/453)

Although these sentences were also uttered only seconds from each other in the same context by the same speaker, they could be argued not to constitute a minimal pair in the same way as (31–32), since (33b) may actually correspond to (33c):

(33) c. *I don't sass **any** old people.*

Most linguists (e.g. Labov 1972a; Feagin 1979; Cheshire 1982) analyze *no* as NEG + *any*, so that (33b) should derive from (33c) rather than from (33a). This analysis would unify the account of negative concord in (31b), (32b) and (33b), and is apparently supported by the following sentence-pair:

(34) a. *He **didn't** use **no** kind of bad words before me.* (SE/006/1759)

    b. *They **don't** use **any** kind of word.* (SE/011/390)

Since *any* in (34b) is the only viable alternative to *no* in (34a), this example offers an especially strong argument for the conversion of *any* to *no*.

Nevertheless, (33b) could vary with *both* (33a) and (33c), provided that (33a) and (33c) have the same denotational meaning (see Weiner and Labov 1983). Kadmon and Landman (1993: 360) argue that *any* widens the previously given domain of quantification, by extending the interpretation of the common noun it modifies. Under this assumption, the NP in (33c) has a wider denotation than that in (33a). But since these sentences involve a mass noun, which applies to a set and thus already has wide interpretation, there is arguably no difference in referential meaning between (33a) and (33c).

In contrast, singular indefinite count nouns (denoting a single person or thing) do not, by definition, allow a wide interpretation, unless accompanied by the determiner *any*. The apparent denotational difference between singular indefinite count nouns with and without *any* has led most linguists (e.g. Cheshire 1982: 65–6; Labov 1972a: 806) to argue that the latter cannot be involved in negative concord. Nonetheless, we adopt the (admittedly controversial) view (along with Howe (1995: 57–65) and Tottie (1991: 306)) that negative concord can also occur with the indefinite *a* + NP. In short, we argue that negative concord can occur with a wider range of elements than has previously been assumed, since negative concord to count nouns with *no* can vary with *any* and Ø as well as with *a*. It can also occur with *one, hardly, either, ever* and *ary*, as in (35–39):

(35)   *She couldn't speak **not one** word in Spanish.*   (SE/006/178)

(36)   *You couldn't **hardly** talk on your – on your phone.*   (ANSE/009/102)

(37)   *I didn't believe in it **neither**.*   (ANSE/009/475)

(38)   ***Nobody never** got mad with each other.*   (ANSE/038/933)

(39)   *If I weren't **not nary** one.*   (ESR/012/305)

Crucially, negative concord with all of these forms is variable. In the following sections, we determine whether the distribution of this variation in Early AAE more closely matches that of other vareties of English or of EBCs.

4.4.2   Negative concord to indefinites in the same clause

A preliminary comparison of negative concord to indefinites in the same clause suggests that modern AAVE operates the same way as creoles (i.e. through

Table 4.8   Rates of clause-internal negative concord with indefinites in SWNE, NWNE, AAVE (Labov et al. 1968), and varieties of Early AAE

	Nonstandard English			Early AAE		
	SWNE	NWNE	AAVE	ANSE	SE	ESR
N	718	42	654	492	222	153
%	75%	81%	98%	89%	66%	80%

categorical application). In their study of New York AAVE, Labov et al. (1968: 277) found categorical application of negative concord to indefinites in the same clause:

(40)   *Down here nobody don't know about no club.*   (Labov 1972a: 786)

By contrast, negative concord to indefinites in the same clause, while variable, has never been obligatory in other varieties of nonstandard English, whether regional (Cheshire 1982; Feagin 1979; Wolfram and Christian 1975, 1976) or historical (Austin 1984; Jack 1978; Nagucka 1978; Traugott 1992).

In table 4.8, which displays frequencies of negative concord in Early AAE and those reported for other varieties, we can see that it is by far the preferred variant in all nonstandard varieties of English, African American or otherwise. Yet the three varieties of Early AAE show far more variability, especially when compared with the categorical use of negative concord that Labov et al. (1968: 277) found for AAVE. In fact, our overall results are much closer to their findings for the white Inwood working-class teenagers they studied, as well as to Feagin's (1979) findings for white urban working-class Alabamans. The lower rates in Early AAE suggest that the categorical use of negative concord is another development of contemporary AAVE, rather than a prior creole legacy. Moreover, Wolfram's (1969) study of Detroit AAVE, in which pre-adolescents and teens use far more negative concord than working-class adults (see also Baugh 1983: 82), suggests that this development is fairly recent. Note that while the high rate of negative concord among African American youths is unparalleled even in nonstandard white varieties of English, it is premature to attribute this development to the divergence of AAVE from American English, since the use of negative concord is also increasing in other nonstandard varieties (Wolfram and Christian 1975: 161).

Table 4.9 Rates of clause-internal negative
concord with verbs in Early AAE

	ANSE	SE	ESR
N	22	25	5
%	**55**	**60**	0

4.4.3 Negative concord to verbs in the same clause

Informal inspection of the variability of clause-internal negative concord to verbs lends support to the creole-origin hypothesis. Bickerton (1981: 65) explicitly states that the *optional* application of negative concord with verbs, as in (41), is a prototypical feature of creole languages:

(41) *Nonbadi non sii am.*
"Nobody saw him."   (Guyanese Creole; Bickerton 1984: 185)

One piece of evidence against this hypothesis is the attestation of this structure in "restricted northern and most southern vernaculars" (Wolfram 1991: 293):

(42) a. *None of em didn't hit the house.*   (Feagin 1979: 229)

b. *And neither of the boys can't play a lick of it.*   (Feagin 1979: 236)

This type of negative concord also has a long history in English, optionally applying in OE (Nagucka 1978: 61) and ME (Jack 1978: 62), as illustrated in (43):

(43) *. . . ne a moment of an hour ne shal nat perisse of his tyme.*
". . . nor shall a moment of an hour of his time perish."   (ME; *Canterbury Tales*; Jack 1978: 60)

As table 4.9 shows, except for the lack of variability in the ESR (attributable to the small number of tokens), clause-internal negative concord with verbs is highly variable in Early AAE, as illustrated in (44):

(44) a. *nobody here went*   (SE/003/625)

b. *nobody didn't go*   (SE/003/626)

Our findings generally confirm Labov's (1972a: 806) observation that negative concord is never obligatory to the preverbal position (i.e. to auxiliaries, *do*, and modals). Since this type of negative concord is variable in all the comparison varieties, and since there is no linguistic conditioning which is distinctive for creoles, we conclude that it cannot be diagnostic of a creole origin.

4.4.4   Negative concord to verbs outside the clause

Although Labov et al. (1968) found several examples of negative concord to verbs outside the main clause, such as his (in)famous example in (45), they are vanishingly rare in contemporary AAVE.

(45)   *It ain't no cat can't get in no coop.*   (Labov 1972a: 773)

That this one sentence should have drawn so much attention within variationist linguistics is somewhat surprising, given the quantitative orientation of the field. In all likelihood, the original attention given (45) was due to the belief that this structure occurs only in AAVE (Labov et al. 1968; Labov 1972a, 1972b, 1972c). Subsequently, Wolfram and Christian (1976: 113) have reported one sentence with negative concord to a verb in another clause, in white Appalachian English, shown in (46), and Feagin (1979: 229) has reported three examples in white Alabama English, shown in (47), though these examples have not garnered the attention bestowed on (45).

(46)   *I wasn't sure that nothing wasn't gonna come up at all.*   (Appalachian English; Wolfram and Christian 1976: 113)

(47)   a.   *I'm not gonna stay home when I ain't married; me and my kids can go on campin' trips.*

   b.   *We ain't never really had no tornadoes in this area here that I don't remember.*

   c.   *But our church did not have any young people that I can't remember.*   (Alabama English; Feagin 1979: 229)

Thus, clause-external negative concord to verbs is vanishingly rare even in those varieties (African American or otherwise) in which it does occur (see also Wolfram 1991: 293).

Early AAE is no exception in this regard: this type of negative concord does not occur in the ESR, but it does occur three times in the SE data and seven times in the ANSE data. These occurrences are of two different types. The first involves spreading to a lower clause. As examples (48–52) show, it is not only rare but also highly heterogeneous. In the five sentences, there are three different pleonastic negators (*n't/not, no, don't*) in both finite and non-finite lower clauses.

(48) *But don't you think that I'm not gon' take it. Not me, no.* (SE/007/1291)
      "But don't you think that I'm gon' take it. Not me, no."

(49) *Well isn't nobody wouldn't go out.* (ANSE/030/812)
      "There wasn't anybody who would go out."

(50) *If he ain't the right man what not to suffer with people, he don't do nothing with the people.* (SE/011/1016)
      "If he [the bishop] is not the right [kind of] man to suffer with people, . . ."

(51) *I didn't come no scare you to death.* (ANSE/039/820)
      "I didn't come to scare you to death."

(52) *They ain't going to don't take out the Mayfish.* (SE/001/495)
      "They aren't going to take out the Mayfish."

The second type involves *upward* spreading to a verb in a higher clause, as shown in (53–5).

(53) *I don't think some of them ain't no better than the one that don't go to church.* (ANSE/009/743)

(54) *I don't think they ain't gonna ch– not gonna change.* (ANSE/00h/98)

(55) *I didn't think it wasn't no phone then.* (ANSE/030/451)

The surrounding discourse context makes it clear that a single negation is intended in each of these sentences. Crucially, the verb in the higher clause is always *think*, which is a negative-raising verb like *believe, suppose, want*, etc. (Horn 1989). Negative-raising verbs allow negation to move from a lower clause (where it logically belongs) to a higher clause, as shown in (56):

(56)   a.   *I think it **ain't** like old time.*   (ANSE/019/411)

     b.   *I **don't** think they is.*   (ANSE/009/317)

Therefore, in Early AAE, the negative may also be *copied* (rather than *raised*) from the lower clause to the higher clause (but cf. Howe 1995: 98). As such, we can consider it part of the second type of clause-external negative concord with verbs.

In other words, clause-external negative concord to verbs, whether of the first or second type, is shared by Early AAE and select varieties of nonstandard English. Given the conspicuous nature of this feature and the fact that it has not been reported in EBCs, this commonality is best explained by a shared origin for all these varieties.

4.4.5   Summary

Of the three types of negative concord we have examined, two (clause-internal) are shared across all varieties, and one (clause-external) is shared by AAVE and nonstandard English but is unattested in EBCs. We have shown that the categorical use of clause-internal concord to indefinites in contemporary AAVE, argued to be a creole legacy, is in fact a recent and spectacular development. Since there is no distinctly creole linguistic conditioning of variable clause-internal concord, it cannot be a creole diagnostic. The simplest explanation for these findings is a shared origin in Old and Middle English, since it is unlikely that such conditioning would have developed again during the process of creolization.

4.5   Negative Postposing and Negative Inversion

Since negative postposing and inversion are unambiguously English, the creole-origin hypothesis predicts that they should be either absent from Early AAE or present but used in ways that differ from English.

4.5.1   Negative postposing

In English, preverbal negation can be omitted if the VP contains a negative word, as in (57):

Table 4.10   Distribution of negative postposing by verb in Early AAE

	have	47%
	be	26%
	got	6%
Lexical verbs:	*know*	4%
	give	3%
	make	3%
	get, forget, hurt, tell, think, talk, hurt, turn, need	

Total N = 78

(57)   *I have **nowhere** to go.* (versus *I **don't** have anywhere to go.*)

Tottie (1991) found negative postposing in widespread use in her large-scale study of colloquial English, while Déprez (1995a, 1995b) and Winford (p.c.) confirm that negative postposing is generally absent from EBCs.

Negative postposing is used in all three varieties of Early AAE, though to varying degrees: six examples in the ANSE data, 54 in the SE data, and 12 in the ESR. It generally occurs within the same clause and, as table 4.10 shows, with the predicates *be*, as in (58), *have*, as in (59), and *got*, as in (60).

(58)   *There **no** lights on the road.*   (ANSE/032/258)

(59)   *We had **no** home.*   (ESR/008/108)

(60)   *They got **no** hills.*   (SE/007/1155)

Only a few instances of negative postposing are found with other predicates, shown in (61–3).

(61)   *The child **know** nothing about it.*   (ANSE/027/1317)

(62)   *I needs **nobody**.*   (SE/002/476)

(63)   *'give him **none**.*   (ESR/013/233)

The quantitative behavior of negative postposing in Early AAE is remarkably consistent with its behavior in colloquial English: Tottie (1991: 233) reports that it occurs most with *be* and *have* (and, therefore, *got*), just as we find in our data. She also finds (1991) that the lexical verbs involving the most negative postposing are *do*, *know*, *give* and *make*, which the few instances of postposing with lexical verbs in Early AAE also parallel. In other words, negative postposing in Early AAE operates in the same way as in other varieties of English.

4.5.2   Negative inversion

Negative inversion is rare in both Early AAE and nonstandard English, but Labov et al. (1968) found a number of examples in AAVE, as illustrated in (64):

(64)   a.   *Can't nobody tag you then.*   (Labov et al. 1968, ex. 366)

      b.   *Won't nobody catch us.*   (Labov 1972a: 811)

Negative inversion is also found in SWNE (e.g. Feagin 1979), Appalachian English (Wolfram and Christian 1975, 1976) and Ozark English (Christian et al. 1988), as shown in (65) and (66):

(65)   *Didn't nobody get hurt or nothin'.*   (Christian et al. 1988: 169)

(66)   *Wouldn't nobody be out there but jus' what would go with us.*

                                                   (Feagin 1979: 234)

Feagin (1979: 252) also reports the variable use of negative inversion in the upper class of Anniston, Alabama. In contrast, no mention is made of negative inversion in creoles (e.g. Bickerton 1975, 1981, 1984).

Negative inversion is very rare but present in Early AAE: the ANSE data and the ESR each include four unambiguous cases of negative inversion, as illustrated in (67–8), while the SE data have none.

(67)   *Didn' no white people stay in Africa.*   (ESR/012/51)

(68)   *Can't no one get there.*   (ANSE/019/564)

Thus, we conclude that negative inversion was transferred to Early AAE via nonstandard English.

4.6 Discussion and Conclusion

Prompted by claims that negation in contemporary AAVE is a creole diagnostic, our examination of four features of negation in Early AAE, which is likely to have figured among the precursors of contemporary AAVE, demonstrates that these varieties generally parallel each other in the distribution of negative features, suggesting a common grammar of negation. Examples of those few constructions which are not shared, no doubt a result of either individual innovation or regional differences in the models to which the early African Americans were exposed (see Tagliamonte and Smith, this volume), can also be found in SWNE, suggesting that they were part of a common negation system that the Early AAE speakers acquired.

Of more direct pertinence to the creole-origins question is our method, which allowed us to compare both the occurrence and the linguistic conditioning of negative constructions in Early AAE, AAVE, nonstandard varieties of English, and EBCs. Some features, such as clause-internal negative concord to verbs, occur in all comparison varieties. Other features, such as the preference for *ain't* over *have + not*, could conceivably serve as the basis for a creole-origin argument. But features such as *ain't/ be + not* variation and *ain't/ didn't* variation clearly pattern the same both in Early AAE and in nonstandard English. Given the clear parallels in the patterning of some features between Early AAE and varieties of English, and the concomitant absence of any clear parallels between Early AAE and creoles, it is hard to defend the creole-origin argument on the basis of these results.

This conclusion is further supported by the complete absence from EBCs of other features, all of which exist in different varieties of English (African American or otherwise): clause-external negative concord to verbs, negative postposing and negative inversion. Over and above their mere existence, the linguistic conditioning of these features is unambiguously English. As such, no distinct creole behavior is ever observable within the negation system of Early AAE (or, for that matter, contemporary AAVE, at least insofar as this is reported by the studies cited here). Rather, comparison of these results with nonstandard and historical varieties of English argues that the variable patterns in negation in Early AAE can be traced directly to colonial English and, in the case of negative concord, to the very origins of the English language.

In addition, we have been able to show for some negative constructions that their frequent or near-categorical usage in contemporary AAVE is a recent and spectacular development. The categorical use of clause-internal negative concord to indefinites is one such construction. A more general development, the

expansion of *ain't* in AAVE, can be seen in the higher rates of *ain't* in the
have + not and *didn't* environments, and in the variation of *ain't* with *don't*
(probably derived from prior *have/got* variation). These innovations reveal the
danger of relying on a method which does not include detailed comparisons
with each of the putative source varieties: what appears to be the relic of a prior
creole upon investigation turns out to be a recent development. The key result
of our comparison is the discovery that the negation system of Early AAE
displays no distinct or unambiguous creole behavior. This discovery suggests
that, at least as far as negation is concerned, early African Americans simply
learned and spoke the colonial English they were exposed to, apparently without approximation or creolization.

Notes

* The data and analysis presented in this paper are derived from Howe (1995), earlier
versions of which were presented at NWAVE 24 in Philadelphia and at NWAVE
26 in Québec City and appeared as Howe (1997). We thank Don Winford for his
helpful comments on a preliminary version of Howe (1995). Financial support was
provided by the Social Sciences and Humanities Research Council of Canada to the
second author in the form of doctoral fellowship #752–97–1759.

1 Winford appears to have reversed positions on this issue – more recently, he characterizes the negation system in AAVE as "thoroughly nonstandard English in character" (Winford 1998: 109) – though he does not explain what evidence led him to this
reversal.
2 The codes in parentheses identify the corpus, speaker, and location of the token.
Corpora include:

    SE: Samaná English   (Poplack and Sankoff 1987)
    ESR: The Ex-Slave Recordings   (Bailey et al. 1991)
    ANSE: African Nova Scotian English   (Poplack and Tagliamonte 1991)
    SWNE: Southern White Nonstandard English   (Feagin 1979)
    NWNE: Northern White Nonstandard English   (Labov et al. 1968)

3 Winford (p.c.) argues that the "non-English" system in a bisystemic account is not
necessarily a creole system.
4 Also referred to as redundant negation (Ramsey 1892), negative attraction (Jespersen
1917), negative agreement (Labov et al. 1968; Kaplan 1989: 17–18), cumulative
negation (Barber 1997), pleonastic negation (Curme 1977; Martin 1992), negative
spread (den Besten 1986) and (most commonly) double or multiple negation (van der
Wouden 1994: 93).

References

Austin, F. (1984) Double negatives and the eighteenth century. In N. Blake and C. Jones (eds), *English Historical Linguistics: Studies in Development*, CECTAL Conference Papers Series, No. 3, Sheffield: University of Sheffield, 138–49.

Bailey, C.-J. N. (1973) *Variation and Linguistic Theory*. Washington, DC: Centre for Applied Linguistics.

Bailey, G., and Maynor, N. (1989) The divergence controversy. *American Speech*, 64: 12–39.

Bailey, G., Maynor, N., and Cukor-Avila, P. (eds) (1991) *The Emergence of Black English: Texts and Commentary*. Amsterdam: John Benjamins.

Barber, C. (1997) *Early Modern English*. Edinburgh: Edinburgh University Press.

Baugh, J. (1983) *Black Street Speech: Its History, Structure and Survival*. Austin: University of Texas Press.

Baugh, J. (1988) Language and race: Some implications for linguistic science. In F. J. Newmeyer (ed.), *Linguistics: The Cambridge Survey*, Cambridge: Cambridge University Press.

Bickerton, D. (1975) *Dynamics of a Creole System*. New York: Cambridge University Press.

Bickerton, D. (1981) *Roots of Language*. Ann Arbor: Karoma.

Bickerton, D. (1984) The language bioprogram hypothesis. *Behavioral and Brain Sciences*, 7: 173–221.

Blake, R. (1997) Defining the envelope of linguistic variation: The case of "don't count" forms in the copula analysis of African American Vernacular English. *Language Variation and Change*, 9 (1): 57–79.

Bolton, W. F. (1982) *A Living Language: The History and Structure of English*. New York: Random House.

Cheshire, J. (1982) *Variation in an English Dialect: A Sociolinguistic Study*. Cambridge: Cambridge University Press.

Cheshire, J. (1991) Variation in the use of *ain't* in an urban British English dialect. In P. Trudgill and J. K. Chambers (eds), *Dialects of English: Studies in Grammatical Variation*, Singapore: Longman Singapore, 54–73.

Christian, D., Wolfram, W., and Dube, N. (1988) *Variation and Change in Geographically Isolated Communities: Appalachian English and Ozark English*, American Dialect Society, No. 74. Tuscaloosa, AL: University of Alabama Press.

Curme, G. (1977) *A Grammar of the English Language*. Essex, CT: Verbatim.

DeBose, C. E. (1992) Closely-related language varieties in contact. Paper presented at SPCL, Philadelphia, PA.

DeBose, C. E. (1994) A note on *ain't* vs. *didn't* negation in African American Vernacular. *Journal of Pidgin and Creole Languages*, 9 (1): 127–30.

DeBose, C. E., and Faraclas, N. (1993) An Africanist approach to the linguistic study of Black English: Getting to the roots of the tense-aspect-modality and copula systems in Afro-American. In S. S. Mufwene (ed.), *Africanisms in Afro-American Language Varieties*, Athens, GA: University of Georgia Press, 364–87.

den Besten, H. (1986) Double negation and the genesis of Afrikaans. In P. Muysken and N. Smith (eds), *Substrata versus Universals in Creole Languages*, Dordrecht: Foris, 185–230.

Déprez, V. (1995a) A minimalist account of negative concord. Paper presented at the Brown University, Harvard University, and CUNY Syntax Colloquium.

Déprez, V. (1995b) Negative concord in French and Haitian Creole. Paper presented at the University of Ottawa Negation Colloquium.

Fasold, R. W., and Wolfram, W. (1975) Some linguistic features of the Negro dialect. In P. Stoller (ed.), *Black American English: Its Background and Its Usage in the Schools and in Literature*, New York: Dell, 49–89.

Feagin, C. (1979) *Variation and Change in Alabama English: A Sociolinguistic Study of the White Community*. Washington, DC: Georgetown Press.

Fischer, O. (1992) Syntax. In N. Blake (ed.), *The Cambridge History of the English Language, Vol. II: 1066–1476*, Cambridge: Cambridge University Press, 207–408.

Gramley, S., and Pätzold, K.-M. (1992) *A Survey of Modern English*. London: Routledge.

Heim, I. (1984) A note on NP and Downward Entailingness. In C. Jones and P. Sells (eds), *Proceedings of NELS 14*, Amherst, MA: GLSA Linguistics Department.

Holm, J. (1988) *Pidgins and Creoles, Volume 1: Theory and Structure*. Cambridge: Cambridge University Press.

Horn, L. (1989) *A Natural History of Negation*. Chicago: University of Chicago Press.

Howe, D. M. (1995) Negation and the history of African American English. Unpublished M.A. thesis, University of Ottawa.

Howe, D. M. (1997) Negation and the history of African American English. *Language Variation and Change*, 9 (2): 267–94.

Jack, G. B. (1978) Negation in later Middle English prose. *Archivum Linguisticum*, n.s. 9: 58–72.

Jespersen, O. (1917) *Negation in English and Other Languages*. Copenhagen: A. F. Host.

Jespersen, O. (1940) *A Modern English Grammar on Historical Principles, Part V*. Copenhagen: Ejnar Munksgaard.

Kadmon, N., and Landman, F. (1993) Any. *Linguistics and Philosophy*, 16: 353–422.

Kaplan, J. P. (1989) *English Grammar: Principles and Facts*. Englewood Cliffs, NJ: Prentice-Hall.

Labov, W. (1972a) Negative attraction and negative concord in English grammar. *Language*, 48: 773–818.

Labov, W. (1972b) *Sociolinguistic Patterns*. Philadelphia: University of Pennsylvania Press.

Labov, W. (1972c) *Language in the Inner City: Studies in the Black English Vernacular*. Philadelphia: University of Pennsylvania Press.

Labov, W. (1981) Resolving the neogrammarian controversy. *Language*, 57: 267–308.

Labov, W., Cohen, P., Robins, C., and Lewis, J. (1968) *A Study of the Nonstandard English of Negro and Puerto Rican Speakers of New York City*. Final Report, Cooperative Research Project No. 3288, United States Office of Education.

Ladusaw, W. (1992) Expressing negation. In C. Barker and D. Dowty (eds), *SALT II: Proceedings from the Second Conference on Semantics and Linguistic Theory* (Ohio State

University Working Papers in Linguistics, 40), Columbus, OH: Department of Linguistics, Ohio State University, 237–60.

Ladusaw, W. (1995) Semantic interpretation of negative concord. Paper presented at the University of Ottawa Negation Colloquium.

Lawler, J. M. (1974) Ample negatives. *Chicago Linguistic Society*, 10: 357–77.

Martin, S. E. (1992) Topics in the syntax of Nonstandard English. Unpublished Ph.D. dissertation, University of Maryland.

Montgomery, M. B., and Bailey, G. (1986) Introduction. In M. B. Montgomery and G. Bailey (eds), *Language Variety in the South: Perspectives in Black and White*, Tuscaloosa: University of Alabama Press, 1–29.

Nagucka, R. (1978) *Negatively Phrased Utterances in English: An Essay in Some Aspects of Negation against the Historical Background*. Warsaw: Uniwersytetu Jagiellonskiego.

Poplack, S., and Sankoff, D. (1987) The Philadelphia story in the Spanish Caribbean. *American Speech*, 64 (2): 291–314.

Poplack, S., and Tagliamonte, S. (1989) There's no tense like the present: Verbal -*s* inflection in early Black English. *Language Variation and Change*, 1: 47–84.

Poplack, S., and Tagliamonte, S. (1991) African American English in the diaspora: Evidence from old-line Nova Scotians. *Language Variation and Change*, 3: 301–39.

Prince, A., and Smolensky, P. (1993) *Optimality Theory: Constraint Interaction in Generative Grammar*. Rutgers, NJ: RuCCS Technical Report TR-2.

Quirk, R., Greenbaum, S., Leech, G., and Svartvik, J. (1985) *A Comprehensive Grammar of the English Language*. New York: Longman.

Ramsey, S. (1892 [1968]) *The English Language and English Grammar: An Historical Study of the Sources, Development, and Analogies of the Language and of the Principles Governing its Usages*. New York, NY: Haskell House.

Rickford, J. R. (1977) The question of prior creolization of Black English. In A. Valdman (ed.), *Pidgin and Creole Linguistics*, Bloomington: Indiana University Press.

Romaine, S. (1983) Historical linguistics and language change: Progress or decay? *Language in Society*, 12 (2): 223–37.

Sankoff, G. (1980) A quantitative paradigm for the study of communicative competence. In G. Sankoff (ed.), *The Social Life of Language*, Philadelphia: University of Pennsylvania Press, 47–79.

Sankoff, D. (1982) Sociolinguistic method and linguistic theory. In L. J. Cohen, J. Los, H. Pfeiffer, and K. P. Podewski (eds), *Logic, Methodology, Philosophy of Science, VI*, Amsterdam: North Holland, and Warsaw: Polish Scientific, 677–89.

Sankoff, D. (1988) Sociolinguistics and syntactic variation. In F. Newmeyer (ed.), *Linguistics: The Cambridge Survey*, Cambridge: Cambridge University Press, 140–61.

Schneider, E. (1989) *American Earlier Black English: Morphological and Syntactic Variables*. Tuscaloosa: University of Alabama Press.

Sells, P., Rickford, J. R., and Wasow, T. (1996) Variation in negative inversion in AAVE: An Optimality Theoretic approach. In J. Arnold, R. Blake, B. Davidson, S. Schwenter, and J. Solomon (eds), *Sociolinguistic Variation: Data, Theory, and Analysis. Selected Papers from NWAV 23 at Stanford*, Stanford: CSLI Publications, 161–76.

Tottie, G. (1991) *Negation in English Speech and Writing: A Study in Variation*. San Diego, CA: Academic Press.

Traugott, E. C. (1992) Syntax. In R. M. Hogg (ed.), *The Cambridge History of the English Language, Vol. I: The Beginnings to 1066*, Cambridge: Cambridge University Press, 168–289.

Van der Wouden, A. (1994) *Negative Contexts*. Groningen: Rijksuniversiteit Groningen.

Wang, W. (ed.) (1977) *The Lexicon in Phonological Change*. The Hague: Mouton.

Weiner, J., and Labov, W. (1983) Constraints on agentless passives. *Journal of Linguistics*, 19: 29–58.

Weinreich, U., Labov, W., and Herzog, M. (1968) Empirical foundations for a theory of language change. In W. P. Lehman and Y. Malkiel (eds), *Directions for Historical Linguistics: A Symposium*, Austin: University of Texas Press, 95–188.

Weldon, T. (1993) A quantitative analysis of variability in predicate negation in a dialect of African American Vernacular English. Paper presented at NWAVE 22, Ottawa.

Weldon, T. (1994) Variability in negation in African American Vernacular English. *Language Variation and Change*, 6 (3): 359–97.

Winford, D. (1983) A sociolinguistic analysis of negation in Trinidadian English. In L. D. Carrington (ed.), *Studies in Caribbean Language*, Augustine, Trinidad: Society for Caribbean Linguistics.

Winford, D. (1992) Back to the past: The BEV/creole connection revisited. *Language Variation and Change*, 4: 311–57.

Winford, D. (1998) On the origins of African American Vernacular English – A creolist perspective, Part II: Linguistic features. *Diachronica*, 15 (1): 99–154.

Wolfram, W. (1969) *A Sociolinguistic Description of Detroit Negro Speech*. Washington, DC: Centre for Applied Linguistics.

Wolfram, W. (1976) *Appalachian English*. Arlington, VA: Centre for Applied Linguistics.

Wolfram, W. (1991) *Dialects and American English*. Englewood Cliffs, NJ: Prentice-Hall.

Wolfram, W., and Christian, D. (1975) *Sociolinguistic Variables in Appalachian Dialects*, Final report. Washington, DC: National Institute of Education of the Department of Health, Education and Welfare.

Wolfram, W., and Christian, D. (1976) *Appalachian English*. Arlington, VA: Centre for Applied Linguistics.

Wright, J. (1898–1905) *The English Dialect Dictionary: being the complete vocabulary of all dialect words still in use, or known to have been in use during the last two hundred years*. London: Henry Frowde.

5

Old Was, *New Ecology: Viewing English through the Sociolinguistic Filter**

Sali Tagliamonte and Jennifer Smith

5.1 Introduction

One of the most informative constructs which can shed light on the origins and development of languages is the *relic area* (e.g. Anttila 1989: 294; Hock 1986: 442). Such areas, because of their peripheral geographic location or isolated social and/or political circumstances, tend to preserve features typical of earlier stages in the history of a language. The African American diaspora in the late eighteenth and early nineteenth century led to a large-scale exodus of African American ex-slaves out of the US into widely-dispersed geographical locations. Many of the communities they established have remained relatively isolated from mainstream developments up to the present day. This makes the varieties of English spoken in such areas particularly important since a key issue in the debate over the origins and development of African American Vernacular English (AAVE) is to determine the nature of its grammar at earlier points in time. When such communities have been analyzed, however, the findings have been controversial. Research on some communities reports that they retain features of earlier varieties of English (Poplack and Tagliamonte 1989, 1991, 1994, 1996a, forthcoming; Tagliamonte and Poplack 1988), while others are reported to resemble creoles. For example, Singler (1989, 1991, 1993, 1997) found a number of creole-like features in Liberian Settler English which provided evidence for Winford (1993) and Rickford (1997) to posit a prior creolization of AAVE. Although Winford's more recent research points to different conclusions, other scholars such as Hannah (1997) continue to claim that AAVE may have started from an erstwhile creole.

There are a number of possible reasons for these antithetic findings, not the least of which are the issues of what kind of variety the original African Americans spoke, and what their transplanted ecology was like (Singler 1998). Other reasons may stem from methodological inconsistencies and the fact that most investigations have tended to rely on secondary source materials for comparison. Thus, while there are many studies comparing AAVE with creoles, many of these have had to rely on relatively superficial observations, often invoking data that are not fully informative. The same is true of comparisons with English dialects which have predominantly been based on information provided by the dialect literature. Such reports are notoriously selective, not exhaustive, and tend to report what their authors happen to notice, rather than to provide a more reliable structural analysis. Problems associated with this method are highlighted in recent research by Tagliamonte and Poplack (to appear), who demonstrate that although an association of verbal -*s* with habitual aspect had never been explicitly documented in secondary sources, such an association could be shown to be retained among elderly dialect speakers in southwest England. This highlights the importance of studying a primary source, and more importantly, one which has evolved in a context relatively isolated from mainstream developments, i.e. in a relic area.

We submit that a much-needed and logical extension of the research program studying varieties of AAVE in the diaspora is to explore the relationship of these enclaves to comparably isolated communities of speakers of British ethnicity, particularly at the source where many conservative dialect areas perdure – Britain. Therefore, in this chapter we study a dialect of English spoken in Buckie, northern Scotland, and provide a cross-variety comparison with three varieties of English spoken in Nova Scotia, two varieties of Early African American English (Early AAE) spoken in enclaves, and a neighboring rural variety of Nova Scotian Vernacular English (NSVE) whose speakers are of British ancestry. In comparing the varieties spoken by people of African and British descent whose history is rooted in similar sociohistorical settings, we are able to shed new light on the extent to which ethnicity accounts for the linguistic differences between AAVE and other varieties of English. This study contributes to the larger ongoing research programme exploring the contribution of Early AAE to the origins and development of AAVE (see also Poplack and Tagliamonte 1989, 1991, 1994, forthcoming; Tagliamonte 1996; Tagliamonte and Poplack 1988, 1993).

To be relevant, the trans-Atlantic comparison we undertake here must select a robust linguistic feature characteristic of all the communities under investigation. The frequent use of *was* in contexts where contemporary Standard English grammar requires *were*, e.g. *you was*, *we was*, *they was*, as in (1),[1] fulfills this requirement.

2ND PERSON SINGULAR
(1) a. And then you *was* away onto a fishing station. (BCK:c:216.13)[2]

  b. You *wasn't* gonna do it or anything. (GYV:£:21.27)

  c. You *was* in the choir with Melanie and Nellie. (NPR:p:325.15)

1ST PERSON PLURAL
(1) d. And we *was* the only colour family. We *were* – we *were* just surrounded. (GYE:l:1591.7)

  e. We *wasna* getting a house at the time. (BCK:f:72.13)

  f. We *was* sleeping. (GYV:£:50.9)

3RD PERSON PLURAL
(1) g. They *wasn't* prejudiced up there then. (GYE:m:170.290)

  h. They *was* picking up wood and thing. (NPR:q:375.43)

FULL NP PLURAL
(1) i. My feet *was* sticking up and she pulled me feet up. (GYV:*:143.14)

  j. The books *was* different from the slates that we use. (NPR:q:14.16)

  k. Them people *was* good to me. (GYE:l:138.12)

EXISTENTIAL *there*
(1) l. And there *was* nine years between me and my brother. (GYV:¢:51.17)

  m. Took awhile for to get plentiful and *wasn't* many cars. (NPR:S:352.47)

  n. There *was* some Buckie lassies and Finichty lassies gutting. (BCK:b:320)

Although *was/were* variation is only a subset of a broader range of variability in agreement in English,[3] only the past indicative forms (*was/were*) were variable in *all* the datasets under investigation. Furthermore, this variation can be traced to earlier stages in the history of English and is attested in English-based creoles. For these reasons *was/were* variation presents an ideal linguistic candidate for tracking the origins of linguistic features in AAVE.

As far as British English is concerned, a number of internal linguistic constraints are attested in the historical record, including: (i) highly differentiated patterning across grammatical persons, and (ii) a constraint based on the type of subject. In English-based creoles on the other hand, variation between *was* and *were* is said to figure among the earliest changes associated with decreolization. According to Bickerton (1975), *was* appears first as an irregular lexical insertion, while *were* is acquired later in direct proportion to increasing acquisition of Standard English features. This predicts that the use of *were* in a decreolizing variety would be conditioned primarily by extra-linguistic constraints, particularly sensitivity to the standard language. Therefore, there is no reason to expect irregular insertions of *was* or *were* to pattern systematically at the internal linguistic level.

We now turn to a consideration of the sociolinguistic situation represented by the communities under investigation.

5.2   The Communities

The communities may be differentiated on two major criteria: (i) their geographic location, and (ii) the type of ethnic background of their speakers. North Preston, Guysborough Enclave, and Guysborough Village are three separate communities in Nova Scotia, one of the maritime provinces on the east coast of Canada. North Preston and Guysborough Enclave are situated in widely separated and peripheral locations in the province. Both are almost entirely inhabited by the descendants of African Americans. Guysborough Village, on the other hand, is comprised entirely of British-origin speakers who live in Guysborough, the small town near Guysborough Enclave. The last community is Buckie on the far northeast coast of Scotland (see map 5.1).

5.2.1   *Guysborough and North Preston, Nova Scotia*

The African communities in Nova Scotia function as linguistic enclaves, at least in terms of the amount of direct contact they have had with the populations in proximate cities and towns. Even the people living in Guysborough Enclave and Guysborough Village have had little social contact, despite the fact that the communities are situated within several kilometers of each other. Further details of the settlement history, and a detailed description of the sociocultural situation in Nova Scotia, may be found in Poplack and Tagliamonte (1991, 1994, forthcoming).

Map 5.1   Great Britain, showing position of Buckie, Scotland, in relation to London

5.2.2   *Buckie, Scotland*

Buckie is a traditional fishing community. It has had a long history of cultural cohesiveness, with entire families directly or indirectly taking part in the fishing trade. Unlike similar rural areas in Scotland, Buckie has not suffered from de-population, as the local economy is capable of supporting the community. On the other hand, in-migration has been extremely limited, resulting in a stable population (approximately 8,000), over the last 30 years. In this context, a tradition of endogamy has been effectively maintained up to the present day. The contributions of these three factors account for its peripheral status. Further details of the history and sociocultural situation in Scotland may be found in Smith (in preparation) and Smith and Tagliamonte (1998).

5.2.3   Tapping the vernacular

The primary goal of the fieldwork in each of the target locations was essentially the same – to collect a representative sample of the vernacular norms of each community. In each case the speakers had been born and raised in the community in question and represented the oldest living generation at the time of fieldwork.

The sample, depicted in table 5.1, consists of 30 speakers, all over 70 years of age and divided between men and women.[4] The tape-recorded conversations, which range from 1 to 3 hours, include discussions about local traditions, narratives of personal experience, group interactions and local gossip. With the exception of Guysborough Village, all were conducted by in-group community members.

The occupations of the speakers, who were all retired at the time of the interviews, had been related to traditional or service industries of the community. In Buckie, all the men were fishermen. In North Preston and Guysborough, they had mostly been employed as labourers. Most of the women were house-wives, although in Buckie some had worked in the fishing industry, and in the Nova Scotian enclaves some had been domestics. Level of education among the informants ranged from almost none to 9 years, with most speakers falling into the lower range. The sociological profiles of all the speakers are similar in that their social circles were generally confined to the community in question and involved both work and leisure activities, typical of high-density networks (Milroy 1980). Therefore, although the samples are relatively small for each

Table 5.1   Distribution of speaker samples

Buckie		North Preston		Guysborough Enclave		Guysborough Village	
M	F	M	F	M	F	M	F
4	4	3	3	3	3	4	6

community, the speakers were specifically selected to represent the local community norms.

All four communities are clearly identified by the monolithic ethnic composition of their inhabitants. In North Preston and Guysborough Enclave, the speakers are of African descent; in Guysborough Village and Buckie, the speakers are of British ancestry. These facts provide a unique opportunity to conduct a cross-variety comparison in which ethnic heritage (African American versus British) and geographic location (Canada versus Britain) of the communities are their primary differences, while, with the possible exception of Guysborough Village, they are relatively similar with respect to their peripherality vis-à-vis mainstream populations.

5.3   Sociohistorical Connections

A cross-variety comparison is relevant only insofar as we can establish whether, and to what extent, the varieties under investigation have had any sociohistorical relevance to one another. In the specific case at hand, what relationship is there between the variety of English spoken in Buckie, northern Scotland, and the Early AAE found in North Preston and Guysborough Enclave and the NSVE in Guysborough Village, all in Nova Scotia, Canada? In the sections that follow, we outline some basic facts and relate these to the communities under investigation.

5.3.1   *African and British populations into Nova Scotia via the US*

All three Nova Scotian communities are almost entirely populated with the descendants of migrants to Nova Scotia from the United States in the late eighteenth and early nineteenth century. As detailed earlier in Poplack and Tagliamonte (1991), the first African American input to Nova Scotia was at the end of the American Revolutionary War, when Loyalists – both African and British – were granted lands in Canada. However, most of the African American cohort were from the southern US colonies (Walker 1992: 5). The British Loyalists, on the other hand, came primarily from the north (e.g. New York, Massachusetts) (van Tyne 1902).[5]

Settlers from both ethnic groups were granted land in Guysborough County. While the British Loyalists were given town lots, the African Loyalists were allotted land in the outlying areas (Winks 1971). This unequal distribution of supplies and land accounts for the present-day geographic setting of Guysborough Enclave several kilometers outside the village of Guysborough.

The second wave of African Americans into Nova Scotia came from the Refugee Slave migration in 1815. These migrants were primarily field hands from the southern colonies. As detailed in Poplack and Tagliamonte (1991), the speakers represented in the North Preston corpus are the descendants of these migrants.

Therefore, the three Nova Scotia communities represent two different waves of migration. More importantly, they represent two different inputs. The origins of both of the African American migrations can be traced to the southern US, but the British Loyalists came predominantly from the north.

Next, we shall consider the settlement patterns into the US prior to the migration of these settlers to Nova Scotia in order to elucidate their original source.

5.3.2   British populations into the US

The first migrations into the United States from Britain were between 1629 and 1641 and these were entirely composed of Puritans from East Anglia. Their point of debarkation was extremely localized, i.e. New England, and their numbers were relatively few (at most 20,000) (Fischer 1989). The next wave of migration came from the south of England to Virginia between 1642 and 1675. British colonists from the North Midlands settled in Delaware in 1675, and continued to migrate there for the next fifty years. However, it was not until the eighteenth century (1717–75) that mass migration from Britain took place (Bailyn 1986; Bailyn and DeWolfe 1986; Fischer 1989). During this period nearly a quarter of a million people migrated to North America. Unlike the migrants that had gone before, the vast majority of these people originated from entirely different geographic locations in Britain – the north of Ireland, the lowlands of Scotland, and the northern counties of England, areas referred to as the "border lands" (Fischer 1989). Moreover, in contrast to the early migrants, who had migrated out of religious choice, the eighteenth-century migrations were motivated by economic need and material betterment, and the people were generally from the working classes (Fischer 1989: 611). As illustrated in figure 5.1, these groups exponentially outnumbered any other in-coming population groups from earlier decades.[6]

Figure 5.1 also highlights the extent to which the different geographic origins of speakers in Britain can be correlated with specific locations in the US. The point of debarkation of British emigrants from the "border lands" was the American "backcountry," which included southwestern Pennsylvania, western parts of Maryland and Virginia, North and South Carolina, Georgia, Kentucky,

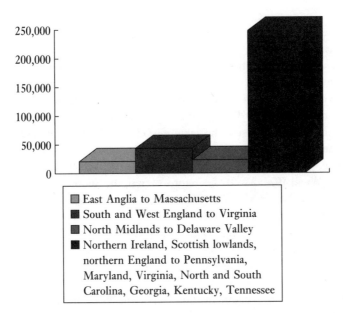

Figure 5.1 Total migration from regions in the UK to regions in the US, 1629–1775

and Tennessee (Fischer 1989). By 1790, they accounted for more than half of the total population of the southern colonies. Moreover, in most counties they represented close to 90 percent of the total number of European migrants. Indeed, Fischer (1989: 635) claims that these emigrants from "North Britain" enjoyed a "cultural hegemony." Thus, in broad terms, settlement of the American colonies was actually highly circumscribed in the seventeenth and eighteenth centuries. British southerners went to the northern US and British "northerners"[7] went to the southern US.

5.3.3 African populations into the US

The first African slaves were brought into the North American British colonies in 1619; however, it was not until the eighteenth century that slaves were imported on a mass scale. As pointed out by Rickford (1997), the proportion of blacks to whites in the main regions of the US differed drastically. Africans constituted only 3 percent and 7 percent of the population in the northern and middle colonies respectively in 1740, but exponentially larger proportions in the South. Crucially, for our purposes, the geographic regions in which the African populations were most numerous are precisely the same geographic regions in which the immigrants from the northern British "borderlands" were most numerous.

Much has been said of the varying ratios of Africans to Europeans during the formative period of the American South (Mufwene, this volume; Rickford 1998). What is not often highlighted however is the fact that the incoming populations of northern British speakers increased along with the African populations during precisely the same period (Wood 1974). Indeed, in most locales the white populations actually outnumbered the blacks by a significant proportion, particularly in the most heavily populated areas (Virginia and North Carolina) (Wood 1974: 38–9). Therefore, even in the South it is logical that the language of the African slaves may have been influenced by the English dialects spoken at the time. In the few cases where the Africans represented a majority in the eighteenth century (i.e. South Carolina),[8] it is still apparent that the white populations increased along with the Africans. Thus, in any southern colony at the time, the predominant British populations were speakers of northern dialects of English.[9]

These historical facts highlight three important observations:

1. Migrants from the more northern regions of Britain came to the US during the same time period as the Africans and both populations increased in parallel.

2. British "northerners" and Africans alike went predominantly to the southern colonies.

3. The vast majority of all British migrants during this time period were speakers of northern dialects of English.

5.3.4 Connections

Thus, while we cannot make direct historical links between Buckie[10] and the Nova Scotian communities, we can establish that the available linguistic models present in the southern US during the time before the African and British ancestors of our speakers migrated to Nova Scotia were overwhelmingly northern (see also, e.g., Montgomery 1989a, 1997).

Given the predictions of the Founder Principle (Mufwene 1996: 122–3), one of the factors influencing the linguistic features to emerge in a contact vernacular is the frequency and nature of structural features of the varieties spoken by the dominant population groups, as these have "selective advantage over competing alternatives." If so, then features of the northern dialect regions of Britain would have been favored in the colonial southern United States.

The fact that British northerners and African Americans can be situated in the southern American colonies during the colonization period, and further that African American populations from this very locale subsequently migrated to Nova Scotia, leads us to posit the following hypotheses regarding the linguistic features in North Preston, Guysborough Enclave, Guysborough Village, and Buckie:

1. The three Nova Scotian varieties may pattern according to characteristics of their differing sociohistorical inputs. Early AAE in North Preston and Guysborough Enclave may reflect a linguistic system comparable to the dialects of English spoken by the British northerners in the southern US colonies. If so, then this may be visible in the details of the linguistic patterning of features in North Preston and Guysborough Enclave, making the two African Nova Scotian varieties similar to each other as well as to the variety of English in Buckie, but not NSVE.

However, given that some researchers contend that "creole varieties were a significant mix of the early contact situation, particularly in the south" (Rickford 1998),

2. Early AAE may have been impervious to the dialects of English spoken by the broader population in the American South and instead may embody the creole-like system said to be typical of people of African descent in North America and the Caribbean. If so, then this may be visible in the details of the linguistic patterning of features in North Preston and Guysborough Enclave, making the two African varieties similar to each other and unlike either Buckie or NSVE.

3. By the same ethnic-identity argument, NSVE and the variety spoken in Buckie may embody patterns which *contrast* with Early AAE either in North Preston and/or in Guysborough Enclave.

4. Of course, Early AAE, NSVE and the variety of English in Buckie may each be unique. If so, they will exhibit divergent linguistic patterns.

Having provided this sociohistorical perspective and its possible ramifications to the emergent varieties in the southern colonial context, as well as a summary of the enclave-like conditions under which both the African Nova Scotian enclaves and Buckie have evolved subsequently, we now establish a time-depth perspective on the use of *was* in the English language before the mass migration into the US. This will answer the crucial question of what the preterit indicative paradigm of *be* was like at that time.

5.4   Historical Precursors of *was*

In the Middle English period a plethora of different variants were in use in the preterit indicative paradigm of the verb *be*, comprising numerous variants in vowel quality, and other variations in the inflectional morphology of the verb. This is amply attested in most accounts of the Middle English period where use of *was* in contexts where contemporary Standard English prescribed *were* was often described as quite frequent (Curme 1977; Jespersen 1954; Pyles 1964; Visser 1970).

5.4.1   Grammatical person

Table 5.2 illustrates the inventory of preterit indicative forms of *be* reported in Forsström (1948), which were culled from a large number of historical texts selected to represent the different geographical regions in Britain.

Use of *was* in 1st and 3rd person contexts was uniform across regions, but in the 2nd person singular it varied according to geographic location. The southern regions of Britain mirrored contemporary standard English norms – the preterit

Table 5.2   Survey of forms of the verb *to be* in Middle English (Forsström 1948)

Preterit indicative	South	Midlands	Northeast, North
1st, 3rd sg	*wes, was*	*was, wes*	*was, wes*
2nd sg	*were, ware, were*	*was* [West Midlands only], *wore, ware*	*was*
Plural	*were(n), ware(n)*	*wore(n), ware(n)*	*wore(n), were(n), ware(n), war(e), were(e)*

indicative was *were* with all the plural personal pronouns (*we, you, they*) as well as 2nd person singular (*thou*). In the West Midlands, a variable system existed: both *was* and *were* were used with 2nd person singular. In the north and northeast, however, *was* was employed almost exclusively with 2nd person singular,[11] as in (2), extracted from northern texts of the Middle English period (Forsström 1948).[12] Moreover, this pattern continued into Early Modern English, as in (3).[13]

(2) a. When *þou was* bowne with a brande my body to shende. (*The Wars of Alexander* ca. 1450: 870)[14]
         "When you were ready with a sword to injure my body."

     b. Caym, Caym, *thou was* wode. (*The Towneley Plays* ca. 1450: 350)
         "Cain, Cain, you were mad."

     c. *Was þou* not at me riȝt now? (*Cursor Mundi* ca. 1300: 3727)
         "Were you not with me just now?"

     d. Ioseph *þou was* mi ioi allan. (*Cursor Mundi* ca. 1300: 4221)
         "Joseph, you alone were my joy."

(3) a. He wreitt to me that ye *ves* in Edinburgh for sick occasiounes. (*Letters of Duntreath*, 1609)

     b. I was glad to hear yesterday that yow *was* come into this country. (*Letters of Duntreath*, 1741)

5.4.2 Type of subject

Perhaps the most famous historical constraint operating on this variation in northern dialects involves a combination of the type of subject of the verb and the adjacency of the subject and verb to each other (Montgomery 1994; Murray 1873). We quote directly from Murray (1873):

> When the subject is a noun, adjective, interrogative or relative pronoun, or when the verb and subject are separated by a clause, the verb takes the termination *-s* in all persons. (Murray 1873: 211)

The past indicative paradigm was included in this stipulation:

> the analogs of the other verbs, in which a form identical with the 3rd pers. sing. was used in the plural in the absence of the pronoun, led to the uses of es, is, in

like cases for ar, er, though only as an alternative form: **in the same way** *was,* *wes,* **intruded upon** *wer, war,* **in the past tense.**   (our emphasis)

Contrastive use of *was* with Full NPs[15] versus plural pronouns is illustrated in (4), where the form *was* appears after Full NPs,[16] as in (4a), but *were* is used after the pronoun *they,* as in (4b), and *we,* as in (4c). Examples are from the Middle English and Early Modern English period.

(4) a.   The bernis both *wes* basit of the sicht.   ("King Hart", Douglas, 1475–1522)

  b.   They *wer* informed that my brother William his soun, should be a ward.   (*Letters of Duntreath,* 1627)

  c.   For ve *ver* all in the mill vuirt.   (*Letters of Duntreath,* 1629)

Secondly, if the subject was separated from the verb (either by one word or by an entire clause), then all verbs ended in *-s,* regardless of whether they were pronouns or not. The effect of non-adjacency may be observed in (5):

(5) a.   They [toke shyppynge and sayled to Dover and] *was* there by noone. (ca. 1523–5, Ld Berners, Froiss III, 357)

  b.   Thousands and thousands [at that banquet] *was* spent.   (ca. 1569, Preston, Cambises (in Manley, Spec. II) 199, 949)

Although Murray describes this as a "Scotch usage," he equates it with the general northern dialect of Britain from the thirteenth century (Murray 1873: 212). However, the favoring effect of plural NPs apparently spread southward. Indeed, the great number of examples of *was* with plural nouns in the sixteenth and seventeenth centuries reported in Visser (1970: 71–2), attests to the pervasiveness of this pattern in all areas of Britain.

5.4.3   Existentials

Another feature of English during this period was the use of *was* in plural existential constructions. This is attested as far back as the Old English period (Forsström 1948: 207; Quirk and Wrenn 1960; Visser 1970), as in (6).

(6) a.   There *was* many Dukes, Erles and Barons.   (Ld Berners, Huon 2, 22, 1533)

b.   And þere *was* in þat tyme many gode holy men and holy heremytes.
(ca. 1400, Mandev. 30, 30) (examples from Visser 1970)

However, this use was not any more frequent than other uses of *was* from this
early period (Visser 1970), and was not geographically delimited.

5.4.4   Summary

In sum, use of *was* where contemporary Standard English requires *were* was a
prominent feature of British English dialects from at least the Middle English
period, perhaps even as far back as Old English (Brunner 1970; Forsström
1948; Mossé 1952). Two internal conditioning factors may be extrapolated from
the literature:

1.   *Was* occurred more often with plural NPs than with pronouns.   (Murray
1873; Visser 1970)

2.   *Was* was used almost exclusively in 2nd person singular in the north, while
southern dialects used *were*.   (Brunner 1970; Forsström 1948; Mossé 1952)

The fact that both tendencies were robust features of British English during the
period which pre-dates the migrations into colonial United States provides us
with an excellent operational tool to explore the origins of the contemporary
varieties under investigation.

5.5   Contemporary Research on *Was*

In light of this historical variation between *was* and *were*, it is not surprising to
find numerous contemporary reports of *was/were* variation in Britain, the United
States, and elsewhere (e.g. Cheshire 1982; Christian et al. 1988; Feagin 1979;
Hazen 1996; Montgomery 1989b; Schilling-Estes and Wolfram 1994).

5.5.1   Grammatical person

Use of *was* is reported with all the plural pronouns in one dialect or another
(Britain forthcoming; Cheshire 1982; Eisikovits 1991; Feagin 1979; Milroy and

Milroy 1993). The examples in (7) and (8) show that 2nd person singular, 1st and 3rd person plural may all appear with *was*, both in contemporary dialects and in Early AAE, NSVE and Buckie. However, very few studies consider whether or not there is differential use of *was* across the grammatical paradigm.

(7)   a.   You *was* with me, *wasn't* you?   (Southern Britain, Reading; Cheshire 1982: 44)

      b.   We *was* in an ideal place for it.   (Southern United States, Alabama; Feagin 1979: 204)

      c.   They *was* really friendly.   (Australia; Eisikovits 1991: 250)

(8)   a.   So if you *was* catched, oh-me.   (BCK:g:975.25)

      b.   We *wasn't* allowed to do that.   (NPR:p:24)

      c.   They *was* pretty strict on to us.   (GYE:i:319.5)

5.5.2   *Type of subject*

The contemporary literature reveals that plural NPs can appear with *was* (Christian et al. 1988; Eisikovits 1991; Feagin 1979; Schilling-Estes and Wolfram 1994; Wolfram and Sellers forthcoming), as in (9). Where frequencies for NPs and the plural pronoun *they* are reported separately, it can be observed that NPs have more *was* than pronouns (Feagin 1979; Schilling-Estes and Wolfram 1994; Wolfram and Sellers forthcoming).[17] Compare (10) from the corpora under investigation.

(9)   a.   Logs, sticks and rocks *was* rolling.   (Ozark and Appalachian English; Christian et al. 1988: 114)

      b.   The doors *was* closed and everything.   (Hyde County, North Carolina; Wolfram and Sellers forthcoming)

(10)   a.   War time weddings *was* all called fae the North-Church. (BCK:a:1202)

       b.   My prayers *was* always answered.   (GYV:£:37.22)

       c.   Them two big dogs *was* here.   (NPR:q:586.9)

5.5.3 Existentials

There are frequent reports in the contemporary literature of the robust use of *was* in plural existential constructions, as in (11) (Christian et al. 1988; Eisikovits 1991; Feagin 1979; Montgomery 1989b). This patterning is reported regardless of geographic location, rural or urban status, or social characteristics of the speakers (Atwood 1953; Feagin 1979; Meechan and Foley 1994; Tagliamonte 1998).[18] Compare (12) from the corpora under investigation.

(11) a. There *was* about twenty somethin' boys. (Feagin 1979: 207)

     b. . . . to see if there *was* any inhabitants. (Christian et al. 1988: 114)

     c. There *was* three little kids in there. (Eisikovits 1991: 251)

     d. There *was* lots and lots of pubs that have been up and down. (Tagliamonte 1998)

(12) a. There *was* no snow ploughs then. (GYV:S:4.13)

     b. After ten or eleven mile there *was* places you could shoot your nets. (BCK:b:16.32)

     c. There really *was* ghosts here. (NPR:S:197.74)

     d. There *was* seven. (GYE:S:396.6)

5.5.4 A negation effect

In the process of conducting this analysis we also found that the distinction between negative as opposed to affirmative contexts, as in (13), exerted a strong effect on the realization of *was*.[19]

(13) a. You *wasn't* allowed to use their toilets. (NPR:p:367.51)

     b. They *wasn't* in no comas. (NPR:t:1118.49)

This suggests that negation may have been another internal constraint on the use of *was* in contexts of standard *were*, although it is not, to our knowledge, mentioned either in the historical literature or in the contemporary dialect literature.

5.5.5   Summary

The cumulative findings from contemporary research demonstrate the pervasiveness of *was* in contexts of contemporary standard *were*, at least in relatively insular dialects. While there is little information as to how this use is distributed across the grammatical paradigm, two internal conditioning factors may be extrapolated from the literature:

1. *Was* tends to occur more often with plural NPs than pronouns.   (Feagin 1979; Schilling-Estes and Wolfram 1994; Wolfram and Sellers forthcoming)

2. *Was* is very highly favored in plural existential constructions.   (Christian et al. 1988; Eisikovits 1991; Feagin 1979; Montgomery 1989b)

  In the remainder of this chapter, we present a methodologically consistent cross-variety comparison of *was*, in which we test the contribution of all these internal factors. In addition, we consider the difference between male and female speakers as a means to determine the extent to which the use of *was* may be patterning according to extra-linguistic pressures in the communities.

5.6   Results

5.6.1   Distributional analysis

Figure 5.2 shows the overall distribution of *was* in contexts of Standard English *were* in Early AAE, NSVE and the variety spoken in Buckie, Scotland. The rates of *was* range from a high of 67 percent in the Early AAE spoken in Guysborough Enclave, to a low of 30 percent in NSVE, Guysborough Village. Notice that no dividing line can be drawn between communities with respect to overall frequency of *was*, nor geographical location, nor ethnicity of the population. Early AAE, as spoken in Guysborough Enclave, one of the African isolates in Nova Scotia, and Buckie, the Scottish fishing town, stand together in having higher rates of *was*. Indeed, the varieties of English with British ancestry are interspersed with the African samples.

  However, overall frequencies such as those in figure 5.2 obscure internal linguistic patterns which may provide clues to the origins and function of *was*. Therefore we turn to an analysis of the data using the logistic regression capabilities of the variable rule program (Rand and Sankoff 1990) in order to

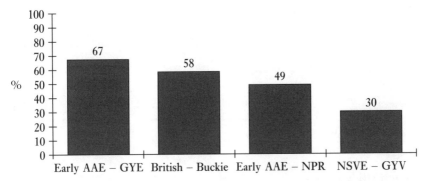

Figure 5.2   Overall distribution of *was* in contexts of Standard English *were* in four communities

model the combined effect of GRAMMATICAL PERSON, the TYPE OF SUBJECT constraint, and the effect of NEGATION. An important methodological advantage gained by using this procedure is that it permits assessment of precisely how each of the factors are contributing to the process under investigation and the magnitude of each of the individual factors (Sankoff 1982).

Because overall rates of *was* and *were* vary across communities, we stress here the *patterns* across the independent internal linguistic factors. Our hypothesis is that if a variable phenomenon is influenced by the same linguistic features (e.g. grammatical person and number) across varieties, and if specific categories of these features of interest to us (e.g. 2nd person singular) are ranked similarly across varieties, then this will be evidence that they share a similar grammar (see also Poplack and Tagliamonte 1989, 1994, 1996a, 1996b).

5.6.2   Multivariate analysis

Table 5.3 shows the results of four independent variable rules analyses of the contribution of factors selected as significant to the probability of *was* in all the communities. As is standard, higher numbers can be interpreted as favoring *was*, whereas lower ones disfavor it. The higher the figure, the greater the contribution of that factor to the use of *was*.[20]

The results for GRAMMATICAL PERSON make clear that some communities highly favor the use of *was* in certain contexts. First, consider plural existential constructions. The factor weights across the board reveal that this context highly favors the use of *was* across all communities. Although this is a pan-community effect, the relationship of existential contexts to the rest of the

Table 5.3 Four independent variable rule analyses of the contribution of factors selected as significant to the probability of *was* (factor groups selected as significant in bold)

		Early AAE		
Community	**BCK**	**GYE**	**NPR**	**NSVE**
Country	UK	CDA	CDA	CDA
Ethnicity	(British)	(African)	(African)	(British)
Corrected mean:	.84	.65	.52	.43
Total N:	302	237	230	276
Grammatical person				
Plural existential	.69	.77	.60	.78
2nd p. singular	.70	.58	.65	.11
3rd p. plural	.48	.42	.54	.45
1st p. plural	.36	.51	.37	.09
Type of subject				
Full NP	81%	.60	.61	33%
Pronoun	KO = 0%	.43	.43	KO = 0%
Negation				
Negative	KO = 100%	.92	.95	.44
Affirmative	58%	.39	.36	.51
Sex				
Female	.71	.53	.45	.52
Male	.38	.46	.54	.48

grammatical persons differs markedly between NSVE and the other varieties. The propensity of *was* is relatively high nearly everywhere in Buckie and Early AAE, both in Guysborough Enclave and in North Preston, while a contrast between existential contexts on one hand, and non-existential contexts on the other, may only be observed in NSVE. In this variety, frequent use of *was* in existential constructions as opposed to other grammatical subjects is similar to reports for contemporary varieties. However, this pattern differs markedly from reports in the historical literature where existentials, although among the contexts for use of *was*, are never singled out as behaving idiosyncratically from other grammatical contexts (see also Tagliamonte 1998; Visser 1970).

Setting aside the existential contexts, the probability of *was* in Buckie and Early AAE patterns according to a very similar hierarchy – 2nd person singular > 3rd person plural > 1st person plural.[21] Most notably, *was* is highly favored in 2nd person singular, with factor weights of 0.70, 0.58, 0.65 respectively representing the highest factor weight of all in Buckie and Early AAE in North Preston, and the second highest in Guysborough Enclave. This pattern clearly sets these communities off from Guysborough Village, where the contribution of 2nd person singular is one of the lowest factor weights. Recall that this is the same context which favored *was* in northern varieties in the Middle English period (see table 5.2).

A parallel constraint hierarchy can be observed across all the varieties with respect to TYPE OF SUBJECT. In each case, NP subjects exhibit a higher probability of use of *was* than with *they*. Thus, every variety retains precisely the same direction of effect attested all over Britain in the historical record, although in Buckie and NSVE it is categorical.[22]

The effect of NEGATION is consistent across Buckie and Early AAE in North Preston and Guysborough Enclave: the *was* variant is favored in negative, as opposed to affirmative contexts. In Buckie this is categorical and it is near categorical in Early AAE. In contrast, NSVE has little to differentiate either affirmative or negative – 0.51 versus 0.44 – and indeed, the direction of effect is the opposite of that of the other communities.

Finally, we note the consistent SEX effect across all varieties (except Early AAE in North Preston), showing that females actually favor the nonstandard variant *was* over males, an effect which is statistically significant only in Buckie. This direction of effect reveals that the use of *was* is not stigmatized, and suggests that it is an inherent part of each of the varieties.

5.7 Discussion

We have described in some detail the historical and contemporary literature on the use of *was* in contexts where contemporary Standard English requires *were* and suggested that this linguistic variable provides a useful tool for the investigation of cross-variety linguistic behavior. The findings we have presented allow the following observations.

First and foremost, use of *was* in all the varieties we have investigated here, including Early AAE, is the result of systematic internal linguistic conditioning. This argues against it being an alien intrusion in the Early AAE grammar as might be expected from an irregular lexical insertion in a creole system, as per hypothesis 2 in section 5.3.4. Moreover, there is no evidence that it is disfavored by female speakers as might be expected of a socially stigmatized variable sensitive to pressure from the standard language. Indeed, sex is not selected as significant in either of the African enclaves. For both these reasons, it can hardly be seen as the result of decreolization.

Table 5.4   Comparison of similarities and differences in internal linguistic features across communities

	BCK	Early AAE		NSVE
		GYE	NPR	
2nd person singular	✔	✔	✔	✘
NP > PRONOUN	✔	✔	✔	✔
Negation	✔	✔	✔	✘

In section 4, we detailed how at least some of the set of constraints on the use of *was* can be reconstructed from historical accounts of the history of the English language. Two prominent internal linguistic constraints emerge. The first is associated with British dialects more generally – full NP subjects favor *was*. This effect is observed across all the varieties.[23] The second is associated with northern British dialects only – *was* favored in 2nd person singular. These effects are observed in Buckie and Early AAE in North Preston and Guysborough Enclave. This argues for *was* being not only a viable part of the grammar, but one whose patterning can be tracked back in time, in this case to British English dialects (see also Montgomery 1994: 94).

A third constraint we considered was the effect of NEGATION – *was* is favored in negative contexts. This effect is also consistent across Buckie, and Early AAE in North Preston and Guysborough Enclave. The fact these communities also share this NEGATION effect suggests that this too may have been one of the set of conditioning factors on *was/were* variation in earlier varieties of British English, despite the fact that it is not mentioned in the historical dialect literature (see Tagliamonte and Poplack to appear).

These similarities and differences are summarized in table 5.4, where the shared patterns are represented by check marks and the differences by Xs. Buckie and Early AAE in Guysborough Enclave and North Preston share all three internal linguistic measures, while NSVE shares only one. How can this be explained?

Recall that our overview of migrations into Nova Scotia during the late eighteenth and early nineteenth century revealed that the ancestors of the Nova Scotians, both African and British, had gone to Nova Scotia by way of the American colonial context, whose major population input was from Britain. Thus, they had all been in a situation where they may have acquired British patterns. The fact that they all retain the favoring effect of plural NPs, which was pervasive in Britain in the sixteenth and seventeenth centuries, is consistent with this general scenario.

Further examination of the British and African migrations into the United States during the eighteenth century revealed that speakers of northern varieties of British English were in the majority in the southern American colonies during the time that African slaves were imported *en masse* into the same area (section 5.3.2). As the Founder Principle predicts, we suggest that this predisposed the varieties which emerged from this context to select linguistic patterns typical of the northern regions of Britain, particularly since the population groups from these areas were greater in number than the Africans in most locales, and had relatively more prestige.

Given this background, it is not surprising that Early AAE exhibits the favoring effect of 2nd person singular which is typical both of the variety in Buckie and other northern varieties of British English. Thus, the unexpected and consistent parallels between Buckie and the African Nova Scotian English enclaves become interpretable if we think of all of them as *retaining* conservative features of northern varieties of British English.

NSVE on the other hand, whose speakers' ancestors originated in the northern United States, came from a geographic location that was settled primarily by migrations from the southern regions of Britain. The speakers of these dialects would surely have had the favoring effect of plural NPs, since this effect is attested all over Britain, but not the patterning of *was* with 2nd person singular subjects typical of the north. These are precisely the results displayed in table 5.4.

We conclude that the use of *was* in Early AAE is the synchronic remnant of older "border land" patterns, which would have embodied both the favoring effect of 2nd person singular *and* the favoring effect of plural NPs.

Finally, what is perhaps most important about these findings is that they raise doubts about the extent to which ethnicity is the basic underlying factor which best accounts for linguistic differences between AAVE and other varieties of North American English. If it was, then why would these African American enclaves in Nova Scotia, Canada, so closely resemble a northern Scottish fishing town? The fact that they differ in ethnic background, but are similar with respect to their status as relic areas, suggests that the differences between varieties have more to do with the socio-demographic conditions under which they evolved in the first place and the sociocultural conditions which have brought them to the present day. This could not be more clearly demonstrated than in the quantitative details of linguistic variation we have shown here, which do indeed "preserve linguistic history over several centuries and several continents" (Labov 1980: xvii).

Table 5.5 Total numbers per cell in each community, including knockouts

	BCK UK (British)	GYE CDA (African)	NPR CDA (African)	NSVE CDA (British)
Total N:	302	237	230	276
Grammatical person				
Plural existential	54	28	14	128
2nd p. singular	45	25	21	29
3rd p. plural	72	132	125	84
1st p. plural	131	52	70	35
Type of subject				
Full NP	72	54	47	84
Pronoun	118	78	71	125
Negation				
Negative	15	36	39	25
Affirmative	405	201	191	251
Sex				
Female	106	130	97	127
Male	196	107	133	149

Notes

* We gratefully acknowledge the financial support of the Economic and Social Research Council (ESRC) of Britain for grants to Tagliamonte (R000221842) and Smith (R00429734633). We thank David Britain, Salikoko Mufwene, Richard Ogden, and Anthony Warner for very helpful comments on earlier versions of this manuscript.

1 No 2nd person plural contexts existed in the data.
2 Codes in parentheses refer to the community, speaker identification, and transcript line number of the utterance. The communities in Nova Scotia are North Preston (NPR) and Guysborough Enclave (GYE), the ANSE locales, and Guysborough Village (GYV), a sample of Nova Scotian Vernacular English (NSVE). In Scotland the community is Buckie (BCK).
3 Variation in present indicative forms of *be*, e.g. *you is*, *we is*, *they is*, as well as *-s* variation on other verbs, e.g. *you goes*, *we goes*, *they goes*, also exist in some dialects.

4   The speech samples we analyzed in this study are actually small subsets of a much larger body of material (see Poplack and Tagliamonte 1991, forthcoming; Smith in preparation).

5   Some of the British settlers had come from North and South Carolina and Georgia, however their numbers were minimal (approximately 7 percent) (Troxler 1974).

6   We note that the historical record is not entirely consistent in its estimates of the size of migration waves from Britain, which sometimes reveal discrepancies in estimates in the magnitude of 300,000 persons over the same 50-year period (Fischer 1989: 609).

7   We use the term "northern" to refer to the emigrants from Scotland, northern Ireland and northern England.

8   In South Carolina the race distribution is skewed by the extreme disproportion of black and white populations on the coastal rice fields (generally 9 to 1 in the eighteenth century) (Wood 1989). As elsewhere, whites were the majority in the hinterlands (Mufwene 1996: 96, 99, 109).

9   The north of England and Scotland come under the more general dialect of Northumbria in the historical literature (Aitken 1979; Murray 1873: 6). Indeed, it is important to keep in mind that the border between Scotland and northern England is a political, rather than linguistic, divide. Moreover, there is a strong Scottish influence in northern Ireland (Montgomery 1989a).

10 While it is true that migrants to North America did not originate as far north as the present-day town of Buckie, this is due to the fact that the population of the Moray Firth coast in general was very sparse at this time. More crucial for our purposes is the fact that the people of Buckie speak a Lowland Scots dialect (Murray 1873: 29) which is thus representative of the dialect region of relevance.

11 Indeed, the only exception to this pattern found by Forsström (1948: 214) occurs in a rhymed position and thus cannot be taken as a counter-example. If so, then there are, in fact, *no* exceptions to the pattern in this early body of northern materials, i.e. the use of *was* with 2nd person singular was categorical.

12 Interestingly, the favoring context of 2nd person singular has a parallel in the development of the present indicative paradigm. In northern varieties of English the -*s* ending is thought to have arisen due to influence from a Germanic verbal inflection in the same grammatical person (Holmqvist 1922) (see also discussion in Stein 1986).

13 In the late sixteenth century, a *was/were* distinction is said to have arisen in the south differentiating 2nd person singular, which was marked with *was*, and 2nd person plural, which was marked by *were* (Pyles and Algeo 1993) mirroring the northern pattern. One explanation put forward for this development is that it maintained the number distinction between *thou/you* which had fallen out of use (Petyt 1985). However, this southern use was very restricted. It correlates strongly with specific writers and may thus be interpreted as a stylistic device. Moreover, in certain quarters it was condemned as "an enormous Solecism" (Pyles and Algeo 1993: 191). By the end of the nineteenth century, 2nd person singular *was* had all

but disappeared in literary texts. In contrast, transition from *thou* to *you* in northern British dialects does not appear to have affected the *form* of the verb in preterit *be*. The extant *was* maintained in 2nd person singular.

14   Variable orthography of 2nd singular as "thou" and "þou" is typical of this period.

15   Collective or conjoined NPs are also reported to have been particularly disposed to *was* in the historical record (e.g. Visser 1970), as well as in contemporary varieties (e.g. Christian et al. 1988; Hazen 1996). However, investigation of these types in the data failed to reveal any consistent pattern.

16   Despite the categorical tone of these descriptions, it is important to note that Murray considers the use of *was* in these contexts "only as an alternative form" (Murray 1873: 213), and this is confirmed in Montgomery's (1994) study of texts from the fourteenth to the late seventeenth centuries.

17   Example (9a) illustrates an additional characteristic which favors *was*, namely a conjoined NP (see note 16). This highlights the extent to which *was/were* variation is a product of multi-causal internal factors.

18   Existential constructions are discussed at length in the literature and will not be elaborated here (see, for example, Haegeman 1994; Henry 1995; Meechan and Foley 1994; Milsark 1977).

19   In the North American scene, whether the context is affirmative or negative has been reported to differentiate the use of *were* in contexts of standard *was* in Ocracoke English (Schilling-Estes and Wolfram 1994) and several communities in North Carolina (Wolfram and Sellers forthcoming). These studies have consistently demonstrated that *weren't* is frequent in negative contexts, as in the following example:

> It *weren't* us with the funny accent; it *was* them.   (Schilling-Estes and Wolfram 1994: 298)

Interestingly, this effect is not limited to North America. Studies carried out in Britain (Milroy and Milroy 1993) report that nonstandard use of *were* is favored in negative constructions in many dialects (see also Britain forthcoming; Hughes and Trudgill 1979: 63–5). For example, Cheshire's (1982) research in Reading, southeast England, found nonstandard *were* in affirmative contexts only 4 percent of the time, while in negative contexts it increased to approximately 40 percent. In the corpora under investigation however, use of *were* in contexts where standard contemporary English requires *was* is rare. Moreover, there is no tendency toward use of *were* in negative contexts. The following examples are the norm:

> a.   Some of my teachers *was* good, and some of them *wasn't*.   (GV:S:7.27)
>
> b.   They *was* out here *wasn't* they?   (GE:S:46.43)

20   Separate analyses in which Grammatical Person and Type of Subject were run as a combined factor group did not alter the results. Total Ns for BCK and GYV do not include 3rd person pronoun *they* as this was a knockout value. The adjacency

constraint attested in the historical record (see section 5.4.2.) could not be tested due to the very small number of non-adjacent contexts. Total Numbers per cell in each community, including knockouts, are displayed in table 5.5, at the end of the chapter.

21 The exception is 1st person plural in GYE, which has a heightened factor weight for *was* in comparison with BCK and NPR. We have no explanation for this other than to suggest it represents a subsequent process of analogical extension (see also Milroy and Milroy 1993; Smith in preparation).

22 This result parallels that found by Montgomery (1994: 92) for Scottish texts from the late fourteenth to the late seventeenth century.

23 Although Buckie and Guysborough Village have categorical *were* with 3rd person pronouns; it must be kept in mind that plural NPs are the *only* location where *was* occurs in Guysborough Village. In Buckie, on the other hand, *was* is robust in every context except *they*. Thus, the relevant finding is the fact that NPs have such high rates of *was* in Guysborough Village even where *was* rarely appears anywhere else. The exception, of course, is existential constructions which we discussed in sections 5.4.3 and 5.5.3.

References

Aitken, A. J. (1979) Scottish speech: A historical view with special reference to the Standard English of Scotland. In A. J. Aitken and T. McArthur (eds), *Languages of Scotland*, Edinburgh: W. and R. Chambers, 85–118.

Anttila, R. (1989) *An Introduction to Historical and Comparative Linguistics*. Amsterdam and New York: John Benjamins.

Atwood, E. B. (1953) *A Survey of Verb Forms in the Eastern United States*. Ann Arbor: University of Michigan Press.

Bailyn, B. (1986) *The Peopling of British North America*. New York: Alfred A. Knopf.

Bailyn, B., and DeWolfe, B. (1986) *Voyagers to the West: A Passage in the Peopling of America on the Eve of the Revolution*. New York: Alfred A. Knopf.

Bickerton, D. (1975) *Dynamics of a Creole System*. New York: Cambridge University Press.

Britain, D. (forthcoming) *Was/weren't* levelling in Fenland English. *Essex Research Reports in Linguistics*.

Brunner, K. (1970) *An Outline of Middle English Grammar*. Oxford: Blackwell.

Cheshire, J. (1982) *Variation in an English Dialect: A Sociolinguistic Study*. Cambridge: Cambridge University Press.

Cheshire, J., et al. (1989) Urban British dialect grammar: The question of dialect levelling. *English World-Wide*, 10 (2): 185–225.

Christian, D., Wolfram, W., and Dube, N. (1988) *Variation and Change in Geographically Isolated Communities: Appalachian English and Ozark English*. Tuscaloosa, AL: American Dialect Society.

Curme, G. O. (1977) *A Grammar of the English Language.* Essex, CT: Verbatim.

Eisikovits, E. (1991) Variation in subject–verb agreement in Inner Sydney English. In J. Cheshire (ed.), *English Around the World: Sociolinguistic Perspectives,* Cambridge: Cambridge University Press, 235–56.

Feagin, C. (1979) *Variation and Change in Alabama English: A Sociolinguistic Study of the White Community.* Washington, DC: Georgetown University Press.

Fischer, D. H. (1989) *Albion's Seed: Four British Folkways in America.* New York and Oxford: Oxford University Press.

Forsström, G. (1948) *The Verb "to be" in Middle English: A Survey of the Forms.* Lund: C.W. K. Gleerup.

Haegeman, L. (1994) *Introduction to Government and Binding.* Oxford: Blackwell.

Hannah, D. (1997) Copula absence in Samaná English: Implications for research on the linguistic history of African-American Vernacular English. *American Speech,* 72 (4): 339–72.

Hazen, K. (1996) Dialect affinity and subject–verb concord: The Appalachian Outer Banks. *SECOL Review,* 20 (1): 25–53.

Henry, A. (1995) *Belfast English and Standard English: Dialect Variation and Parameter Setting.* New York and Oxford: Oxford University Press.

Hock, H. H. (1986) *Principles of Historical Linguistics.* Amsterdam: Mouton de Gruyter.

Holmqvist, E. (1922) *On the History of the English Present Inflections Particularly -th and -s.* Heidelberg: Carl Winter.

Hughes, A., and Trudgill, P. (1979) *English Accents and Dialects: An Introduction to Social and Regional Varieties of British English.* London: Edward Arnold.

Jespersen, O. H. (1954) *A Modern English Grammar on Historical Principles, Part VI: Morphology.* London: George Allen and Unwin.

Labov, W. (ed.) (1980) *Locating Language in Time and Space.* New York: Academic Press.

Meechan, M., and Foley, M. (1994) On resolving disagreement: Linguistic theory and variation – *There's bridges. Language Variation and Change,* 6 (1): 63–85.

Milroy, J., and Milroy, L. (1993) *Real English: The Grammar of English Dialects in the British Isles.* New York: Longman.

Milroy, L. (1980) *Language and Social Networks.* Baltimore: University Park Press.

Milsark, G. L. (1977) Towards an explanation of certain peculiarities of the existential construction in English. *Linguistic Analysis,* 3: 1–31.

Montgomery, M. B. (1989a) Exploring the roots of Appalachian English. *English World-Wide,* 10: 227–78.

Montgomery, M. B. (1989b) The pace of change in Appalachian English. *English World-Wide,* 10 (2): 227–8.

Montgomery, M. B. (1994) The evolution of verbal concord in Scots. In A. Fenton and D. A. MacDonald (eds), *Proceedings of the Third International Conference on the Languages of Scotland,* Edinburgh: Canongate Academic Press, 81–95.

Montgomery, M. B. (1997) Making transatlantic connections between varieties of English. *Journal of English Linguistics,* 25 (2): 122–41.

Mossé, F. (1952) *A Handbook of Middle English.* Baltimore: Johns Hopkins University Press.

Mufwene, S. S. (1996) The Founder Principle in creole genesis. *Diachronica*, 13 (1): 83–134.

Murray, J. A. H. (1873) *The Dialect of the Southern Counties of Scotland: Its Pronunciation, Grammar and Historical Relations*. London: Philological Society.

Petyt, K. M. (1985) *Dialect and Accent in Industrial West Yorkshire*. Amsterdam and Philadelphia: John Benjamins.

Poplack, S., and Tagliamonte, S. (1989) There's no tense like the present: Verbal -*s* inflection in Early Black English. *Language Variation and Change*, 1 (1): 47–84.

Poplack, S., and Tagliamonte, S. (1991) African American English in the diaspora: The case of old-line Nova Scotians. *Language Variation and Change*, 3 (3): 301–39.

Poplack, S., and Tagliamonte, S. (1994) -*S* or nothing: Marking the plural in the African American diaspora. *American Speech*, 69 (3): 227–59.

Poplack, S., and Tagliamonte, S. (1996a) The grammaticization of gonna in six varieties of English: A cross-linguistic comparison. Paper presented at NWAVE 25, University of Nevada, Las Vegas, USA.

Poplack, S., and Tagliamonte, S. (1996b) Nothing in context: Variation, grammaticization and past time marking in Nigerian Pidgin English. In P. Baker (ed.), *Changing Meanings, Changing Functions. Papers Relating to Grammaticalization in Contact Languages*, Westminster, UK: University of Westminster Press, 71–94.

Poplack, S., and Tagliamonte, S. (forthcoming) *African American English in the Diaspora*. Oxford: Blackwell.

Pyles, T. (1964) *The Origins and Development of the English Language*. New York: Harcourt, Brace and World.

Pyles, T., and Algeo, J. (1993) *The Origins and Development of the English Language*. Orlando: Harcourt Brace.

Quirk, R., and Wrenn, C. L. (1960) *An Old English Grammar*. London: Methuen.

Rand, D., and Sankoff, D. (1990) *GoldVarb: A Variable Rule Application for the Macintosh*, Version 2. Montreal, Canada: Centre de recherches mathématiques, Université de Montréal.

Rickford, J. R. (1997) Prior creolization of African-American Vernacular English? Sociohistorical and textual evidence from the 17th and 18th centuries. *Journal of Sociolinguistics*, 1 (3): 315–36.

Rickford, J. R. (1998) The creole origins of African-American Vernacular English: Evidence from copula absence. In S. Mufwene, J. R. Rickford, G. Bailey, and J. Baugh (eds), *African-American English: Structure, History, and Use*, London: Routledge, 154–200.

Sankoff, D. (1982) Sociolinguistic method and linguistic theory. In L. J. Cohen, J. Los, H. Pfeiffer, and K. P. Podewski (eds), *Logic, Methodology, Philosophy of Science, VI*, Amsterdam: North Holland; and Warsaw: Polish Scientific, 677–89.

Schilling-Estes, N., and Wolfram, W. (1994) Convergent explanation and alternative regularization patterns: *Were/weren't* leveling in a vernacular English variety. *Language Variation and Change*, 6 (3): 273–302.

Singler, J. V. (1989) Plural marking in Liberian Settler English. *American Speech*, 64 (1): 40–64.

Singler, J. V. (1991) Copula variation in Liberian Settler English and American Black English. In W. F. Edwards and D. Winford (eds), *Verb Phrase Patterns in Black English and Creole*, Detroit: Wayne State University Press, 129–64.

Singler, J. V. (1993) An African-American linguistic enclave: Tense and aspect in Liberian Settler English. In H. Aertsen and R. Jeffers (eds), *Historical Linguistics 1989. Papers from the 9th International Conference on Historical Linguistics*, Amsterdam and Philadelphia: John Benjamins, 457–65.

Singler, J. V. (1997) On the genesis, evolution, and diversity of African American English: Evidence from verbal -*s* in the Liberian Settler English of Sinoe. Paper presented at Society for Pidgin and Creole Linguistics, London, UK.

Singler, J. V. (1998) The African-American Diaspora: Who were the dispersed? Paper presented at New Ways of Analyzing Variation (NWAV), Athens, Georgia.

Smith, J. (in preparation) Synchrony and diachrony in the evolution of English: Evidence from the far reaches of Scotland. D.Phil. dissertation, University of York.

Smith, J., and Tagliamonte, S. (1998) *We was all thegither, I think we were all thegither*: Was regularization in Buckie English. *World Englishes*, 17 (2): 105–26.

Stein, D. (1986) Old English Northumbrian verb inflection revisited. In D. Kastovsky and A. Szwedek (eds), *Linguistics across Historical and Geographical Boundaries*, Amsterdam and Philadelphia: John Benjamins, 637–50.

Tagliamonte, S. (1996) Has it ever been PERFECT? Uncovering the grammar of early Black English. *York Papers in Linguistics*, 17: 351–96.

Tagliamonte, S. (1997) Obsolescence in the English Perfect? Evidence from Samaná English. *American Speech*, 72 (1): 33–68.

Tagliamonte, S. (1998) *Was/were* variation across the generations: View from the city of York. *Language Variation and Change*, 10 (2): 153–91.

Tagliamonte, S., and Poplack, S. (1988) How Black English *past* got to the present: Evidence from Samaná. *Language in Society*, 17 (4): 513–33.

Tagliamonte, S., and Poplack, S. (1993) The zero-marked verb: Testing the creole hypothesis. *Journal of Pidgin and Creole Languages*, 8 (2): 171–206.

Tagliamonte, S., and Poplack, S. (to appear) Back to the present: Verbal -*s* in the (African American) English Diaspora. In J. Lipski (ed.), *African American English and its Congenors*, Amsterdam and Philadelphia: John Benjamins.

Troxler, C. W. (1974) The migration of Carolina and Georgia Loyalists to Nova Scotia and New Brunswick. Ph.D. dissertation, University of North Carolina.

van Tyne, C. H. (1902) *The Loyalists in the American Revolution*. New York: Macmillan.

Visser, F. T. (1970) *An Historical Syntax of the English Language*. Leiden: E. J. Brill.

Walker, J. W. S. G. (1992) *The Black Loyalists: The Search for the Promised Land in Nova Scotia and Sierra Leone 1783–1870*. Toronto: University of Toronto Press.

Winford, D. (1993) Back to the past: The BEV/Creole connection revisited. *Language Variation and Change*, 4: 311–57.

Winks, R. W. (1971) *The Blacks in Canada: A History*. Montreal: McGill-Queen's University Press.

Wolfram, W., and Sellers, J. (forthcoming) Alternative regularization patterning and ethnic marking in a tri-ethnic rural southern community. *Journal of English Linguistics*.

Wood, P. H. (1974) *Black Majority: Negroes in Colonial South Carolina from 1670 through the Stono Rebellion.* New York: Alfred A. Knopf.

Wood, P. H. (1989) The changing population of the Colonial South: An overview by race and region, 1685–1790. In P. H. Wood, G. A. Waselkov, and T. M. Hatley (eds), *Powhatan's Mantle: Indians of the Colonial Southeast,* Lincoln and London: University of Nebraska Press, 25–103.

Part III
Syntactic Variables

6

*The Question Question: Auxiliary Inversion in Early African American English**

Gerard Van Herk

6.1 Introduction

Similarities in question formation between creoles and African American Vernacular English (AAVE) have been invoked by proponents of the hypothesis that AAVE is descended from a prior creole. Unlike Standard English (StdE), where questions require inversion of the auxiliary verb and subject, questions in creole languages are said to resist inversion (Alleyne 1980; Crowley and Rigsby 1987; Holm 1988). In fact, Bickerton (1981: 70) asserts that creoles exhibit no "difference in syntactic structure between questions and statements." Contemporary AAVE (Alleyne 1980; Burling 1973; Dillard 1972; Holm 1988; Labov, Cohen, Robins and Lewis 1968) displays both non-inverted forms, as in (1), and inverted forms, as in (2).

(1)   Why she ain' over here?   (Dillard 1972: 63)

(2)   Can he go?   (Dillard 1972: 63)

If the non-inverted forms, as in (1), are a remnant of a prior plantation creole, they must have been more common in Early African American English (AAE). To my knowledge, only two studies have tested this hypothesis by examining data that may be representative of Early AAE: the speech of African Americans born in the pre-Emancipation era, or of descendants of former American slaves in linguistic enclaves like Samaná in the Dominican Republic. The examination by Schneider (1982) of the Ex-Slave Narratives, transcripts of interviews with African Americans born in the mid-1800s (Rawick 1979), revealed both inverted and non-inverted question forms, with inverted (StdE-like) forms in the majority. On the other hand, DeBose (1996) claimed, on the basis of analysis of 100 questions culled from his corpus of Samaná English (SE), that non-inversion in SE reflects its prior-creole status. Such non-inversion is instantiated in (3a) to (3d), taken from DeBose (1996).

(3) a. We ain' got no coffee fo share wit that man?

     b. Why I didn't see you?

     c. From where you is?

     d. Where you was?

6.2   Methods and Issues

The present study set out to replicate DeBose's findings in three corpora (two diaspora, one baseline) of Early AAE which we consider to be precursors of contemporary AAVE: the Ex-Slave Recordings (ESR) (Bailey, Maynor and Cukor-Avila 1991), SE (Poplack and Sankoff 1987), and African Nova Scotian English (ANSE) (Poplack and Tagliamonte 1991). This replication, however, ran into a number of theoretical and methodological problems, which raise enough issues of general relevance to warrant detailed discussion.

6.2.1   Defining the variable context

I first exhaustively searched each of the three corpora and extracted every question, for an initial total of 3,343 questions, as in table 6.1. However, as the creolist diagnostic proposed is lack of subject–auxiliary *inversion*, it was first necessary to restrict the data to questions involving a subject and an (optionally deleted) auxiliary – that is, to define the variable context. A first interesting finding is that more than two-thirds of all questions across corpora qualify as what Rickford et al. (1991) have termed "non-count." That is, they are outside that variable context. These consist of repetition requests, as in (4), tag questions (5), fixed expressions (6), fragments (7), echo questions (8), and comprehension checks (9).

(4)   How? Hmm? Huh? Eh?   (SE/021/523, 530, 537, 555)[1]

(5)   They fought for Jiminez, eh?   (SE/001/369)

Table 6.1 Defining the variable context in Early African American English

		ESR	ANSE	Sámaná	Total
Informants	N	11	36	21	68
All questions	N	75	2465	803	3343
Non-count	N	54	1645	606	2305
(examples 4–10)	%	72	66	75	68
Aux. deletion	N	13	320	105	438
(examples 11–12)	%	17	13	13	13
Variable context	N	8	500	92	600
	%	10	20	11	18

(6)   a.   Ain't true?   (SE/005/283)

     b.   You don't believe?   (SE/003/394)

(7)   The hotel?   (SE/001/939)

(8)   Interviewer: Who was the last one, uh . . .
     Informant: Who was the last one I knew?   (SE/016/697)

(9)   Interviewer: Do you think that's bad?
     Informant: If I think it's bad?   (SE/016/355)

Question (9) is a shorter form of "(Are you asking me) if I think it's bad?" Note that another, similar question type could easily be mistaken for a non–inverted ("creole") form:

(10)   Interviewer: What did you learn with Horacio?
      Informant: Why I didn't learn with Horacio?   (SE/016/552)

As in (9), it is clear from the full context that (10) is a shorter form of "(Are you asking me) why I didn't learn with Horacio?"

    Unlike DeBose, who reported only five unsuitable questions in his data, our peeling away of incomplete and, especially, anomalous questions reduces the corpus by a full 68 percent, or 2,305 tokens (table 6.1). In nearly half of the remaining 1,038 questions, however, the auxiliary is deleted altogether, rendering them ineligible for the study of auxiliary inversion. Such questions, exemplified in (11), are ambiguous as to underlying form, i.e., it is imposs-ible to determine whether the original auxiliary was inverted or not prior to deletion. Underlying example (11), for instance, could be (11a) (StdE) or (11b) (creole).

(11)   And where you-all come from?   (SE/008/359)

    a.   Where *did* you-all come from?

    b.   Where you-all *did* come from?

Some auxiliary deletions are yet more difficult to spot. DeBose (1996) classes among uninverted "auxiliaries" sentences such as (12a) and (12b).

(12)   a.   You been to Oregon?

    b.   Where you gon' stay?

Such question forms are also found in the present corpus, e.g. (13).

(13)   What we going to do?   (SE/003/427)

Going to here *is* an auxiliary, but not the one that is eligible for inversion in StdE – witness the ungrammaticality of (13a).

(13)   a.   *What going we to do?

The example in (13) actually results from the deletion of *are*, which might have arisen from an underlying StdE (13b) or creole (13c) form.

(13)   b.   What *are* we going to do?

    c.   What we *are* going to do?

The auxiliaries in DeBose's examples (12a)–(12b) cannot invert, either, since they do not qualify as what traditional grammars (e.g. Quirk and Greenbaum 1972) refer to as "operator auxiliaries." This is evidenced by their ungram-maticality when inverted, at least in contemporary English, as in (14) and (15).

(14)   *Been you to Oregon?

(15)   *Where gon' you stay?

Non-operator auxiliaries make up six of DeBose's ten cited examples of non-inversion. This problem alone seriously damages any argument that questions in SE pattern like those in creoles by failing to invert. Once the ineligible questions – exemplified in (12) – are removed from the database, only nine of all the questions cited by DeBose are eligible for inversion (i.e. fall into the variable context), and only four of them – fewer than half – are non-inverted.

The present study also requires the exclusion of questions with deleted auxiliaries (N = 438). As can be seen in table 6.1, this leaves a total of 600 questions eligible for inversion, and hence for study: i.e. those containing an overt auxiliary. Such questions make up between 10 and 20 percent of the actual questions in each corpus, and less than 18 percent of our original 3,343. The variable context for this study thus includes all "pure" verbal auxiliaries (16). In addition, it includes true copulas – i.e. *be* used other than as a verbal auxiliary, as in (17). In other words, we include any, and only, forms eligible for inversion.

(16) To who *was* they going? (SE/002/313)

(17) Where your riches *is*? (SE/001/814)

6.2.2 *Variation and diagnosticity*

At first glance, the research question here is remarkably simple. It is presumed that StdE always inverts auxiliaries in questions, and creoles never do. If Early AAE were to show near-categorical inversion, this would be proof that it is descended from StdE; if it shows near-categorical non-inversion, it is descended from a creole (with inversion in contemporary AAVE due, according to DeBose (1996), to influence from, or "code-switching" to, StdE). In reality, neither the facts of English in general, nor the behavior of Early AAE in particular, support this simple agenda. As Crowley and Rigsby (1987) have pointed out, yes/no questions, which do not invert in creoles, need not invert in English, either. Witness (18), uttered by a speaker of Standard Ottawa English.

(18) It's near Billings Bridge? (OT/244/A005)

The problem is one of *diagnosticity* of the variable. If both creole and StdE systems allow non-inverted yes/no questions, non-inversion in such questions cannot constitute evidence either of a prior creole or of English acquisition, as summarized in table 6.2. A preponderance of inverted forms, however, does

Table 6.2 Unequal diagnosticity: acceptability of inversion in question types by language

Feature	Question type	StdE	Creole
Non-inversion	yes/no	✔	✔
	Wh-	✘	✔
Inversion	yes/no	✔	✘
	Wh-	✔	✘

count as evidence against a creole origin, since the creole-origin hypothesis predicts a near-complete absence of such forms. Failure to consider this distinction between question types marks the analyses of both DeBose (1996), which supports a prior-creole origin for AAVE, and Schneider (1982), which does not.

The data, too, are unwilling to conform to categorical preconceptions. Non-inversion is neither categorical nor totally absent. The apparent exception is the Ex-Slave Recordings, where non-inverted forms do not occur; however, this may be due to the scarcity of any questions in that corpus. Of all questions eligible for inversion in the two diaspora corpora, a slight majority in SE showed no inversion, as compared with only 7 percent in ANSE (see table 6.3). As both creoles and English permit non-inversion in yes/no questions, we might expect the greatest number of non-inverted forms to show up in such an environment. This is indeed the case. Yes/no questions showed 69 percent non-inversion in SE, and 19 percent in ANSE. In *Wh*-questions, where the creole diagnostic is non-inversion, we see far less non-inversion: 39 percent in SE, and a mere 3 percent in ANSE.

Clearly, if both StdE and creoles feature categorical question-formation rules, neither can be the model for the system displayed in table 6.3. Quantitative studies of English-based creoles (EBCs) or English, however, might reveal that question formation in those systems is actually more variable than the literature would have us believe.

An example drawn from the literature on contemporary AAVE questions illustrates how variability can disappear in the telling. Holm (1988) describes AAVE as a "semi-creole" featuring non-inversion in *Wh*-questions only, citing Burling (1973). Burling, however, describes AAVE non-inversion in both *Wh*- and yes/no questions, and rightly points out that non-inversion in yes/no questions is not limited to AAVE: "Black nonstandard English hardly differs from standard colloquial English in its formation of simple [i.e. yes/no] questions except that it omits auxiliaries more easily and more often" (Burling 1973:

Table 6.3 Non-inversion in Early African American English by question type

Question type	ESR N	ESR %	Samaná N	Samaná %	ANSE N	ANSE %	Prediction StdE	Prediction Creole
yes/no	6	0	61	69	156	19	✔	✔
Wh-	2	0	31	39	344	3	✗	✔
All	8	0	92	59	500	7		

65). Burling's only examples of AAVE non-inversion in *Wh*-questions, in turn, are drawn from Labov et al. (1968: 293–94), who conclude (from the preponderance of StdE-like forms (70–75 percent) and from memory tests) that AAVE's "basic pattern for direct questions is WH – [+T] – NP – the flip-flop [inversion] rule applies in the same way as [StdE], although there is a sizeable amount of variation in the application of the rule" (Labov et al. 1968: 296). In yes/no questions, Labov et al. (1968: 293) describe "many clear cases of the flip-flop rule operating," along with "a very large number of utterances which do not show the flip-flop rule." That is, they propose a variable system with a preponderance of StdE forms in *Wh*-questions, but a good deal of non-inversion in yes/no questions – the opposite of the rule proposed by Holm (1988). The description in Holm (1988) appears to result from denying forms resembling StdE a place in the core grammar of AAVE, thus greatly circumscribing the potential bounds of this grammar. We may find that descriptions of creole and other grammars have similarly been limited by the exclusion of variability, especially that which includes forms resembling those of StdE.

6.2.3 A variable model: Early Modern English

Unlike traditional descriptions of StdE and creole grammars, the history of English does provide a variable model for question formation. This is the adoption in Early Modern English (Early ModE) of periphrastic *do*, thoroughly quantitatively described in Ellegård (1953), Kroch (1989a, 1989b), and Stein (1988, 1991, 1992). The increasing use of *do*-support between the late fifteenth and eighteenth centuries was a form of non-inversion. Question formation evolved from Old English lexical verb inversion, as in (19), to fronting of the dummy auxiliary with (non-inverted) Subject–lexical Verb–Object order, as in (20).

Table 6.4 Factors shown to condition non-inversion in Early Modern English

Variable context	Factor group	Favoring factor	Source
All questions	Negation	Negative	Ellegård 1953
Affirmative yes/no & Adverbial questions	Question type	Yes/no (post-1600)	Stein 1988, 1992 Kroch 1989a Ellegård 1953
Affirmative *Wh*-questions	Causativity	Causative	Stein 1988, 1992 Ellegård 1953
	Transitivity	Transitive	Kroch 1989a Ellegård 1953
	Subject type	NP	Kroch 1989b
Non-copula *Wh*-questions	Question type	Adverbial (pre-1600)	Stein 1988, 1992 Kroch 1989a Ellegård 1953

(19) How great and greuous tribulations [O] *suffered* [V] the Holy Appostyls [S]?   (Kroch 1989b)

(20) Where *doth* [AUX] the grene knyght [S] *holde* [V] hym [O]?   (Kroch 1989b)

There is much debate among scholars of earlier English with respect to the applicability and fit of competing theoretical models to describe the motivation for the great increase in Early ModE of non-inversion. There is more agreement, however, on the facts that these competing theories attempt to describe. Non-inversion follows a clear hierarchy of conditioning factors, as summarized in table 6.4. First, in all Early ModE questions, non-inversion is favored by negatives (Ellegård 1953). In affirmative questions, non-inversion is favored by the yes/no question type (Stein 1988), especially in the later, post-1600 period (Kroch 1989b). Causatives (the *why?* and *wherefore?* questions) favor non-inversion to a greater degree than the other *Wh*-questions (Stein 1988). Non-inversion is further favored by transitives and NP subjects, which are linked (Kroch 1989b): transitives having subjects of a weight equal to or greater than their objects favor non-inversion. In the earlier, pre-1600, period, non-inversion is favored by adverbial over *Wh*-object questions (Ellegård 1953; Kroch 1989b; Stein 1988). Phonological constraints on non-inversion (Stein 1988) will not be further considered here, as they are derived from the *you/thou* distinction in Early ModE, a distinction which is absent from these Early AAE corpora.

This chapter will show that the extension of non-inversion from lexical verbs, as in (20), to auxiliaries, as in (21) to (32) and (34) to (36) in table 6.5, taken from Early AAE, is part of a single process of regularization of word order in questions. The climate for such extension appears to have existed: vernacular non-inversion raced ahead of prescribed usage. Non-inversion had reached the 50 percent mark by the late sixteenth century (Ellegård 1953), while contemporary prescriptivist works like Edw. Coote's *The English Scholemaster*, published in 1596, used only fully-inverted lexical verbs (Visser 1970). Nearly two centuries later J. Pickbourn's *A Dissertation on the English Verb* (1789) conceded that the *do* form was by then "almost universally employed," although we detect a hint of disapproval in the qualification "at least by prose writers" (1789: 26, in Visser 1970: 1545).

Further, as suggested by the mention of pre- and post-1600 periods above, it should be possible to identify by purely linguistic means the period in which the proposed extension of non-inversion to auxiliary verbs could have occurred. Early ModE (Ellegård 1953; Stein 1988) is said to have more non-inversion in adverbial questions than in *Wh*-object questions. However, Kroch (1989a: 224) clarifies: Ellegård found that yes/no and adverbial questions "showed almost the same frequency of *do* use in the first part of the change. . . . In the second half of the change, adverbial questions behaved like *Wh*-object questions, but Ellegård continued to group them with yes/no questions." If non-inversion in Early AAE occurs with approximately equal frequency in adverbial and yes/no questions, but less frequently in *Wh*-object questions, the extension dates to the early period, pre-1600. If, on the other hand, adverbials show less non-inversion than yes/no questions, at a rate closer to that of *Wh*-object questions, the extension would be dated to the later, post-1600 period. Further, when *Wh*-subject questions, which categorically invert, are removed from the equation in Stein (1988), the sole unambiguously *Wh*-object form (*whom*) shows a high rate of non-inversion. Thus, a constraint hierarchy derived from post-1600 Early ModE might even permit a *higher* rate of non-inversion in *Wh*-object questions than in adverbials.

6.2.4   *Operationalizing and coding for variable constraints*

Just as we earlier removed layers of non-application contexts to circumscribe the variable context, so here we must distinguish the contexts in which the factors hypothesized to constrain variable inversion may apply. The constraints

Table 6.5 Early Modern English constraints operationalized to code Early AAE questions

Factor group	Factor	Example
Negation	Negative question	(21) He *don't* know the pastor? (SE/003/965)
	Affirmative	(22) *Did* you-all know about this Reverend Putton? (SE/003/502)
Question type	Yes/no	(23) *Is* there any hills to work in? (SE/006/1154)
	Adverbial	(24) But *when* you'll be coming back again? (SE/004/701)
	Causative	(25) *Why* you-all are English-speaking people and you speak Spanish with the children? (SE/003/175)
	Wh-object	(26) *What* do you mean by real beer? (ANSE/032/856)
Subject type	NP	(27) What *Ella* must have done with it? (SE/011/1024)
	Pronoun	(28) What did *you* say? (ANSE/038/940)
Object type	NP	(29) Where are you gonna get *turkey*? (ANSE/018/791)
	Pronoun	(30) How do you use *it*? (ANSE/003/714)
	Intransitive	(31) Where are you going? (ANSE/006/376)
Auxiliary type	Modal	(32) How *could* we pray when we were running? (ANSE/025/447)
	Copula	(33) repeats (17) Where your riches *is*? (SE/001/814)
	have	(34) You *have* heard from him? (SE/003/235)
	Verbal aux. *be*	(35) repeats (16) To who *was* they going? (SE/002/313)
	do	(36) What *do* you call them? (ANSE/007/758)

on Early ModE non-inversion apply in four different contexts, as seen in the first column of table 6.4. Should these constraints also account for the Early AAE data, they will only apply to like subsets of the data (thus explaining the different Numbers in our subsequent analyses).

The constraints described in table 6.4 were operationalized as a coding system for the 92 SE and 500 ANSE questions in which auxiliary and subject were present (as the eight ESR questions categorically inverted, they were not part of any further variationist analysis). As described in table 6.5, each question was coded for the presence or absence of negation (21)–(22), and for type of question (23)–(26), of subject (27)–(28), and of object (29)–(31). In addition, questions were coded for auxiliary type (32)–(36), to test the hypothesis that Early ModE non-inversion of *lexical* verbs would result in non-inversion being favored by semantically-heavier modals (Kroch 1989a: 218) and by true copulas, which, as the only verb in the question, could be seen as syntactically heavier.

The contribution of these factors to the probability of non-inversion was independently analyzed in SE and ANSE by means of Goldvarb, a variable rule application for the Macintosh (Rand and Sankoff 1990).

6.3   Results

The constraints on non-inversion of the Early AAE auxiliaries show striking similarities to those on lexical verb non-inversion in Early ModE, as detailed in sections 6.3.1 to 6.3.6 below.

6.3.1   Negation favors non-inversion

In Early ModE, negation favored non-inversion in all question types. As table 6.6 shows, negation also favors non-inversion in both varieties of Early AAE. In SE, negation rendered all other factors statistically non-significant in this variable context.

6.3.2   Yes/no questions favor non-inversion

In Early ModE affirmative questions, non-inversion was more highly favored in yes/no than in *Wh-* adverbial questions (*where*, *when*, *why*, *how*) (Stein 1988), at least in the post-1600 period (Kroch 1989a). Once we remove *do* auxiliaries, which categorically invert in this environment in both corpora, we find the same robust effect to hold for Early AAE: in both varieties, yes/no questions favor non-inversion (table 6.7).

Table 6.6 Variable rule analysis of the contribution of Early Modern English factors to the probability of non-inversion in Early African American English questions

	Variable context: all questions	
	Samaná English	ANSE
Corrected mean	.623	.029
Total N	92	500
Negation		
Negative	.79	.92
Affirmative	.29	.43
Range:	*50*	*49*
Question type		
Yes/no		.81
Wh-	[ ]	.36
Range:		*45*
Factors not selected:		
Question type (yes/no vs. *Wh-*)	X	
Causativity	X	X
Transitivity	X	X
Subject type	X	X
Auxiliary type	X	X
Question type (adverbial vs. *Wh-*object)	X	X

6.3.3   Causatives favor non-inversion

Negation and the yes/no question type, the strongest factors favoring non-inversion in Early ModE (and, as demonstrated above, in Early AAE), are linked semantically by Stein (1988). He suggests that this is because both negative and yes/no questions focus on the truth value of an entire proposition, rather than on the information contained in its component parts, and that this might be why such propositions are considered as a whole – that is, without inverting. Stein further extends this description to the *Wh*-questions that he says most closely resemble yes/no questions – causatives. In Early ModE, causative questions favored non-inversion more than other *Wh*-questions. The sole SE causative – example (25) above – does match the Early ModE prediction. In

Table 6.7 Variable rule analysis of the contribution of Early Modern English factors to the probability of non-inversion in Early African American English affirmative yes/no and *Wh*-adverbial questions

	Variable context: all affirmative yes/no and *Wh*-adverbial questions	
	Samaná English	ANSE
Corrected mean	.594	.040
Total N	26	293
Question type		
Yes/no	.72	.81
Wh-	.26	.39
Range:	*46*	*42*
Auxiliary type		
have/be		.74
Copula		.42
Modal		.40
Range:		*34*
Factors not selected:		
Causativity	X	X
Transitivity	X	X
Subject type	X	X
Auxiliary type	X	
Question type (adverbial vs. *Wh*-object)	X	X

ANSE affirmative questions, a strong favoring effect for causativity in the marginal percentages was not revealed to be significant by a variable rule analysis (see table 6.8). As this apparent lack of significance may have been due to the relative rarity of this question type, rather than to the actual magnitude of the effect, we will not rely solely on the stepwise option in the multiple regression procedure incorporated in the variable rule program (Rand and Sankoff 1990). To get a better view of the hierarchy of constraints associated with causativity (and transitivity) across ANSE and SE, table 6.8 displays an analysis in which all factors are "forced" into the regression, as shown in iteration #1 of the stepdown analysis (Poplack and Tagliamonte 1989). Factors not selected as statistically significant are enclosed in square brackets.

Table 6.8   Variable rule analysis of the contribution of Early Modern English factors to the probability of non-inversion in Early African American English affirmative *Wh*-questions

	Variable context: all affirmative *Wh*-questions	
	Samaná English	ANSE
Corrected mean	.183	.023
Total N	**28**	**344**
Causativity		
Causative	100% (KO)	[.77]
Non-causative	37%	[.47]
Transitivity		
Transitive	.73	[.52]
Intransitive	.18	[.47]
Range:	*55*	
Subject type		
Pronoun	.91	3%
NP	.03	0% (KO)
Range:	*88*	
Auxiliary type		
Modal	.90	[.38]
Copula	.81	[.42]
have/be/do	.01	[.59]
Range:	*89*	
Factors not selected:		
Causativity	X	X
Transitivity		X
Subject type		X
Auxiliary type		X
Question type (adverbial vs. *Wh*-object)	X	X

A closer investigation of ANSE causatives revealed that many causatives had been removed with negative questions (to which they are semantically linked by Stein 1988). A separate analysis in which negation and causatives were considered together revealed that ANSE causatives, especially negative causatives, strongly favored non-inversion (table 6.9). This matches the Early ModE predictions. The "no data" cell in table 6.9 shows that *all* negative *Wh*-questions in these

Table 6.9 Factors contributing to non-inversion in all *Wh*-questions in African Nova Scotian English

		Causative	Non-Causative
Total N		363	
Factor-group:			
Negation/causativity			
Negative		.96	no data
Affirmative		.90	.39
	Range	*57*	
Subject			
First person		.89	
Third person		.70	
NP		.63	
Second Person		.19	
	Range	*70*	

Factors not selected:
Transitivity, auxiliary type

Early AAE corpora are causatives. This further illustrates the strong link between negation and causativity in *Wh*-questions, supporting Stein's proposed semantic analysis.

Given the strong link between negation and causativity, it is not surprising that most published examples of *contemporary* AAVE non-inversion represent precisely this type of negative causative question, as in examples (37) and (38).

(37) a. *Why* you *don't* like him?   (Labov et al. 1968: 294)

   b. *Why* I *don't* need no grease?   (Labov et al. 1968: 294)

(38) *Why* she *ain'* over here?   (Dillard 1972)

Further proof of a residual causativity distinction in contemporary English (and its effect on inversion) might be adduced from the causative *how come?* form, as in example (39). This is the only type of question in vernacular (white and black) English where *non*-inversion is categorical.

(39) How come the children *don't* play like that?   (ANSE/005/263)

Further research might reveal that the causativity distinction that appeared to remain active in Early AAE may also be active (though little noticed) in contemporary English. Examining the co-occurrence of negation and causativity is one possibility; a link between negation or rhetorical emphasis and the choice of the non-inverted *how come?* form is another.

6.3.4 *Transitivity favors non-inversion*

Non-inversion in Early ModE was further favored by transitivity and a heavy NP subject, which are also linked. To paraphrase Kroch (1989b), an object, if present, dislikes a subject of its own weight or heavier intervening between it and the verb. This is related to processing – the preferred question is as close to SVO (Subject–Verb–Object) order as possible. Table 6.8 shows that in SE, transitivity favors non-inversion, as predicted, but only in *Wh*-questions. In ANSE, we find a favoring transitivity effect (3 percent > 1 percent) in the marginals, but it is not selected as significant.

In both corpora, however, non-inversion is highly disfavored with NP subjects; it is absent in this context in ANSE. This seems to be contrary to the constraints on Early ModE. Recall, though, that it is the *relationship* between subject type and transitivity that constrains non-inversion in Early ModE (Kroch 1989b: 167). NP subjects are only expected to favor non-inversion when they are followed by an NP or pronoun object. When we combine subject and object types into the favoring Early ModE configuration (object + subject of equal or greater weight), and the disfavoring environment (everything else), as in table 6.10, the apparent counter-evidence disappears. In fact, although the data are

Table 6.10 Subject–object relationship contribution to non-inversion in Early African American English

	Samaná	ANSE
N:	13	198
Favors non-inversion in		
Early Modern English	100% (1/1)	5% (1/20)
$(S_{NP} + O_{NP}, S_{NP} + O_{pro}, S_{pro} + O_{pro})$		
Disfavors non-inversion in		
Early Modern English	25% (3/12)	2% (2/178)
$(S_{pro} + O_{NP},$ all intransitives)		

again too sparse to achieve statistical significance, the marginals parallel the Early ModE hierarchy.

6.3.5   Lexically heavy auxiliaries favor non-inversion

For effects due to type of auxiliary, we have of course no direct comparative base in Early ModE – *do*-periphrasis naturally involves *do* (and a lexical verb). We can, however, extrapolate from theoretical work on Early ModE. Recall that the point of *do*-periphrasis was to maintain Subject–*lexical* Verb–Object order. Thus, we would expect non-inversion to occur preferentially with the auxiliary verbs that most closely resemble full lexical verbs. These include modals, whose meaning of possibility makes them semantically heavier than other auxiliaries, and copulas, which are the only verbs in the sentences in which they appear. This is exactly what table 6.8 indicates for SE. Modals (at 0.90) and copulas (at 0.81) favor non-inversion far more than other auxiliaries. This finding also suggests that modals in AAVE retain some lexical identity,[2] and so are farther behind on the grammaticization continuum than modals in other varieties of English. Such lexical weight is also evidenced by their appearance in AAVE (and Southern nonstandard English) as second verbs, as in example (40):

(40)   You *might could* hang a doghouse there.   (Feagin 1979: 156)

6.3.6   Do adverbials favor non-inversion?

The literature on Early ModE describes adverbial *Wh*-questions favoring non-inversion over *Wh*-object questions in the pre-1600 period, with no effect or perhaps even a slight favoring effect for *Wh*-object questions in the post-1600 period. The paucity of such questions in our Early AAE data in this variable context precludes a multivariate analysis – SE has too few questions in these contexts (N = 19), and ANSE has too little non-inversion (N = 11). The marginal percentages, however, again parallel the constraints proposed for the post-1600 period. Given the assumption that the syntax of AAE would have been set in the 1600s and 1700s, this finding is exactly as expected.

6.3.7   Summary of results

We have seen a clear shared hierarchy of non-inversion in the two varieties of Early AAE for which there is sufficient data to permit analysis, paralleling patterns attested for Early ModE. Moreover, the contexts in which Early ModE non-inversion was farthest advanced are precisely those which exerted significant effects on non-inversion in Early AAE. In both Early ModE and Early AAE, non-inversion is most likely with negative questions. In affirmative questions, it is more likely in yes/no than in *Wh*-questions. In *Wh*-questions, it is more likely with causatives. In the remaining *Wh*-questions, an easily-processed Subject–lexical Verb–Object order is maintained through non-inversion with transitives, and in SE, with modals and copulas. These parallels to the complex system of Early ModE question formation are striking, and are beyond coincidence.

6.4 Discussion

The results of the present study are suggestive with respect to both methodological issues and the creole-origins debate.

6.4.1 *Methods revisited*

From a methodological standpoint, the diagnosticity of any variable used to claim possible creole origins for AAVE must be adequately weighed. In the case at hand, non-inversion in yes/no questions, despite its inclusion in earlier work, is clearly not uniquely diagnostic of creole languages. On the contrary, we have seen that non-inversion is possible in this context in both Early Modern and contemporary English.

We also require a good deal of quantitative work on other language varieties. The work of Kroch, Ellegård, and Stein on the evolution of *do*-support in Early ModE has furnished the basis to explain the grammar from which constraints on Early AAE question formation derive. For purposes of comparison, it would be instructive to know what factors constrain variability in contemporary AAVE, in mesolectal EBCs, and in other vernacular varieties of English. A completely different constraint hierarchy in an uncontestably decreolizing variety would be compelling evidence against the creole origins of AAVE. Given, however, the undisputed contribution of English to both AAVE and EBCs, as well as the possible influence of linguistic universals, to be discussed below (section 6.4.2), we would expect at least some of the constraints operating in Early AAE to be shared by AAVE and EBCs. We have already discussed the tendency to dismiss variability in AAVE as code-switching or contact-induced change. Is the "categorical" non-inversion claimed for EBCs due to a similar reluctance to acknowledge long-standing inherent variability?

Likewise, other vernacular varieties of English share a source language with AAVE and EBCs. Here, too, quantitative work may reveal variability that has been obscured by prescriptivist assumptions. Already, preliminary results from a small sample of vernacular English as spoken in Ottawa (Canada) suggest some similar conditioning (Van Herk 1996). As in Early AAE, negation strongly promotes non-inversion. An example is (41).

(41)   So you *didn't* come home stum– stumbling drunk?   (OT/244/A084)

Further research, both linguistic and sociohistorical, might enable us to more clearly trace the path by which Early ModE non-inversion of lexical verbs was extended to Early AAE auxiliaries. It may be that the extension had already occurred in those regional varieties or registers that served as the models for first-generation AAVE, and the variable system was perfectly acquired. If so, traces of the system in contemporary British regional varieties, which have yet to be examined in this regard, may still persist. This does not rule out the possibility that the extension may have been a linguistic innovation by the first generations of African Americans, who expanded Early ModE domains of variability to allow the expression of semantic distinctions carried over from their native languages. If this is the case, linguistically principled comparison with movable question particles in West African languages might help explain why Early AAE developed constraints that parallel and extend so precisely those of Early ModE.

A simpler methodological point should also be made: we need more questions. In the present study, three complete corpora have been mined. However, small corpora like the Ex-Slave Recordings hardly lend themselves to quantitative study of already infrequently-occurring features like questions. Even in the 2,465 questions in the ANSE corpus, the highly-restricted contexts for some of the constraints described here of necessity continue to result in small samples. In any corpus, we are also left with a problem that results from the standard format of the sociolinguistic interview. One does not elicit many questions by asking them.

6.4.2   Inversion and the creole-origins debate

The results of this study offer both quantitative and qualitative arguments against the prior-creole hypothesis, at least insofar as it relates to question formation.

A first important finding is that once the variable context is accurately circumscribed, the inverted forms reveal themselves as a substantial share of
the total, far too common for each occurrence to be explained away, as others
have done, as tape noise, fixed or frozen expressions, or idiosyncratic use. In
yes/no questions, where inversion is optional, even in mainstream or StdE,
inverted questions form a strong minority in SE, and a majority in ANSE. In
Wh-questions, where non-inversion is a creole diagnostic, inversions represent
a majority in SE, and nearly all attested cases in ANSE. Likewise, the number
of different auxiliary forms in the corpora of Early AAE, including SE, mitigates
against an alternative proposal in DeBose (1996), made on the basis of his SE
corpus, that the inverted "auxiliary" is actually a creole-like interrogative marker
that coincidentally resembles the English auxiliary form. It stretches credibility
to imagine an interrogative marker that changes to become identical to each
different English auxiliary form, as the variation attested here would require.

Secondly, the occurrence of non-inversion in Early AAE is clearly rule-
governed. The challenge has been to discover the system giving rise to those
rules. This chapter has shown that the variable constraints conditioning that
system are the same ones that constrained subject–verb inversion in Early
ModE, and that those constraints have been extended to auxiliaries. Here, the
standard creole-origins argument will not do – it requires categorical non-
inversion, and even if it admitted variation, certainly makes no provision for the
negation or causativity distinctions which we have seen to operate in Early
AAE. The mere existence of non-inversion in other systems, including EBCs,
does not suffice to qualify them as potential antecedents for Early AAE. Rather,
it is the structure of the grammar, as revealed by the patterning of the linguistic
factors conditioning non-inversion, that must be the diagnostic.

In this context, it is telling that the Early ModE hierarchy described here is
also evident in the corpus of SE analyzed in DeBose (1996), which advocates a
prior-creole origin. In that paper, all four cited examples with non-inverted
eligible auxiliaries feature either negation or copulas, as we can see by repeating
examples (3a) to (3d).

(3)   a.   We ain' got no coffee fo share wit that man?
      b.   Why I didn't see you?
      c.   From where you is?
      d.   Where you was?   (DeBose 1996)

Both negation and true copulas are, of course, factors that favored non-
inversion in Early ModE.

What of the possibility that the similar constraint hierarchies in Early Modern and African American Englishes reflect some deep, universal tendencies,

Table 6.11   Factors influencing non-inversion in different sociolinguistic contexts

	Child acquisition	SLA	Early AAE/ModE
Negation	favors	favors	favors
Yes/no	*disfavors/neutral*	*disfavors*	*favors*
Causative	favors	neutral	favors
Copula	neutral	*disfavors*	*favors/neutral*

which operated on Early AAE creole speakers even as they attempted to acquire the acrolect? There *are* some clear similarities between the constraint hierarchy described here and parts of those proposed for acquisition of both first languages (Bellugi 1971; Labov and Labov 1976; Stromswold 1996) and second (Pienemann et al. 1988). There are also, however, clear differences, as summarized in table 6.11.

In child language acquisition, it has been claimed that yes/no questions either disfavor (Bellugi 1971) or are neutral (Stromswold 1996) with respect to non-inversion – the opposite of the strong favoring effect found in Early Modern and African American Englishes. In second-language acquisition, Pienemann et al. (1988) find that second-language learners invert yes/no questions before *Wh*, and copulas before other auxiliaries. If the variation found in SE were actually "acrolectal code-switching," i.e. use of a system acquired after acquisition of a creole language, yes/no questions and copulas should disfavor non-inversion. Instead, as we have seen, they favor it. These discrepancies suggest the observed variation is less a partial second-language acquisition profile and more part of a system acquired from birth.

That system, as described in this chapter, shows striking and complex parallels to the grammar of Early ModE *do*-support, which figures among the first variable systems studied in variationist sociolinguistics. The continued existence of variability in AAE question formation over centuries affords us a rare chance to develop and test explanatory factors that can serve as tools for analysis of other language varieties. Discovery and analysis of variation in question formation in other varieties of English and in EBCs will no doubt further develop our understanding of this little-studied but fascinating aspect of African American English.

Notes

*   This paper has been greatly improved by the comments on earlier versions made by audience members at NWAVE 1997, SPCL 1998, and CLA 1998. All remaining

errors are my own. I am grateful to the government of Ontario for financial support in the form of an Ontario Graduate Scholarship.

1   Codes in parentheses refer to the corpus (SE = Samaná English, ANSE = African Nova Scotian English, ESR = Ex-Slave Recordings), speaker identification number, and transcript line number of the utterance.
2   The lack of a parallel finding for ANSE may relate to the great majority of ANSE questions resisting inversion through auxiliary *deletion*, rather than non-inversion. In Van Herk (1998) I investigate constraints on auxiliary deletion, the strongest of which forbids deletion of modals.

References

Alleyne, M. C. (1980) *Comparative Afro-American: An Historical-Comparative Study of English-based Afro-American Dialects of the New World*. Ann Arbor: Karoma.
Bailey, G., Maynor, N., and Cukor-Avila, P. (1991) *The Emergence of Black English: Texts and Commentary*. Amsterdam and Philadelphia: John Benjamins.
Bellugi, U. (1971) Simplification in children's language. In R. Huxley and I. Elisabeth (eds), *Language Acquisition: Models and Methods*, New York: Academic, 95–119.
Bickerton, D. (1981) *Roots of Language*. Ann Arbor: Karoma.
Burling, R. (1973) *English in Black and White*. New York: Holt, Rinehard & Winston.
Crowley, T., and Rigsby, B. (1987) Question formation. In T. Shopen (ed.), *Languages and Their Status*, Cambridge, MA: Winthrop, 153–207.
DeBose, C. E. (1996) Question formation in Samaná English. Paper presented at NWAVE 25, Las Vegas, Nevada.
Dillard, J. L. (1972) *Black English: Its History and Usage in the United States*. New York: Random House.
Ellegård, A. (1953) The auxiliary *do*: The establishment and regulation of its use in English. *Gothenburg studies in English*. Stockholm: Almqvist and Wikwell.
Feagin, C. (1979) *Variation and Change in Alabama English: A Sociolinguistic Study of the White Community*. Washington, DC: Georgetown University Press.
Holm, J. (ed.) (1988) *Pidgins and Creoles, Volume I: Theory and Structure*. Cambridge: Cambridge University Press.
Kroch, A. (1989a) Reflexes of grammar in patterns of language change. *Language Variation and Change*, 1 (3): 199–244.
Kroch, T. (1989b) Function and grammar in the history of English: Periphrastic *do*. In R. Fasold and D. Schiffrin (eds), *Language Change and Variation*, Washington, DC: Georgetown University Press, 133–72.
Labov, W., Cohen, P., Robins, C., and Lewis, J. (1968) *A Study of the Non-standard English of Negro and Puerto Rican Speakers in New York City*, Co-operative Research Report 3288, vol. I. Philadelphia: US Regional Survey.
Labov, W., and Labov, T. (1976) Das Erlerner der Syntax von Fragen. *Lili: Zeitschrift für Literaturwissenschaft und Linguistik*, 6 (23–4): 47–82.

Pienemann, M., Johnston, M., and Brindley, G. (1988) Constructing an acquisition-based procedure for second language assessment. *Studies in Second Language Acquisition*, 10: 217–43.

Poplack, S., and Sankoff, D. (1987) The Philadelphia story in the Spanish Caribbean. *American Speech*, 62 (4): 291–314.

Poplack, S., and Tagliamonte, S. (1989) There's no tense like the present: Verbal -*s* inflection in Early Black English. *Language Variation and Change*, 1 (1): 47–84.

Poplack, S., and Tagliamonte, S. (1991) African American English in the diaspora: The case of old-line Nova Scotians. *Language Variation and Change*, 3 (3): 301–39.

Quirk, R., and Greenbaum, S. (1972) *A University Grammar of English*. London: Longman.

Rand, D., and Sankoff, D. (1990) *GoldVarb: A Variable Rule Application for the Macintosh*, Version 2. Montreal, Canada: Centre de recherches mathématiques, Université de Montréal.

Rawick, G. P. (ed.) (1979) *The American Slave: A Composite Autobiography*. Westport, CT: Greenwood.

Rickford, J. R., Ball, A., Blake, R., Jackson, R., and Martin, N. (1991) Rappin on the copula coffin: theoretical and methodological issues in the analysis of copula variation in African American Vernacular English. *Language Variation and Change*, 3 (1): 103–32.

Schneider, E. W. (1982) On the history of Black English in the USA: Some new evidence. *English World-Wide*, 3 (1): 18–46.

Stein, D. (1988) Semantic similarity between categories as a vehicle of linguistic change. *Diachronica*, 5 (1–2): 1–17.

Stein, D. (1991) Semantic aspects of syntactic change. In D. Kastovsky (ed.), *Historical English Syntax*, Berlin: Mouton de Gruyter, 355–66.

Stein, D. (1992) *Do* and *tun*: A semantics and varieties-based approach to syntactic change. In M. Gerritsen and D. Stein (eds), *Internal and External Factors in Syntactic Change*, Berlin: Mouton de Gruyter, 131–55.

Stromswold, K. (1996) Analyzing children's spontaneous speech. In D. McDaniel, C. McKee, and H. S. Cairns (eds), *Methods for Assessing Children's Syntax*, Cambridge, MA: MIT Press, 23–53.

Van Herk, G. (1996) Question inversion in Ottawa English. Unpublished manuscript, University of Ottawa.

Van Herk, G. (1998) Auxiliary verbs in Early African-American Vernacular English questions: Non-inversion, deletion, and inherent variability. Paper presented at CLA, Ottawa, Canada.

Visser, F. T. (1970) *An Historical Syntax of the English Language*. Leiden: E. J. Brill.

7

It's All Relative: Relativization Strategies in Early African American English

Gunnel Tottie and Dawn Harvie

7.1 Introduction

Although relativization is an area of grammar that has been treated by several researchers of African American Vernacular English (AAVE) (Martin and Wolfram 1998; Montgomery 1991; Schneider 1989; Smith 1969; Tottie and Rey 1997) it has received relatively little attention in the debate over the origins of this variety as a prior creole or as a dialect of English. Perhaps because most of its variants are neither particularly stigmatized, nor stereotypically associated with AAVE, it has not become a center of controversy as have other more salient variables, such as the copula (Walker 1997, and this volume), negation (Howe 1995, 1997; Howe and Walker this volume), verbal -s (Poplack and Tagliamonte 1991b; Tagliamonte & Poplack to appear), and the plural (Poplack and Tagliamonte 1994; Poplack et al. this volume). By contrast, relativization may be called a covert variable (cf. Tottie and Rey 1997).

The three most robust variants of the relative marker in Early African American English (Early AAE) are *that*, *what*, and zero, as illustrated in (1) to (3):

(1) Knocked every tooth **that** he had in his head.   (ANSE/038/166)[1]

(2) She want to do things **what** her age don't give to do, you know.
(SE/003/288)

(3) He said millionaires dies an' leave all Ø they got.   (ESR/012/127)

In this chapter, we build on Tottie and Rey's (1997) analysis of relativization in the Ex-Slave Recordings (ESR; Bailey et al. 1991), extending it to two other varieties of Early AAE: African Nova Scotian English (ANSE; Poplack and Tagliamonte 1991a) and Samaná English (SE; Poplack and Sankoff 1987). Our examination of the system of relativization, particularly zero relatives, in Early AAE is intended as a contribution both to the origins debate and, more generally, to the understanding of the system of relativization in English.

The origins debate concerns the attempt to explain differences between AAVE and other varieties of English, and to determine whether these differences can be attributed to one of the following sources: (i) underlying grammatical structures which derive either from the original languages spoken by the African slaves or from a plantation creole; or (ii) variable (nonstandard) features acquired from the English varieties to which they were originally exposed; or (iii) to some combination of the two.

In this chapter we demonstrate that the systems of relativization in three varieties of Early AAE are fundamentally similar to those of other varieties of English, both standard and nonstandard. The similarities concern the availability and patterns of use of the relative markers *that*, *what*, and zero, and more particularly the use of zero forms. Although we will concentrate on zero relatives, we will also discuss the use of *what* as a relative marker.

As a background to our own investigation, we first discuss relative markers in contemporary AAVE in section 7.2, and in English-based creoles (EBCs) in section 7.3. We discuss the use of zero relative markers in the history of English in section 7.4, and the use of *what* as a relativizer in English in section 7.5. In section 7.6 we present our data and methodology, and in sections 7.7 to 7.9 we detail the results of our investigation.

7.2 Relative Markers in Contemporary AAVE

As shown by Schneider (1989) and Tottie and Rey (1997), very little work has been done on relativization in contemporary AAVE. The exceptions known to us are Smith (1969), McKay (1969), Light (1969), Dillard (1972), Labov and Cohen (1973), and Martin and Wolfram (1998). With the exception of McKay, none of the studies offer accountable quantitative data, and some of the information is contradictory. Labov and Cohen (1973: 227) surprisingly assert that *which* is the prevalent relative pronoun in AAVE. Light (1969), known to us only through Schneider (1989: 218), claims that there are no subject zeros in AAVE (although he does quote one in an example).

Among other authors there is some consistency in pointing out two nonstandard features of AAVE relativization, namely the use of *what* and zero subjects. Thus Smith (1969) points to the occurrence of these features but gives no overview of the system. Dillard (1972: 68ff) notes that "the relative clause patterns [in Black English or AAVE] are also a great deal different [from Standard English (StdE)]." He reports that there are both zero object and zero subject relatives in AAVE, referring to the latter as "the typical . . . relative pronoun of Black English and related varieties" (Dillard 1972: 59). Dillard quotes (4) and (5) below as examples of subject relatives.

(4)   That's the chick Ø I keep tellin' you about Ø got all that money.   (Dillard 1972: 60)

(5)   He got a gun Ø sound like a bee.   (Dillard 1972: 68)

Dillard futher notes that subject zeros are also found in Jamaican Creole and other African American dialects but fails to mention that this construction is found in a number of nonstandard varieties of English. He also states that if there is an overt relative pronoun in AAVE it is *what*, noting that it is found in a creole (Gullah), but again failing to mention that it occurs in many nonstandard varieties of English. (See also section 7.5.) In a similar vein, Martin and Wolfram (1998: 38f) especially stress the existence of subject zeros in AAVE, claiming that this distinguishes AAVE from other varieties of English. They also point to the preference for *that* over *who* and the existence of object zero constructions.

    Unfortunately, the only accountable study of relatives in contemporary AAVE, McKay (1969), is based on the speech of a single informant, comprising a mere 56 restrictive relative clauses.[2] In McKay's data, zero is the most frequently used relativizer, with 54% of all cases, more than half of which are subjects; *that* comes second with 38%, and *what* accounts for 9%; except for quotations from the Bible, *who* and *which* do not occur.

    The accounts reported here thus point to the existence of an AAVE system almost entirely lacking the relativizers *who* or *which*, but with *that*, *what*, and zero as prominent members. Among these, *what* and subject zero stand out as nonstandard. However, it is important to point out that large-scale quantitative research in this area is still missing.

7.3   Relative Markers in English-based Creoles

We begin by addressing the question of whether relative markers, especially zero relatives, in AAVE are likely to derive from creole usage.

Based on "the fact that in a number of creoles [Guyanese Creole, Seychelles Creole, some Portuguese creoles] there still exist conservative dialects or restricted sentence types in which relative pronouns are deletable in subject position – or rather, more probably, were never inserted," Bickerton (1981: 63) speculates that creoles may have been "born without surface relativizers" and that speakers subsequently introduced surface relativizers as a means of avoiding ambiguity. (This development would then parallel that sketched for Standard English by Bever and Langendoen (1971) as regards subject zeros.)

However, zero relatives are reported to exist in only six of the thirty-three EBCs surveyed by Hancock (1987) (viz. Bahamian, Belizean, Guyanese, Hawaiian Creole, Liberian English, and Providencian), while the other twenty-six are said to have only overt relativizers. In addition to Gullah (cf. Mufwene 1986), zero relatives are also reported for Tok Pisin by Sankoff and Brown (1976), Romaine (1988) and Aitchison (1992). They are also attested in contemporary AAVE.

Bickerton (1981) cites relativization as one of five variables that distinguish Hawaiian Pidgin from Hawaiian Creole English. He focuses on relative constructions especially in connection with pronoun-copying, an aspect that we will not treat here. He quotes examples like (6) and (7) (Bickerton 1981: 35):

(6) da gai Ø gon lei da vainil fo mi bin kwot mi prais
"The guy WHO is going to lay the vinyl for me had quoted me a price."

(7) yu si di ailan Ø get koknat
"You see the island THAT has coconut palms on it."

It would be useful to have a comprehensive view of relativization strategies in EBCs, but we have as yet been unable to locate any fully accountable quantitative studies. A good qualitative survey is provided by Mufwene (1986), who gives an account of relativization in Gullah, listing the variants *wat*, *wuh*, *weh*, *who* and zero as subject relatives (plus *fuh* in non-finite constructions), and the same variants except *wuh* as object relatives. For other NP positions, or functions of the relativizer, see further Mufwene (1986).

However, given the fact that EBCs do not seem to share a common system of relativization, it is difficult to argue that zero relatives in Early AAE, which we will see in what follows to be systematically constrained, have a creole origin. In the remainder of this study we test the alternative hypothesis, that the variable use of zero relatives in Early AAE was acquired from contemporaneous varieties of English. We begin with a brief diachronic account of the use of zero relativization in English, both in the standard language and in regional dialects.

7.4 Zero Relative Markers in the History of English

Many studies confirm that although overt relatives were by far the most frequent type, zero forms have existed since the very earliest attestation of English (cf. Traugott 1992: 224, 228; and Mitchell 1985: vol. 2, 186ff). In Old English, subject relatives were the norm, but object relatives also did occur, although examples of this type are frequently ambiguous, as examples (8) and (9) demonstrate:

(8) . . . se fæder hyre sealde ane þeowene, Ø Bala hatte.   (Mitchell 1985: vol. 2, 186)
"and her father gave her a (maid)servant, *who* was called Bala"

(9) buton anre hide Ø ic gean into þære cyrcean þam preoste þe þar gode þeowaþ.   (Mitchell 1985: vol. 2, 188)
"except for one hide *that* I give to the church, to the priest who serves God there"

In Middle English, zero relatives in subject function were still the predominant type, but zero object relatives were becoming more frequent (cf. Fischer 1992: 306ff). Illustrative examples from Chaucer's *Canterbury Tales* are (10) and (11):

(10) Withinne our yeerd, wheer as I saugh a beest
Ø Was lyk an hound . . .
"In our yard, where I saw a beast Ø was like a dog . . ."
(Chaucer, *The Nun's Priest's Tale*, line 4089)

(11) Greet was the wo Ø the knyght hadde in this thoght . . .
"Great was the woe Ø the knight had in his mind . . ."
(Chaucer, *The Wife of Bath's Tale*, line 1083)

In Early Modern English (Early ModE), zero relativization increased overall, mostly in object relatives and relativizers functioning as prepositional complements, whereas subject zero relatives fell into disuse in StdE (Dekeyser 1984: 65). That they survived in the spoken language in the Early ModE period is clear from plays:

(12) I have a neece Ø is a merchants wife.   (Ben Jonson, *Every Man Out of His Humour*, I, ii, 1600)

(13) I bring him news Ø will raise his drooping spirits.   (Dryden, *All for Love*, I, 113, 1678)

Early grammarians, among them Bishop Lowth, noted and commented on the existence of zero relativization. That famous prescriptivist observed: "The Relative is often understood, or omitted: as, 'The man I love,' that is, 'whom I love'." Lowth does not mention subject zeros but criticizes object zero constructions, saying: "The construction is hazardous, and hardly justifiable, even in Poetry" (Lowth 1762/1775: 175, fn 2). However, in this area, prescriptive judgments had no effect; object zeros continued to increase in the standard language as well as in nonstandard varieties. The question of whether subject zeros declined in the standard language because of the ambiguity of structures such as *The girl knew the man became sick*, as Bever and Langendoen (1971) argue, remains controversial. Romaine (1982: 78) argues that this ambiguity is only a problem in the written language and that "[i]n the spoken language tonic placement would probably disambiguate most doubtful cases." The difficulty of using them in writing may certainly have played a part in their disappearance.

Zero relatives in subject function are attested in most present-day nonstandard and regional dialects of English. Dialect maps of England show that in data elicited in the frame *I know a man . . . will do it for you*, the overall majority of respondents all over England supplied a zero subject relative in preference to all other alternatives (cf. Orton et al. 1978: Map S5; and the discussion in Poussa 1985: 99ff). Zero subjects were especially frequent in the Southwest and the Northeast of England, but were also recorded in most other areas. Studies of specific dialects give support for this usage in different dialects. Thus, for instance, Van den Eynden (1993) records a total of 129/480 or 27% zero relatives in her Dorset corpus. Of these, 29% have subject function, and of all subjects, 14% are zero forms. Macaulay (1991) observes an interesting social class difference in the use of zero in subject function in the dialect of Ayr in Scotland. In his middle-class sample, 5/180 (<3%) of all restrictive relative clause subjects were zeros, but in the lower-class sample, as many as 53/221 (24%) were. Similarly, Hackenberg's data (1972) show that lower-class speakers of Appalachian English had more zero subjects (35% with both personal and non-personal antecedents) than higher-class speakers, who had 11–13% respectively (see Ball 1996: 242).

7.5 *What* as a Relative Marker in English

What has also existed as a relative marker at least since the beginnings of Middle English, especially after *all* and *nothing*.[3] Some examples from Middle English and Early ModE taken from Curme (1977) follow:

(14)   Til she had herd all **what** the frere sayde   (Chaucer, *The Somnours Tale*, 493)

(15)   Every lover thoughte, That all was well **what** so he seyde and wroughte   (Chaucer, *Troilus and Criseyde*, III, 1799)

(16)   anything **what** thou wilt   (Ben Jonson, *Every Man Out of His Humour*, V, iii, AD 1600)

(17)   To persue everything **what** went into the "Post"   (H. Sydnor Harrison, *Queed*, ch. VII)

Curme (1977: vol. II, 215) also observes that "[I]n popular speech . . . *what* may point back to a definite antecedent, even to one representing a person or persons" as in the examples below (1977: vol. II, 215). Notice also example (20), which is not an example of popular speech:

(18)   I can't see that the man **what**'s willing to remain poor all his life has any pride at all   (George Moore, *Esther Waters*, ch. VI)

(19)   This is them two sisters **what** tied themselves together with a handkercher   (Dickens, *Our Mutual Friend*, I, ch. III)

(20)   That **what** we falsely call a religious cry is easily raised by men who have no religion   (Dickens, *Barnaby Rudge*, Preface)

In present-day English, *what* as a relative marker meaning "who, which, that" in headed relative constructions is stigmatized as "now *dial.* or *vulgar*" by the OED (2nd edn, s.v. C I 7a). However, it is documented in a large number of nonstandard British dialects. The dialect survey maps (Orton et al. 1978; and Viereck and Ramisch 1991) do not do justice to the widespread use of *what* as a relativizer, but it is well documented in a large number of specialized dialect studies, such as Ihalainen (1980), and Van den Eynden (1993). In these studies, *what* is a minor variant; thus, for instance, the rural Dorset dialect described by Van den Eynden (1993) has 27% zero, 39% *that*, and 7% *what* (N = 480). *What* also occurs in the English spoken in Reading by teenagers (Cheshire 1982) and in present-day Yorkshire English (Tagliamonte, personal communication). In vernacular American dialects, its occurrence is reported by Wolfram and Christian (1976: 121) in Appalachian English, although it is not reported to be a frequent variant either in that variety or in other nonstandard dialects (cf. Ball 1996: 241 and 253, fn 11 and 12).

However, there are also careful dialect studies that report *what* to be a major variant in the relative marker paradigm in the eastern parts of England. Poussa (1993) shows, on the basis of extensive elicited material, that *what* is the preferred relative marker in Norfolk, and she reports similar findings by Ojanen (1982) for Cambridgeshire. Kekäläinen (1985) also demonstrates that in Suffolk, *what* is the most frequently used relative marker. Extremely interesting in this context is also Forby (1830/1970). This early dialectologist, whose manuscript was finished in 1825, reports the frequent use of *what* as a relative pronoun equivalent to *who* and *which*. Forby (1830/1970: 138) states: "*What* is very often used for the relatives *who* or *which*. Ex. 'The woman *what* came yesterday.' 'The pigs *what* I bought last Tuesday.' "[4] As it is difficult to find historical data on nonstandard and dialectal forms that have never been part of the standard language this is particularly valuable evidence for the availability of *what* in varieties of English that may have served as input to Early AAE.[5]

As is clear from this and the previous section, both *what* and zero relative markers in subject function are well-established variants in the relative marker paradigm in nonstandard British and American dialects.

7.6 Data and Methods

The data used in this study were extracted from three datasets on Early AAE: African Nova Scotian English Corpus (ANSE; Poplack and Tagliamonte 1991a), the Samaná English Corpus (SE; Poplack and Sankoff 1987) and the Ex-Slave Recordings (ESR; Bailey et al. 1991). Every relative clause was extracted from taped conversations with 12 speakers of ANSE, 12 speakers of SE, and 10 speakers from the Ex-Slave sample, resulting in a total of 245 tokens for ANSE, 406 tokens for SE, and 116 tokens for ESR.

Relative markers are a fairly infrequent phenomenon. Based on Bailey et al. (1991), we calculate that the ESR consist of about 37,000 words, meaning that the frequency here would be 116/37,000 or 3 per one thousand words. The interviews with the 12 ANSE speakers included in this study consist of a total of approximately 239,000 words; the frequency here is 245/239,000 or 1 per thousand words. The interviews with the 12 SE speakers consist of a total of approximately 151,000 words, yielding a frequency of 406/151,000 or 2.7 per thousand words.

7.6.1   Circumscribing the variable context

Because of the widely varying practices of previous studies of relative markers, we specify here exactly the types of constructions under study. We begin with those that we do not consider, and continue in 7.6.2 with the factors we examined for possible conditioning effects on the choice of relative marker, especially zero. Each of these factors represents a hypothesis proposed to explain variability in relativization strategies in other studies of relative markers in English.

7.6.1.1   Exclusions

Among the constructions not considered in this study are non-restrictive relative clauses, where the antecedent was already a fully determined NP head, as in (21). We also excluded adverbial relative constructions, where the relativizer was *where*, *when*, or *why*, or an alternant of these relativizers.

(21)   Anderson **who** was then you know [inc][6] a old president they call Lilis
        he– that's where you– see Peter-van- married his sister.   (SE/001/50)

We excluded instances of *whiz*-deletion, such as (22), where both the relative marker and the auxiliary *be* are deleted. These constructions, although found in StdE, are not normally classified as relative clauses by researchers because grammarians have usually focused on finite constructions, and because of the lack of variability in these constructions. *Whiz*-deletion also involves issues of auxiliary-deletion (Van Herk 1998). Thus none of the studies cited in this chapter discuss this phenomenon except Huddleston (1971).

(22)   And there's alot of people Ø [who are] gonna be hungry this winter.
        (ANSE/030/2620lt)

There were many instances of ambiguity, such as (23) and (24), where the clause is ambiguous between a relative clause and a subordinate clause introduced by the complementizer *that*. The utterance in (24) could be paraphrased as: "I don't want any crow *who/that/Ø* comes around and tells me . . ." or "I don't want any crow to come around and tell me. . . ." We also excluded constructions that were ambiguous between restrictive and non-restrictive relativization.

(23) Well, we had to do that because there wasn't nothing much to eat. I saw one time **that** we were so hungry, off the potato skins, all the pota– all the potato skins off potato and we used to take them.   (ANSE/016/90)

(24) I don't want no crow Ø come around telling me [inc].   (ANSE/039/1175c)

The utterance in (25) was excluded because it is impossible to tell, even with more context, exactly what is meant, and in (26), hesitation makes it difficult to determine whether there is a relative clause.

(25) Whatever was home **what** had anything drinking.   (ANSE/030/1512)

(26) And so different things Ø do we– one has and you take that pee and you drinks that with– let it be whatever– some other medicine whatever it is according to the m– according to whatever it is you know. (SE/002/863)

We also excluded non-headed relatives, such as (27), which are invariant.

(27) That's **who** brought me up.   (ANSE/016/893)

For the purposes of this study we thus consider only restrictive, non-adverbial relative clauses, henceforth, "relative clauses", as in (28). We do this for two reasons: firstly, most of the variability occurs in this context, and secondly, this is the preferred site for zero relatives.

(28) That's for cold, or anything Ø you have around your body.   (ANSE/031/156t)

7.6.2   Selecting and coding factors

Previous work on relative constructions in English is extremely heterogeneous. Material, methods of data collection and classification, as well as explanatory factors chosen for study, show a rich and sometimes bewildering array of varieties and factors. Thus, to name but a few of them, Quirk (1957) studied educated spoken British English, Huddleston (1971) written scientific British English, Taglicht (1973) written British non-fiction, Olofsson (1981) written American English, fiction as well as non-fiction, Romaine (1982) Scots and Middle Scots,

Guy and Bayley (1995) spoken and written American English, Tottie (1995) written British and American English, and Ball (1996) compared spoken British and American English (in addition to re-analyzing many other types of data). Olofsson (1981) looked only at relative constructions with non-personal (i.e. non-human) antecedents, and Ball (1996) at personal and non-personal relative markers but only in subject function. Some writers included relative markers in adverbial function or in some adverbial functions (e.g. Olofsson 1981; Quirk 1957; Romaine 1982), but others excluded them (e.g. Macaulay 1991). Spoken material was either broadcast or surreptitiously recorded (Quirk 1957), re-corded with the knowledge of at least some of the participants (Guy and Bayley 1995), or collected in sociolinguistic interviews (Macaulay 1991). Most writers chose, as we do, to examine only restrictive relative clauses.

Among the variables examined for possible effects on the choice of relative marker are humanness of the antecedent (and thus of the referent of the relat-ive marker as well), grammatical function of the relative marker in the relative clause, various properties of the antecedent such as definiteness, quantification, or superlative premodifiers, length of the relative clause, adjacency of anteced-ent and relative marker, position of relative clause (final or medial), and subject of the relative clause. Extra-linguistic factors such as class or gender have also been included (Adamson 1992; Cheshire 1982; Macaulay 1991; Tottie and Rey 1997). Variable rule methodology was used by Adamson (1992), Guy and Bayley (1995), Tottie (1995), and Tottie and Rey (1997) to assess the contribution of these and other factors. For the present study, we coded our material for those factors that seemed most revealing on the basis of earlier studies and for which the data were sufficient to permit investigation according to the methods described below. Each example was coded for the relative marker, speaker, and function of the relative marker, as well as for those factor groups listed in (29). References are given in parentheses to the presentation of relevant results in section 7.8.

(29)   FACTOR GROUPS:

Matrix clause factors:
- Grammatical category of antecedent NP head (7.6.2.1, 7.8.1)
- Adjacency of antecedent NP head and relative marker (7.6.2.2, 7.8.2)
- Humanness of antecedent NP head (7.6.2.4, 7.8.4)

Relative clause factor:
- Category membership of subject of relative clause (7.6.2.3, 7.8.3)

Each of the factor groups above comprises several factors which will be dis-cussed below.

7.6.2.1   Grammatical category of antecedent NP head
The grammatical category of the antecedent NP head has been claimed to play an important role in the choice of relative marker in several studies. Huddleston (1971) showed a correlation between definiteness of the antecedent and zero relativization, but Taglicht (1973) found no such effect, and Tottie (1995: 212) showed that such an effect could not be supported by a variable rule analysis. Olofsson (1981) showed a correlation between "special antecedents," including superlatives and pronouns, and zero relativization.

Each token was coded for pronoun, as in (30a), indefinite NP, as in (30b), and definite NP, as in (30c).

(30)   a.   Ain't doing *nothing* Ø God want to do.   (ANSE/016/240t)

       b.   The doctor told me I got something in the head but I do say 'twas *a cold* Ø I caught in that head, you know.   (SE/003/592)

       c.   The clothes, I mean nothing like *the clothes* Ø you wear today. (ANSE/002/22t)

7.6.2.2   Adjacency of antecedent NP head and relative marker
The adjacency of the relative marker to its antecedent NP has been given a good deal of attention by grammarians. Jespersen (1965) noted that zero relatives must be adjacent to their antecedent, and this has been empirically confirmed for educated spoken British English (Quirk 1957; Taglicht 1973) and standard American English (Guy and Bayley 1995; Olofsson 1981). The factors in this factor group are simply adjacent, as in (31a), and non-adjacent, as in (31b).

(31)   a.   Yes, all that kind of foolishness, that's *all* Ø we got.
                                                        (ANSE/016/272)

       b.   They had a *fella* here Ø had a property.   (SE/019/375)

7.6.2.3   Category membership of subject of relative clause
The grammatical category of the subject of the relative clause has also been shown to be important for the choice of relative marker. Zero relatives have been shown to co-occur with personal pronoun subjects ("light subjects") in American English (Olofsson 1981) as well as British English (Quirk 1957; Taglicht 1973).

This factor group was coded for personal pronoun, as in (32a), definite NP, as in (32b), indefinite NP, as in (32c), and proper name, as in (32d).

(32) a.   All Ø *he* do is go calling people– girls and thing and Amy– doing the
           same thing with Mildred.   (ANSE/030/496c)

      b.   Yes, yes, when we had worms they used to dig the worms, and put
           them in a st– old stockings Ø *the women* used to wear like in the–
           mostly like nylon stocking but they were kind of heavy and tie
           it– live worm to our stomach.   (ANSE/002/55t)

      c.   That's the first– the first education Ø *any pers– any person* have.
           (SE/019/861)

      d.   I have the heart **what** *God* give me.   (SE/014/323)

7.6.2.4   Humanness of antecedent NP head
The humanness of the antecedent has been a key factor in the choice of relative marker since the beginning of the Early ModE period. Its main importance concerns the choice between *who* and *which*, but Quirk (1957) shows that
for educated spoken British English, zero relatives have mostly non-human
antecedents, and this is confirmed by Tottie (1997: 204). This factor group is
divided into non-human, (33a), and human, (33b).[7]

(33) a.   There wasn't *nothing* Ø she could let out of there 'cause it were
           cooked.   (ANSE/030/2742lt)

      b.   On the way– he's *the only one* Ø be on that land.   (ANSE/031/398)

7.7   Overall Results

In our presentation of the results of our investigation, we will not proceed in
exactly the same way as Tottie and Rey (1997) for several reasons. First,
contrary to our expectations at the outset of our work, each set of speakers –
Nova Scotia, Samaná and Ex-Slave – turned out to have different overall preferences for relative markers. Secondly, we present results for zero relatives in
subject and non-subject function separately, rather than pooling them as done
by Tottie and Rey (1997). We do this for two reasons. Firstly, this enables us to
avoid interaction between the factors testing humanness of the antecedent and
syntactic function of the relative marker in the relative clause. The basic assumption is that factor groups contribute independent effects to the probability that
a zero relative will be selected. However, as in so many other cases, notably
the copula (Walker, this volume), and the plural (Poplack et al., this volume),

Table 7.1 Cross-tabulation of humanness and syntactic function of the relative marker in the relative clause for zero in ANSE, SE, and ESR

	ANSE		SE		ESR	
	Subject	Object	Subject	Object	Subject	Object
Human	78	13	223	37	56	13
Non-human	28	109	48	83	2	36

this turns out not to be the case. On the contrary, as table 7.1 illustrates, subjects are correlated with humanness, and objects are correlated with non-humanness (Ball 1996; Montgomery 1991; Schneider 1989; Tottie and Rey 1997), so that, given a particular antecedent, it is impossible to tell whether the effect in question is due to the syntactic function of the relative marker in the relative clause or to the humanness of antecedent. Attempts to factor out this interaction result in further overlap among the interaction term (human subject, human object, non-human subject, non-human object) and other factors, subject of the relative clause in particular.

Secondly, we wanted to maximize comparability with previous research on zero relatives, which has dealt mostly with dialects without subject zeros.

However, making separate analyses of subject and non-subject relatives results in some cells becoming too small to support a variable rule analysis. In what follows, we therefore focus on the *proportions* of zero in each of the contexts we have identified, basing our discussion on marginal percentages. In section 7.7.1, we first present the overall distribution of variant relative markers in all syntactic functions, followed by their overall distribution in non-subject and subject function, respectively. Section 7.8 presents relative marker usage in non-subject function according to the factor groups discussed in section 7.6, and section 7.9 discusses the use of relative markers in subject function.

7.7.1 Overall distribution of variants

Table 7.2 shows the overall distribution of relative markers in all three varieties of Early AAE. We see that the three relative markers *that*, *what*, and zero predominate in each of the varieties of Early AAE, but that overall, a different one is favored by each: *that* in ANSE (43%), *what* in SE (53%), and zero in ESR (59%). Indeed, these three markers accounted for 99% of the total in

Table 7.2 Overall distribution of relative markers in non-adverbial restrictive relative clauses in ANSE, SE, and ESR

	ANSE	SE	ESR
Zero	37%	19%	59%
	91	78	68
That	43%	21%	33%
	105	86	38
What	19%	53%	9%
	47	214	10
Who	0%	6%	–
	1	24	0
Which	0%	1%	–
	1	4	0
Total	245	406	116

ANSE, 93% in SE, and were the only ones recorded in ESR. These figures should be compared with those reported by Schneider (1989) based on the written Rawick data (N = 786): 39% zero, 26% *that*, and 28% *what*.[8] The StdE variants *which* and *who* are rare in both ANSE and SE and do not occur at all in ESR (see, e.g., Ball 1996). It is interesting to note that *who* occurs as often as 6% in SE; *whom* does not occur in any of the varieties.

Examples of the favored relativizers in each variety were given in (1) to (3) above. Although zero relatives were not the preferred variant in ANSE or SE, they are still robust with 37% in ANSE and 19% in SE.

Tables 7.3 and 7.4 show the distribution of relative markers in non-subject and subject function, respectively. A comparison of tables 7.3 and 7.4 shows, as expected, that the distribution of variant pronouns is different in different syntactic functions. In non-subject function, zero is the preferred variant not only in ESR but also in ANSE, with 76% and 48%, respectively, and though *what* predominates in SE, zero is three times as frequent in non-subject function as in subject function. In subject function, *that* is the preferred variant in both ANSE and ESR, with 59% and 48%, respectively. *What* is still the preferred variant in SE, with 55%. Zero is a strong competitor in ESR, where it is used in as many as 41% of all cases, and robust (23%) in ANSE, though it accounts for only 11% in SE.

Table 7.3   Overall distribution of non-subject relatives

	ANSE	SE	ESR
Zero	48%	36%	76%
	67	48	44
That	30%	15%	17%
	42	20	10
What	21%	48%	7%
	29	65	4
Who	–	1%	–
	0	1	0
Which	1%	1%	–
	1	1	0
Total	139	135	58

Table 7.4   Overall distribution of subject relatives

	ANSE	SE	ESR
Zero	23%	11%	41%
	24	30	24
That	59%	24%	48%
	63	66	28
What	17%	55%	10%
	18	149	6
Who	1%	8%	–
	1	23	0
Which	–	1%	–
	0	3	0
Total	106	271	58

Both in their alternation among *that*, *what*, and zero and, to some extent, in their distribution, the three varieties of Early AAE thus parallel other standard and nonstandard varieties of English in Britain as well as in the United States. *That* needs hardly any comment, as its widespread use in both speech and writing on both sides of the Atlantic is well documented (see, e.g., Guy and Bayley 1995; Tottie 1997). The same holds for zero in non-subject function. As we have seen above in section 7.5, *what* is well represented in English regional dialects, constituting a major variant in northern East Anglia, where there is also strong historical evidence for its frequency in the eighteenth century, as discussed in section 7.5 above. The widespread use of zero in subject function is well documented in nonstandard dialects like Appalachian English and Scottish English. Thus none of the characteristics of the relative markers of Early AAE studied here is either unique to them or traceable to what has been documented for creoles.

7.8   Zero Relative Markers in Non-subject Function

The overwhelming majority (between 85 and 95 percent) of relative markers in non-subject function were direct objects in all three varieties of Early AAE, with a sprinkling of prepositional complements and isolated examples of indirect objects and notional subjects.

7.8.1   *Grammatical category of antecedent NP head*

Contrary to the findings of Huddleston (1971), but in accordance with the findings of Taglicht (1973) and Tottie (1995) for other varieties of English, table 7.5 shows that definite NP heads do not correlate with zero relatives in our material. On the contrary, definite NPs show a lower-than-average incidence of zero in SE. Pronominal antecedents have the highest incidence of zero in all three varieties (although the differences between pronominal and other antecedents are small in ANSE), a fact that should be compared with the finding that pronouns such as *anything* and *anyone* have been shown by Olofsson (1981: 94ff) to favor zero relatives in written American English. The examples in (34) are thus typical instances.

(34)   a.   She did bake and fix for *anything* Ø you wanted, you could have went to her, yes ma'am.   (SE/002/1122)

     b.   Ain't doing *nothing* Ø God want to do.   (ANSE/016/240t)

Table 7.5 Distribution of zero according to the grammatical category of the antecedent NP head (non-subject relatives only)

	ANSE	SE	ESR
Total N	139	135	58
Total zero relatives	67	48	44
Pronoun	55% 17/31	50% 8/16	89% 16/18
Definite NP	48% 34/71	24% 18/76	74% 20/27
Indefinite NP	43% 16/37	51% 22/43	62% 8/13

Table 7.6 Distribution of zero according to adjacency of the antecedent NP head and the relative marker (non-subject relatives only)

	ANSE	SE	ESR
Total N	139	135	58
Total zero relatives	67	48	44
Adjacent	50% 66/131	37% 47/127	84% 43/51
Non-adjacent	13% 1/8	13% 1/8	14% 1/7

7.8.2   *Adjacency of antecedent NP head and relative marker*

Table 7.6 demonstrates that the adjacency of the relative to its antecedent is as relevant to the diaspora varieties of English as it is to British English (Quirk 1957) and standard American English (Guy and Bayley 1995; Olofsson 1981). As table 7.6 shows, in all three varieties of Early AAE the majority of zero relatives are adjacent to the antecedent NP head and account for a high proportion of the relative markers.

Examples of zero relatives adjacent to an antecedent NP head are found in (35):

(35) a.   And I wanted to do the same thing Ø she was doing. (ANSE/002/
           15t)

      b.   Only one Ø they stayed with is Romana. (SE/001/520)

Where antecedent and relativizer were non-adjacent, zero relatives did also occur, as in (36a), but overt relativizers were mostly used, as in (36b) and (36c).

(36) a.   Because they had a next old lady, stayed up on that hill, Ø they call
           Semiraya. (SE/002/1010)

      b.   A old lady, you know, **what** had knowed medicines and thing.
           (SE/002/637)

      c.   I'm scared to death of hell, 'cause I been seeing it so much and it must
           be alot back here **that** God left for me to do. (ANSE/016/60)

7.8.3   *Category membership of subject of relative clause*

Consistent with findings concerning the importance of the grammatical cat-egory of the subject of the relative clause in British English (Quirk 1957; Taglicht 1973) as well as American English (Olofsson 1981), table 7.7 reveals that personal pronouns, so-called light subjects, also clearly favor zero relative for SE and ESR, though in ANSE, category membership does not affect choice of relative. This is exemplified in (37a) and (37b).

(37) a.   Personal pronouns:
           I was a child Ø they raising there and you know I didn't– uhm.
           (SE/003/273)
           Old friend Ø I got there in town. (SE/002/782)
           That was the example Ø she leave for her children. (SE/017/256)

      b.   Definite NP:
           Old white horse Ø my father got from uh– George-Buddy down
           Cherry-Brook. (ANSE/014/72t)
           And we gave him a little bit of the medicine **what** the doctor had
           sent. (SE/002/644)
           My first name, first name **what** my mother name me, is Mitchell,
           Mitchell Watkins. (ESR/012/10)

Table 7.7 Distribution of zero according to the category membership of the subject of the relative clause (non-subject relatives only)

	ANSE	SE	ESR
Total N	139	135	58
Total zero relatives	67	48	44
Definite NP	50%	9%	40%
	7/14	1/11	2/5
Personal pronoun	49%	37%	79%
	60/123	46/123	41/52
Indefinite NP	–	100%	100%
	0/0	1/1	1/1
Noun	0%	–	–
	0/2	0/0	0/0

Table 7.8 Distribution of zero according to humanness of the antecedent NP head (non-subject relatives only)

	ANSE	SE	ESR
Total N	139	135	58
Total zero relatives	67	48	44
Non-human	48%	34%	80%
	57/118	31/92	33/41
Human	48%	40%	65%
	10/21	17/43	11/17

7.8.4 Humanness of antecedent NP head

Table 7.8 shows that humanness of antecedent NP head does not exercise a consistent effect on relative choice in Early AAE. Only ESR shows a weak tendency, established for educated spoken British English (Quirk 1957; Tottie 1997: 472f.), to favor zero as a relative marker with non-human antecedents; SE shows a weak tendency to the contrary, and there is no effect at all in ANSE.

7.8.5   Summary of factors determining the use of
zero relatives in non-subject function

We see that among the factors singled out by previous researchers as favoring zero relativization, the varieties of AAE studied here have much in common with other dialects of English, including varieties of standard English. The most robust similarities in non-subject relative function concern the type of antecedent and adjacency of the antecedent and relative marker, while category membership of the relative clause subject was a determining factor in two of the three Early AAE varieties. Only humanness of the antecedent fails to show a consistent effect in this material; this factor requires further investigation to determine whether it is indeed predictive of relative marker choice.

7.9   Zero Relative Markers in Subject Function

As already pointed out in section 7.4, zero relatives in subject function are well established in nonstandard varieties of English. The speakers of Early AAE documented here ranged between 11% (SE) and 41% (ESR), with ANSE falling between them with 23% (cf. tables 7.4, 7.9, and 7.10).

Turning now to factors determining the use of zero relativization in this context, we cannot expect the same constraints to apply to subject zeros as to object and other non-subject zeros, for several reasons. We have already shown that humanness of the antecedent is tied to subject function of the relative marker; there are pragmatic reasons for this, as humans tend to be agents and non-human entities tend to be patients (cf. Tottie and Rey 1997: 239f). Moreover, the factor group involving the category membership of the subject of the relative clause is void, as the subject is always the relative marker. However, we coded subject relative constructions according to the same schema as the non-subject zeros for the other factor groups and report here on those factor groups which affected the choice of relative, namely grammatical category of the antecedent NP head and adjacency of antecedent and the relative marker.

Table 7.9 shows the distribution of subject zeros according to the grammatical category of the antecedent NP head. In each variety of Early AAE examined, indefinite NP heads clearly favor zero relatives, an effect which is especially robust in SE and ESR.

Table 7.10 shows the distribution of subject zeros in adjacent and non-adjacent constructions. We notice that adjacent constructions are the majority

Table 7.9 Distribution of zero according to the grammatical category of the antecedent NP head (subject relatives only)

	ANSE	SE	ESR
Total N	106	271	58
Total zero relatives	24	30	24
Indefinite NP	25% 6/24	20% 19/93	69% 9/13
Definite NP	22% 15/67	3% 3/115	40% 14/35
Pronoun	20% 3/15	13% 8/61	11% 1/9
Numeral	– 0/0	0% 0/2	0% 0/1

Table 7.10 Distribution of zero according to adjacency of the antecedent NP head and the relative marker (subject relatives only)

	ANSE	SE	ESR
Total N	106	271	58
Total zero relatives	24	30	24
Adjacent	24% 23/96	11% 27/253	45% 22/49
Non-adjacent	10% 1/10	17% 3/18	22% 2/9

in each variety, and that in ANSE and ESR adjacency favors zero relatives. In SE the effect seems to be reversed but notice that numbers are low.

Hackenberg (1972) also considered adjacency as a factor favoring zero relativization in white Appalachian English, but found that zero subject relative markers occurred with practically the same frequency in constructions where antecedent and relative marker were adjacent as in those where they were

Table 7.11 Distribution of different types of subject zero constructions in three dialects of Early AAE and Appalachian English (AppE; Hackenberg, 1972)

	ANSE		SE		ESR		AppE	
	%	N	%	N	%	N	%	N
Existential constructions	21	5	–	–	13	3	40	39
Possessive *have/got*	13	3	63	19	8	2	26	25
It/That clefts	8	2	3	1	–	–	6	6
Other	58	14	33	10	79	19	29	28
Total	100%	24	99%	30	100%	24	101%	98

non-adjacent, or 27% and 32%, respectively. However, he did find that adjacency played a part in existential *there*-sentences: such constructions had 52% zero relatives, whereas non-existentials had only 28% (Hackenberg 1972: 105ff).

It thus seemed of particular interest in this context to look closely at the particular syntactic constructions in which subject zero relatives occur in the dialects of Early AAE that we investigated, and to compare these with favored environments in other varieties of English that allow zero subject relatives. Ball (1996: 257) gives a useful overview of typical constructions here, listing them as follows:

(i)   Existential constructions (with examples from Ayr, Yorkshire, Somerset, Appalachian English, as well as earlier English);
(ii) Possessives with *have* and *get* (with examples from Ayr, Yorkshire, Norwich, and Appalachian);
(iii) *It/That*-Clefts (with examples from Somerset, Appalachian, and 17th century English);
(iv) "Other", as in *Everybody Ø lives in the mountains has an accent all to theirself,* from Appalachian English.   (Wolfram and Christian 1976: epigraph)

We checked the occurrence of these different constructions in our material and compared it with the data found in Hackenberg (1972). This work includes an extremely useful appendix listing all the relative constructions in the material, and it was thus possible to calculate the proportions of the different types of constructions with zero relatives. We report the distribution of zero subject relatives in Early AAE dialects as well as in Hackenberg's data on Appalachian English in table 7.11.

We see that despite the sparseness of the data the four types of constructions listed by Ball (1996) are all attested in Early AAE, although SE has no instances of *there*-constructions, and *it/that*-clefts are absent from the ESR sample. Interestingly, the possessive *have/got* constructions are highly favored in SE, with 63% of the total. The distribution in Hackenberg's data is most similar to that found in ANSE: the most frequent type was the existential *there*-construction, followed by *have/got* constructions and cleft constructions. The residual "other" category accounted for 27% in Hackenberg's data and is large in all three varieties of Early AAE, ranging from 33% in SE to 79% in ESR. This is a mixed bag of constructions that would merit further analysis. However, in order to undertake a valid analysis of the data for subject zero relatives, one would have to re-analyze all subject constructions in search of possible constraints on the different constructions. Time and space preclude such an analysis here; we therefore limit ourselves to giving examples of the three main types of subject zero constructions listed by Ball as well as the residual category.

(38) Existential constructions (including *it*- and subjectless types):
There was a few people Ø could knit gloves. (ANSE/015/173t)
Well isn't nobody Ø wouldn't go out– you didn't go from camp to camp. (ANSE/030/812t)
An' there was a nigger Ø bring them in. (ESR/005/100)
Ain' but one white man Ø try to objec' church and that was Mr. M. (ESR/004/610)

(39) Possessives with *have/get*:
Oh yeah we had a– old man Ø had chicken. (ANSE/038/196t)
And they had one Ø had came to town from before. (SE/002/640)
They had a, they had a preacher Ø treated us fine. (ESR/001/181)

(40) *It/That*-clefts:
That was onliest thing Ø was going back in them years. (ANSE/014/429t)
It was group of fellas Ø used to play guitar and . . . marimba and all those things, used to sing. (SE/019/759)

(41) Residual:
I used to look– look after the children for schoolteacher Ø used to teach school out to East-Preston. (ANSE/002/453)
You know that one Ø be talking proud. (ANSE/009/898t)
One died a single lady and the next one Ø died she was married to a Rhymer, Rhymer. (SE/018/585)

An' the man Ø killed him name Guiteau an' he went back over in his
state where he come from.   (ESR/012/217)
If you go over there an' get that man, the man Ø done the killing . . .
(ESR/012/225)

We also found that we could identify a focusing construction other than the *it/
that*-clefts, as in (42):

(42)   Focusing:
       On the way– he's the only one Ø be on that land.   (ANSE/031/398)
       I was the last one Ø got married home.   (SE/018/609)
       I'm the man Ø straightened up [inc].   (ESR/012/346)

   Much more comparative work needs to be done concerning constraints on
zero relative markers in subject function, both in Early AAE and in other
varieties which feature them, but this must await more systematic reports on
other subject zero dialects. In the interim we note that the distribution and
conditioning of zero subject relatives show surprising parallels across the varieties we have considered, particularly in view of their sparse number in Early
AAE.

7.10   Summary and Discussion

When we started the research for the present chapter, our intention was to
replicate Tottie and Rey's (1997) study of relativization in Early AAE by simply
expanding the dataset to include samples of African Nova Scotian English and
Samaná English. We were proceeding on an assumption that is often made in
studies of AAVE, that there is little variation across North America, and that
regional varieties are fairly similar to one another. However, our findings turned
out to be very different from our expectations in one important respect. We
found that the two additional varieties of Early AAE studied here displayed
markedly different preferences as regards overall choice of relative marker.
Although the three relative markers *that*, *what*, and zero were present in all
three dialects, they occurred in different proportions, with *that* as the preferred
variant in ANSE, *what* in Samaná, and zero in ESR. *Which* was extremely rare
in all three varieties, and *who* – but not *whom* – occurred only in a small
proportion of instances in SE.

Although to our knowledge there are no quantitative accounts of relative markers in Caribbean creoles, it is useful to make a qualitative comparison of our results with the inventory of relativizers given by Mufwene (1986) for Gullah. We note first the presence of *that* in our data, a relative marker that is completely absent from the Gullah system but all-pervasive in standard as well as nonstandard varieties of English on both sides of the Atlantic. Secondly, the Gullah relativizers *wuh* and *weh* are totally lacking in our data (as are the non-finite *fuh*-constructions). Thirdly, although Gullah does have *wat*, *who*, and zero relatives in both subject and non-subject function, the likelihood of these deriving from the lexifier language seems vastly greater than that of Early AAE taking over these elements from a creole system. Thus the use of *what* as a relativizer in ANSE, SE, and ESR must be related to its occurrence in other nonstandard dialects of English. Particularly important is the fact that we have good historical evidence for earlier British dialectal usage: for example, *what* can be shown to have been frequent in East Anglia in the eighteenth century, thus pre-dating the migration of African Americans to Samaná in 1824. Finally, the existence of zero relativization is well documented in standard and non-standard dialects of English. In particular, subject zeros are well documented in many nonstandard varieties of English on both sides of the Atlantic. Indeed, although Martin and Wolfram (1998: 32) are possibly correct in asserting that a "notable difference between AAVE and many other English vernaculars is AAVE speakers' ability to form bare *subject relative clauses*," the findings of this chapter suggest that we could rather stress that this feature constitutes a notable similarity between AAVE and many English vernaculars.

As noted in many of the other studies in this volume, however, the simple existence, or lack thereof, of forms in a variety is not necessarily revealing of the system that gave rise to them. In this context, overall distributions of variants are less revealing than an analysis according to the syntactic function of the relativizer in the relative clause. Thus the same tendency towards a functional split could be found in all three varieties, in that all showed an increased use of zero in non-subject function and a preference for surface relativization in subject function. ANSE and ESR both favored *that* in subject function whereas *what* was favored in both functions in SE.

Beyond the preference for *that* in ANSE and ESR, and for *what* in SE, it is illuminating to compare the distribution of zero and surface relatives in subject and non-subject function in the three varieties of Early AAE, both intra-AAE, and with other varieties of spoken English for which data exist. Based on tables 7.3 and 7.4 above we can summarize the data as in table 7.12. In this table, data for contemporary spoken British and American English are also presented, taken from Tottie (1997; table 4).[9]

Table 7.12 Zero relativization in Early AAE and present-day spoken American and British English

	Subject	N	Non-subject	N
SE	11%	30	36%	48
ANSE	23%	24	48%	67
ESR	41%	24	76%	44
Spoken 20th-c. AmE	2%	124	53%	78
Spoken 20th-c. BrE	5%	183	64%	239

We see, first, that in all three varieties of Early AAE there is a robust increase of zero relativization between subject and non-subject function, amounting to 25 percentage points in SE and ANSE and 35 percentage points in ESR. In fairly standard spoken corpora of British and American contemporary English, zero subject relatives are rare, as expected, but not categorically absent; the increase in zero relativization between subject and non-subject function is drastic, amounting to 50–60 percentage points. It is reasonable to regard the distributions of zero and surface relatives in Early AAE and present-day spoken English as instances of the same constraint, where subject function disfavors and non-subject function favors zero relativization. It seems clear that the distribution that we now have in spoken colloquial English has developed from an earlier stage, where zero subjects accounted for a higher proportion of the total, and which would have been closer to the distributions evinced by Early AAE – see the discussion in section 7.4 above. It is highly likely that the higher degree of literacy of modern standard speakers accounts for much of the discrepancy between their usage of zero relatives in subject function and that of the speakers of Early AAE.

Looking next at constraints on zero relativization, we split up the zero relatives into two groups, having subject and non-subject function, respectively. For the latter kind, the existing literature offers a fair amount of information concerning factors favoring their use in more or less standardized varieties of English. Although we were not able to set up a completely consistent constraint hierarchy across ANSE, SE, and ESR, we found that the three dialects patterned in a remarkably similar way with respect to all but one of the constraints previously examined in the literature. Thus pronominal antecedents and adjacency of the antecedent NP head and the relative marker, two factors that are well established as favoring zero relativization in other varieties of English, were found to also favor the zero relative marker across the three varieties of Early AAE considered, although the effects were stronger for SE and ESR than for ANSE. Personal pronouns as subjects of the relative clause favored zero relativization in two out of the three varieties.

The existing literature has little to say about constraints on the use of subject zero relatives. Testing the same factors as those examined with regard to non-subject relatives, it was possible to show that indefinite NPs as antecedents favored zero relativization across the three varieties, most strongly in SE and ESR, and that antecedent/relative marker adjacency was correlated with zero subject relative marker at least in ANSE and ESR. This indicates that these constraints would be worth testing on other English dialects with zero subjects.

Although few fully accountable studies seem to exist, many studies of subject zero relative constructions point out that they often occur in existential *there*-constructions, possessive *have/have got*-constructions, and *it/that*-clefts (see, e.g., Ball 1996); this holds for British dialects as well as Appalachian English.[10] We were able to show that Early AAE exhibits the same types of constructions (with variation between *there*, *it*, or *ain't* in AAE existential constructions) in much the same distribution as Appalachian English. A wide variety of other types was also attested in Early AAE as in the other varieties. More systematic and accountable quantitative work is needed to establish accurate constraint hierarchies for the zero variant in this function, but it seems clear to us that the similarities between Early AAE and other nonstandard varieties with respect to this feature can hardly be due to chance or indeed be easily attributable to a creole substratum.

We are thus convinced that our data add to the accumulating evidence based on other linguistic factors (such as: negation, Howe 1995; Howe and Walker, this volume; present tense -*s*, Poplack and Tagliamonte 1991b; plural, Poplack and Tagliamonte 1992, 1994; future, Poplack and Tagliamonte 1995, 1996; Tagliamonte 1991; past tense, Tagliamonte and Poplack 1988; to appear; question formation, Van Herk, this volume) that these varieties of Early AAE are descended from the same genetic stock, and that this stock is English, with strong representation of nonstandard features. To this we must add the mounting sociohistorical evidence against the existence of a prior widespread plantation creole as the ancestor of AAE, presented by Mufwene (this volume).

In concluding, we stress that the parallels in relativization strategies we have described obtain *despite* the substantive differences in variant rates in each of the three varieties of Early AAE. An intriguing direction for future research concerns the question why each variety shows the distinct variant preferences it does. In particular, why does ANSE, elsewhere characterized by a preponderance of nonstandard variants (Poplack, this volume), feature so much standard *that*, while SE shows a marked preference for *what*? The fact that education seems to play no role in constraining relative marker selection in Samaná (Harvie 1998) suggests that these preferences were already present in the varieties that served as models for the early slaves. Particularly relevant in this connection is Ball's (1996: 243) observation that there seems to be "no vernacular norm for either BrE or AmE with respect to the distribution of relative markers," but rather, "a wide range of variation both in the relative paradigm and in relative frequencies within a given regional paradigm."[11] This is precisely what we observe in Early AAE.

We need to know more about variable historical, dialectal, and regional patterns of relativization in the British English varieties spoken by the colonists, as well as about migration patterns of British speakers from England to North America, and migration patterns of African Americans within North America, and from North America to the various locales in the diaspora. These lines of research were suggested by Montgomery (1997) and are illustrated by Tagliamonte and Smith (this volume). We also need to study the co-occurrence of relative markers with other features of standard and nonstandard English, a considerable but hopefully not impossible challenge.

Notes

1 Examples are identified by corpus (ANSE: African Nova Scotian English; SE: Samaná English; ESR: Ex-Slave Recordings), speaker number, and transcription line number.

2 McKay designed her study to provide evidence for a transformational account but the quantitative data are retrievable from her presentation.

3 Traugott (1972: 155) maintains that the use of *what*, especially after *all* or *nothing*, existed in Old English, but according to the *OED* (2nd edn, s.v. C 7) Old English examples were calques from Latin. Neither Mitchell (1985), nor Bourcier (1977) make any mention of *hwæt* in headed relatives in Old English.

4 Interestingly, Forby (1830/1970) also mentions left dislocation and the use of *them* for *those* as characteristics of Norfolk and Suffolk dialects. Both of these features are also typical of AAVE.

5 Poussa postulates a different origin of *what* in East Anglia, resulting from *that* by way of a bilabial fricative. Whether this is correct or not is immaterial for the argument of the present chapter.

6 "inc" refers to an incomprehensible portion of the tape-recorded interview.

7 This basically correlates with personal and non-personal, the distinction made in some studies.

8 Notice that the high incidence of *what* in ANSE and SE should be compared with that reported by Schneider (1989: 214). Montgomery (1991) makes a comparison

between a subset of the instances in the Rawick written material and the ESR recordings, and suggests that the paucity of *what* in ESR suggests that the Rawick material could have been introduced by the interviewers (1991: 184). Our results from much larger samples of transcriptions of spoken Early AAE lend some support to the reliability of the Rawick transcriptions with regard to the freqency of *what* as a relativizer. Notice, however, that Schneider only reports 2% zero subjects. This low incidence is even more likely to be due to transcription error or normalization.

9 Tottie (1997) reports on relativizers in subject and direct object function, but the difference between those proportions and those we report for subjects and non-subjects is immaterial here. The data are taken from the Corpus of Spoken American English assembled at the University of Santa Barbara and the British National Corpus.

10 The work of Shnukal (1981) concerning zero subject relatives in Australian English was brought to our attention too late to be considered in our comparisons; however, her data are fully in accordance with ours.

11 Ball restricts her statement to subject relatives, the type she studied; her statement seems to us valid for other functions as well.

References

Adamson, H. D. (1992) Social and processing constraints on relative clauses. *American Speech*, 67: 123–33.

Aitchison, J. (1992) Relative clauses in Tok Pisin: Is there a natural pathway? In M. Gerritsen and D. Stein (eds), *Internal and External Factors in Syntactic Change*, Berlin: Mouton de Gruyter, 295–316.

Bailey, G., Maynor, N., and Cukor-Avila, P. (1991) *The Emergence of Black English: Texts and Commentary*. Amsterdam and Philadelphia: John Benjamins.

Ball, C. (1996) A diachronic study of relative markers in spoken and written English. *Language Variation and Change*, 8 (2): 227–58.

Bever, T. G., and Langendoen, D. T. (1971) A dynamic model of evolution of language. *Linguistic Inquiry*, 2 (4): 433–65.

Bickerton, D. (1981) *Roots of Language*. Ann Arbor: Karoma.

Bourcier, G. (1977) *Les propositions relatives en vieil-anglais*. Paris: Editions Honoré Champion.

Cheshire, J. (1982) *Variation in an English Dialect: A Sociolinguistic Study*. Cambridge: Cambridge University Press.

Curme, G. O. (1977) *A Grammar of the English Language*. Essex, Conn.: Verbatim.

Dekeyser, X. (1984) Relativi[z]ers in Early Modern English: A dynamic quantitative study. In J. Fisiak (ed.), *Historical Syntax*, Berlin: Mouton de Gruyter, 61–87.

Dillard, J. L. (1972) *Black English: Its History and Usage in the United States*. New York: Random House.

Fischer, O. (1992) Syntax. In N. Blake (ed.), *The Cambridge History of the English Language*, Cambridge: Cambridge University Press, 207–408.

Forby, R. (1830/1970) *The Vocabulary of East Anglia*. New York: A. M. Kelley.

Guy, G. R., and Bayley, R. (1995) On the choice of relative pronouns in English. *American Speech*, 70: 148–62.

Hackenberg, R. G. (1972) Appalachian English: A sociolinguistic study. Ph.D. dissertation, Georgetown University.

Hancock, I. (1987) A preliminary classification of the Anglophone Atlantic Creoles with syntactic data from thirty-three representative dialects. In G. G. Gilbert (ed.), *Pidgin and Creole Languages*, Honolulu: University of Hawaii Press, 264–333.

Harvie, D. (1998) Tracking down old relatives: Zero relatives in subject and non-subject function in Early African American English. M.A. thesis, University of Ottawa.

Howe, D. (1995) Negation in Early African American English. M.A. thesis, University of Ottawa.

Howe, D. M. (1997) Negation and the history of African American English. *Language Variation and Change*, 9 (2): 267–94.

Huddleston, R. (1971) *The Sentence in Written English*. Cambridge: Cambridge University Press.

Ihalainen, O. (1980) Relative clauses in the dialect of Somerset. *Neuphilologische Mitteilungen*, 81: 187–96.

Jespersen, O. H. (1965) *A Modern English Grammar, Part III: Syntax (second volume)*. London: George Allen and Unwin.

Kekäläinen, K. (1985) Relative clauses in the dialect of Suffolk. *Neuphilologische Mitteilungen*, 86: 353–8.

Labov, W., and Cohen, P. (1973) Some suggestions for teaching Standard English to speakers of nonstandard urban dialects. In J. S. De Stefano (ed.), *Language, Society and Education*, Worthington, Ohio: Charles A. Jones.

Light, R. L. (1969) Syntactic structures in a corpus of non-Standard English. Ph.D. dissertation, Georgetown University, Washington, DC.

Lowth, R. (1762/1775) *A Short Introduction to English Grammar*. London: printed by J. Hughs for A. Millar and J. Dodsley.

Macaulay, R. K. S. (1991) *Locating Dialect in Discourse: The Language of Honest Men and Bonnie Lasses in Ayr*. Oxford: Oxford University Press.

Martin, S., and Wolfram, W. (1998) The sentence in African-American Vernacular English. In S. Mufwene, J. Rickford, G. Bailey, and J. Baugh (eds), *African-American English*, London and New York: Routledge, 11–36.

McKay, J. R. (1969) A partial analysis of a variety of nonstandard Negro English. Ph.D. dissertation, University of California, Berkeley.

Mitchell, B. (1985) *Old English Syntax*. Oxford: Clarendon Press.

Montgomery, M. (1991) The linguistic value of the Ex-Slave Recordings. In G. Bailey, N. Maynor, and P. Cukor-Avila (eds), *The Emergence of Black English: Text and Commentary*, Amsterdam and Philadelphia: John Benjamins, 173–89.

Montgomery, M. B. (1997) Making transatlantic connections between varieties of English. *Journal of English Linguistics*, 25 (2): 122–41.

Mufwene, S. (1986) Restrictive relativization in Gullah. *Journal of Pidgin and Creole Languages*, 1: 1–31.

Ojanen, A.-L. (1982) A syntax of the Cambridgeshire dialect. Licentiate thesis, University of Helsinki.

Olofsson, A. (1981) *Relative Junctions in Written American English*. Göteborg: Acta Universitatis Gothoburgensis.

Orton, H., Sanderson, S., and Widdowson, J. (1978) *The Linguistic Atlas of England*. London: Croom Helm.

Poplack, S., and Sankoff, D. (1987) The Philadelphia story in the Spanish Caribbean. *American Speech*, 62 (4): 291–314.

Poplack, S., and Tagliamonte, S. (1991a) African American English in the diaspora: The case of old-line Nova Scotians. *Language Variation and Change*, 3 (3): 301–39.

Poplack, S., and Tagliamonte, S. (1991b) There's no tense like the present: Verbal -*s* inflection in Early Black English. In G. Bailey, N. Maynor, and P. Cukor-Avila (eds), *The Emergence of Black English: Texts and Commentary*, Amsterdam and Philadelphia: John Benjamins, 275–324.

Poplack, S., and Tagliamonte, S. (1992) Plural marking in Early Black English. Paper presented at the Canadian Linguistic Association, University of Prince Edward Island, Charlottetown, PEI, Canada.

Poplack, S., and Tagliamonte, S. (1994) -*S* or nothing: Marking the plural in the African American diaspora. *American Speech*, 69 (3): 227–59.

Poplack, S., and Tagliamonte, S. (1995) It's black and white: The future of English in rural Nova Scotia. Paper presented at NWAVE 24, University of Pennsylvania, Philadelphia, USA.

Poplack, S., and Tagliamonte, S. (1996) The grammaticization of *gonna* in six varieties of English: A cross-linguistic comparison. Paper presented at NWAVE 25, University of Nevada, Las Vegas, USA.

Poussa, P. (1985) Historical implications of the distribution of the zero-pronoun relative clause in Modern English dialects: Looking backwards towards OE from Map S5 of the lingusitic atlas of England. In S. Jacobson (ed.), *Papers from the Third Scandinavian Symposium on Syntactic Variation*, Stockholm: Almqvist and Wiksell, 99–117.

Poussa, P. M. (1993) Relativization and settlement history in North Norfolk. Ph.D. dissertation, University of Sheffield.

Quirk, R. (1957) Relative clauses in educated spoken English. *English Studies*, 38: 97–109.

Romaine, S. (1982) *Socio-Historical Linguistics: Its Status and Methodology*. Cambridge: Cambridge University Press.

Romaine, S. (1988) *Pidgin and creole languages*. London: Longman.

Sankoff, G., and Brown, P. (1976) The origins of syntax in discourse. *Language*, 52 (3): 631–66.

Schneider, E. W. (1989) *American Earlier Black English*. Tuscaloosa, AL: University of Alabama Press.

Shnukal, A. (1981) There's a lot mightn't believe this . . . Variable subject relative pronoun absence in Australian English. In D. Sankoff and H. Cedergren (eds), *Variation Omnibus*, Carbondale and Edmonton: Linguistic Research, 321–8.

Smith, R. B. (1969) Interrelatedness of certain deviant grammatical structures in negro nonstandard dialects. *Journal of English Linguistics*, 3: 82–8.

Tagliamonte, S. (1991) A matter of time: Past temporal reference verbal structures in Samaná English and the Ex-Slave Recordings. Ph.D. dissertation, University of Ottawa.

Tagliamonte, S., and Poplack, S. (1988) How Black English *past* got to the present: Evidence from Samaná. *Language in Society*, 17 (4): 513–33.

Tagliamonte, S., and Poplack, S. (to appear) Back to the present: Verbal *-s* in the (African American) English diaspora. In J. Lipski (ed.), *African American English and its Congeners*, Amsterdam and Philadelphia: John Benjamins.

Taglicht, J. (1973) The choice of relative pronouns in written English. *Scripta Hierosolymitana*, 25: 327–36.

Tottie, G. (1995) The man Ø I love: An analysis of factors favouring zero relatives in written British and American English. In G. Melchers and B. Warren (eds), *Studies in Anglistics*, Stockholm: Almqvist and Wiksell, 201–15.

Tottie, G. (1997) Relatively speaking: relative marker usage in the British National Corpus. In T. Nevalainen and L. Kahlas-Tarkka (eds), *To Explain the Present: Studies in the Changing English Language in Honour of Matti Rissanen. Mémoires de la Société Neophilogique de Helsinki*, 52. Helsinki: Société Néophilologique.

Tottie, G., and Rey, M. (1997) Relativization strategies in Earlier African American Vernacular English. *Language Variation and Change*, 9 (2): 219–47.

Traugott, E. C. (1972) *A History of English Syntax: A Transformational Approach to the History of English Sentence Structures*. New York: Holt, Rinehart & Winston.

Traugott, E. C. (1992) Syntax. In R. M. Hogg (ed.), *The Cambridge History of the English Language*, Cambridge: Cambridge University Press, 168–289.

Van den Eynden, N. (1993) *Syntactic Variation and Unconscious Linguistic Change: A Study of Adjectival Relative Clauses in the Dialect of Dorset*. Frankfurt a. M.: Peter Lang.

Van Herk, G. (1998) Auxiliary verbs in Early African-American Vernacular English questions. Paper presented at Canadian Linguistic Association, University of Ottawa, Ottawa, Canada.

Viereck, W., and Ramisch, H. (eds) (1991) *The Computer Developed Linguistic Atlas of England 1*. Tübingen: Niemeyer.

Walker, J. (1997) Rephrasing the copula: Contracted and zero copula in African Nova Scotian English. Paper presented at NWAVE 26, Québec City, Québec, Canada.

Wolfram, W., and Christian, D. (1976) *Appalachian Speech*. Arlington, VA: Center for Applied Linguistics.

Part IV

The Sociohistorical Context

8

Some Sociohistorical Inferences about the Development of African American English

Salikoko S. Mufwene

8.1 Preliminaries

8.1.1 The theses

In the past fifteen years, the evidence that bears on whether or not African American Vernacular English (AAVE) developed by debasilectalization from an erstwhile Gullah-like creole once widely spoken by (descendants of) Africans in the United States has diversified. Much of the addition to the debate has consisted of comparisons of AAVE with Ex-Slave Narratives (e.g., Schneider 1989), with Ex-Slave Recordings (see, especially, the contributions to Bailey, Maynor, and Cukor-Avila 1991; Tottie and Rey 1997), with English varieties of the African American diaspora (e.g., DeBose 1983, 1988; Hannah 1997; Poplack and Sankoff 1984; Poplack and Tagliamonte 1989, 1991, 1994; Rickford 1998; Singler 1989, 1991; Tagliamonte and Poplack 1988, 1993; and other contributions to this volume), with more Caribbean creole data (Baugh 1980; Holm 1984; Rickford and Blake 1990; Winford 1992, 1993, 1998), with the Hoodoo Texts (Ewers 1996), and with older and nonstandard varieties of British English (Poplack and Tagliamonte 1996; Smith and Tagliamonte 1998; Tagliamonte 1996; Tagliamonte to appear; Tagliamonte and Smith 1998; this volume). They have also included considerations of the socioeconomic history of North America (e.g., Mufwene 1996, in press; Rickford 1997; Winford 1997).

This chapter focuses on some aspects of the socioeconomic historical evidence – part of the external ecology of the development of AAVE, Gullah, and their Caribbean kin – to defend the following positions:

1. The socioeconomic history of the United States does not support the hypothesis that AAVE developed from an erstwhile creole, either American or Caribbean.

2. However, this position does not preclude influence, in the way described below, from Caribbean English varieties imported with slaves in the seventeenth and eighteenth centuries on the restructuring of colonial English that produced AAVE.

3. Nor does the recognition of possible Caribbean influence entail that AAVE could not have developed into what it is now without it.

4. Closer examination of sources of the direct origins of slaves during the eighteenth century suggests that influence from African languages was perhaps more determinative than that from the Caribbean.

5. By no means should anyone overlook or downplay the nature of colonial English as spoken by both the English and the non-English in the seventeenth and eighteenth centuries, nor its central role as the target language during the development of AAVE, Gullah, and their Caribbean kin.

The correlation of structural and sociohistorical evidence supports a greater impact of the language of the colonial founder populations than has been suggested by the creole-origins hypothesis, recognizing that the sources of Gullah's and Caribbean English creoles' features are largely the same as AAVE's, as they have developed by similar restructuring processes. Differences among these vernaculars are attributable to variation in the ecologies of the restructuring processes applied to them individually (Mufwene 1996).

8.1.2　The working assumptions

I maintain Mufwene's (1996) interpretation of *restructuring*, namely "system reorganization." That is, materials and principles selected from extant systems are re-articulated into a new system, in which they need not be integrated in the same ways as in the earlier one(s). The sources of these materials and rules need not be the same dialect or language, consistent with the assumption that contact-based varieties (not just those identified as pidgins and creoles) are mixed systems.[1] A question that has been critical in the origins debate is: which particular variety contributed the features (often re-articulated) that are attested in the new vernacular?

Answering the latter and related questions depends very much on how we interpret *influence*. My conception of it is different from Allsopp's (1977) sense of "apport" or importation of elements foreign to the lexifier's system into the emerging vernacular. Often identified with the suffix *-ism*, as in *Africanism*, the apport interpretation is what Carrington (1993) criticizes as marginalizing the contribution of substrate languages to creoles' structures. Although such contributions cannot be precluded by fiat – and there are undoubtedly some such – I interpret African *substrate influence* as the role played by (some) substrate languages in favoring the selection of particular variants from among competing alternatives especially from within the lexifier itself (Mufwene 1993). This is consistent with Thomason's (1983) and Thomason and Kaufman's (1988) notion of convergence, according to which structural characteristics shared by the lexifier and some of the languages that it came in contact with are likely to be selected into the new vernacular's system, notwithstanding other selection principles that Mufwene (1996) tries to work out.

We must note that the Africans intended to speak, subject to non-scholastic second-language acquisition limitations, the vernacular of their new ethnographic ecology. Consistent with Mufwene's (1996) competition-and-selection approach to the development of contact varieties, structural and pragmatic features of the languages that they spoke previously became, along with those of the lexifier, part of a pool from which features were selected into the new vernacular. However, the Africans also knew that their adaptive success depended largely on how closely they approximated the diffused, or less-focused, target (in the sense of LePage and Tabouret-Keller 1985) to which they were exposed.[2] Influence from African languages consisted thus in the natural tendency to select, by the least-effort principle, options that were similar to those of the languages they spoke before, or in interference phenomena from the same languages that the circumstances of their language acquisition did not enable them to eliminate.[3] Such influence need not be interpreted as failure to acquire the lexifier (a conclusion to which Baker (1997) rightly objects) nor as part of a deliberate decision to develop a different medium of inter-ethnic communication (which Baker (1997) mistakenly suggests). Substrate influence and the development of AAVE (or any of its creole kin) as a different vernacular are both accidents of language transmission and acquisition in contact settings.

It is worth emphasizing that forms and principles selected from either the lexifier or substrate languages need not be preserved intact in the new vernacular. In response to the specific contact ecologies of language transmission and acquisition, they have often been adapted slightly or significantly to fit in the new vernacular. Thus, as shown by Poplack and Tagliamonte (1996), *gon(na)* as a future marker does not obey exactly the same weighting of constraints in white vernaculars as in AAVE, despite striking distributional parallelisms across the varieties. The English origin of the construction is not necessarily compromised by (the extent of) African substrate influence on such a development. In this case, selecting *gon(na)* as the future marker from among competing alternatives in the lexifier, they identified its function as (more or less) the same as that of future markers in languages they spoke before, in which future is marked by a morpheme related to, or meaning, "go." The high incidence of copula absence before this particular morpheme in AAVE may very well be a reflection of this identification-cum-re-analysis, especially if *gon(na)* is no longer interpreted morphosyntactically or semantically as a progressive construction – in which the copula is not required either, in the rest of its system (e.g. in *he talkin*). The re-analysis is thus consistent with both the English origin of the construction and substrate influence, as substrate morphosyntactic principles have influenced the usage of a marker selected obviously from the lexifier. Unlike *gonna* (more common in white vernaculars), *gon* (more typical of AAVE) keeps no trace of the coalescence of *going* and the complementizer *to*. Even the connection of *gon* to the main verb *go* is more etymological than anything, which makes the combination *gon* + V morphosyntactically closer to the substrate pattern GO + V than to the original COPULA + *go-ing* + *to* + V > COPULA + *gonna* + V.[4]

African apports need not have been preserved intact either. For instance, the associative plural, as in *Felicia (an) dem* "Felicia and her family/associates", is not quite consistent with the variable morphosyntax of the substrate constructions which favored its development in AAVE. In many of them, it consists of a regular plural marker added to a proper name, literally "Felicia PLURAL". Boretzky (1993) gives very good examples of such adaptations of external apports to some languages.

Below, examining patterns of social interaction at different colonial stages, I highlight periods and settings that would have minimized or enhanced interference, producing among (descendants of) Africans new English vernaculars that either were similar to, or diverged from, those spoken by (descendants of) Europeans. I argue that the time and extent of divergence of African American vernaculars from their white counterparts of the same regions are inversely proportionate to the degree of social integration of the speakers in the majority and/or politically-dominant population. The same principle enables us to make good use of data from enclave communities of the African American diaspora in ways that we cannot of Caribbean creole data. The former originated in the USA, while the latter were brought in at times during which the Africans' English vernaculars that were more American in nature must have already been in place. In fact, speakers of Caribbean varieties must have been under pressure to adapt linguistically to the new ecologies. The obvious genetic connection between them and AAVE justifies comparisons for the purposes of shedding light on the evolution of AAVE. Because the enclave communities are not fully integrated in their host communities, data from them can, like the Ex-Slave

Recordings and the Hoodoo Texts, help us determine whether or not AAVE has debasilectalized since either the nineteenth century or the early twentieth century, hence whether it would have developed from an erstwhile creole. Comparisons with Caribbean creoles are likely to highlight no more than structural similarities or differences between their evolutionary paths and AAVE's, helping us answer the question of whether the socioeconomic ecologies and competition-and-selection principles that produced them are similar. I argue that the answer is affirmative on many counts. I will now start with the socioeconomic historical background.

8.2   The Socioeconomic Ecology of the Development of AAVE

8.2.1   The seventeenth century

8.2.1.1   Early contacts in the Chesapeake and the Caribbean, and between them
A critical date in the development of English in North American colonies is 1619. Twelve years after the founding of the Virginia colony, the oldest English colony in the New World, a Dutch frigate traded 20 Africans to the Virginia governor in exchange for food. The settlers did not quite know how to use them. Those who bought them used them typically as domestics, with the same socioeconomic status of indentured servants as many Europeans (Tate 1965). The survivors managed to buy their freedom in five to seven years and, as free Blacks, they developed their own land and hired their own indentured servants, a number of whom were Europeans (Tate 1965).

Few, if any, major plantations had developed yet. The Africans lived in annexes to the planters' "big house" in Williamsburg or in homesteads outside the original capital. Although they must have gone through interlanguage phases in acquiring colonial English, nothing in this particular kind of social history suggests that the Africans would have developed a pidgin or a creole. The circumstances are not typical of those in which pidgins have developed; contacts with speakers of the lexifier were certainly not occasional and the Africans did not communicate mostly among themselves. Thus, the kind of social setup that would have favored the restructuring and divergence of their new vernacular did not obtain yet. The Africans were scattered and integrated within a European majority.[5]

Overall, the slave population in Virginia grew very slowly during the seventeenth century. Toward the end of this period, it increased more by local births than by importation (Thomas 1997). The Africans constituted no more than 15 percent of the total colonial population by the beginning of the eighteenth century (Tate 1965), and the majority of them still worked as domestics or on small farms. Mostly European indentured servants worked on the tobacco plantations. The status of Africans as indentured servants continued up to about 1675, providing 56 years of founder population that presumably spoke the same kind of English as the Europeans with whom they interacted and worked on a regular basis. The black and mulatto children who were born in the colony had no reason then to speak differently from their white counterparts, together with whom they generally were looked after, while their parents worked in the field or in "the big house." Even after the status of Africans changed to that of slaves for life (from that of indentured servants), the low proportion of Africans and their sparse distribution among Europeans just did not favor the development of separate varieties of English, unless there would be race-based reasons for such a divergence to have taken place.[6]

The above inference is quite consistent with the absence of any reference to Africans speaking English differently in the seventeenth century. Since so much effort had been directed toward lowering the status of Africans since the 1640s (Tate 1965) – reflecting negative attitudes toward them – any divergent speech patterns would have been recorded in writings of the time. The absence of such reports suggests that there was really nothing different that had developed then, while a colonial English distinct from its metropolitan ancestor was in gestation.

During the second half of the seventeenth century, a large proportion of the slaves were imported from Caribbean English colonies, especially from St Kitts, which was founded in 1623 and whose colonization was often interrupted by exoduses caused by difficulties with the tobacco agriculture and by wars with French colonists on the Island during the second half of the seventeenth century (Corcoran and Mufwene 1998), and from Barbados, which was founded in 1627 and became an important colonial distribution point after 1650.

Throughout the seventeenth century, most of the colonial estates were small farms. That is where the majority of the Kittitian slaves were held, maintaining with their masters, and with the indentured servants from Ireland (then only partly anglophone), from other parts of the British Isles, and from continental Europe, relations very similar to those in Virginia (Corcoran and Mufwene 1998). Up to the end of the seventeenth century, the Africans on St Kitts hardly exceeded half the total colonial population. All this suggests that linguistic developments on St Kitts were quite similar to those in Virginia. It is unlikely that the Kittitian slaves imported to Virginia would have brought with them a sociolect that was more divergent from colonial English than what was being developed by the local slaves.

Both on St Kitts and in Virginia, there were undoubtedly handfuls of linguistically less skilled individuals who developed some of the features associated today with basilectal creoles. However, the chances of their influencing the majority's speech must be considered minimal. Corcoran and Mufwene (1998) infer that no creole basilect could have developed on St Kitts before the mid-eighteenth century, primarily because of the colony's protracted and intermittent beginnings and because of the close social rapports between Europeans and Africans on the Island that were imposed by the circumstances of war and other hardship conditions.[7] They conclude that it is more likely for the emergence of Kittitian to have been influenced by linguistic developments on other Caribbean islands than the other way around.

Barbados developed more steadily than St Kitts. By the end of the seventeenth century, the African–European population ratio was 2:1. However, there were more farms than plantations and the early overpopulation of the small Island turned it into a slave distribution point. In other words, many slaves were rerouted to different colonies before they had a chance to participate in the development of the local vernacular. It is true that Candy and Tituba, two slaves recently imported from Barbados by the time of the Salem Witch Trials in Massachusetts in 1692, spoke creole/pidgin-like idiolects (Cassidy 1986). However, we do not know for sure that these were not interlanguages nor how representative they were of Barbadian slaves in general (Mufwene in press).

To be sure, some basilectal idiolects may have started emerging then on Barbadian sugar-cane plantations, where the African–European ratio was lopsided in favor of Africans. The overall ratio was less than 3:1 in 1690. However, in the interest of the local economy, the vast majority of the slaves exported to other colonies were probably newcomers or originated from small farms, which went out of business because they could not cope with the competition from large plantations. While some of these slaves spoke little local vernacular if anything, most of the others probably spoke some variety of colonial English that would not be identified as basilectal creole. Perhaps this variety was not quite different from what was developing already among Virginian slaves. After all, more or less the same African languages and English dialects came in contact in more or less similar socioeconomic ecologies.

Thus, seventeenth-century Barbadian slaves had no stronger chance of influencing the development of the antecedent of AAVE away from Virginia's colonial English than Kittitian slaves. African linguistic influence (as characterized in section 8.1.2) through slaves imported directly from Africa or through those bought from Barbados is apparently what deserves more attention, aside from the fact that we should focus more on how structural features were selected into the new vernaculars from the pools where they competed with each other for similar communicative functions. However, Caribbean English may have contributed to favoring particular options of Virginian colonial English that were more consistent with either the African languages and/or selections that were also favored in the Caribbean.

There are other good reasons why seventeenth-century varieties of Caribbean English vernaculars brought over to North America by African slaves could not have influenced the development of AAVE in the way claimed by supporters of the creole-origins hypothesis. By the Founder Principle (Mufwene 1996), newcomers to the region would have sought to adapt to the local norm(s) rather than to impose their own. Effects of interference from language varieties previously spoken would have been offset by what their offspring spoke, normally the local norms rather than those of their newcomer parents. As explained in Mufwene (1996), children, regardless of whether they were locally born or imported (Lovejoy 1989), slowed down the divergence of Africans' English vernaculars from those of Europeans, because they were more likely to acquire colonial English with minimal restructuring, although, as we must always remember, this target was heterogeneous (diffused, in Lepage and Tabouret-Keller's (1985) sense) and itself developing too.

Given the demographic conditions in the Virginia colony in the seventeenth century, especially the relative integration of most of the Africans in the small land holdings and the importance of the birth rate in the slave population growth, I maintain that Caribbean English vernaculars would have influenced the development of African American English (AAE) varieties either by favoring those options which they shared with the Virginian vernacular or by adding to variation. Increased variation would have exposed those who came or were born later to a more diverse range of choices. Influence from African languages during the massive slave importations of the eighteenth century (see below) could have led to selections that made African American varieties more different from both European-American English vernaculars and the Caribbean varieties themselves. But in no case could we assume that Caribbean slaves brought with them an already developed basilect from which AAE would have developed. Besides, there is no particular reason why the African slaves in North America would have shifted to the Caribbean vernaculars or taken them as their models.

8.2.1.2 What about the other colonies?

Gullah has been left out of the picture so far for several reasons. The South Carolina colony was settled in 1670, from Barbados, precisely during the period when a widespread creole basilectal sociolect was unlikely to have developed on the Island. These colonists, consisting of Europeans who did not find suitable land to exploit in Barbados, came with some of their slaves, who remained a minority until the beginning of the eighteenth century (Wood 1974, 1989). They started with small land holdings and lived in homesteads. Very few of them experimented in rice fields, which needed more numerous laborers, by the end of the seventeenth century. The Africans did not become a majority in South Carolina (2:1, but at a much higher ratio on the coastal plantations) until 1720.

Aside from the fact that there is no evidence of South Carolina supplying slaves to Virginia during the seventeenth century, basilectal Gullah could not have developed before the development of large plantations, under an African majority population (Mufwene 1992) and under the conditions of rapid population replacement explained in Mufwene (1996). According to Perkins (1988), the Chesapeake colonies, not South Carolina, provided the hinterlands colonies (Alabama, Mississippi, and Arkansas) with the founder slave populations to start their cotton plantations.

North Carolina has likewise been omitted because it had a negligible proportion of Africans in the seventeenth century: 2 percent by 1700, according to Wood (1989). In fact it had a late start, in the 1650s, with the first settlers originating in Virginia. Wood (1991) indicates that this colony was settled in part by Germans and Scots-Irish from as far north as Pennsylvania, as well as by Welsh and Scots apparently immigrating directly from the British Isles. They were small farmers. Unable to confront the powerful Native Americans in the coastal area, they settled inland. The possible impact of settlements near the coast, which would develop into tobacco plantations in the eighteenth century, will be discussed in the next section.

Northern colonies have also been kept out of the picture for the following reasons. They were not agricultural colonies and made limited use of slave labor, primarily as domestics or as help on farms. They did not provide the right ethnographic–ecological conditions for the development of a separate African American vernacular, especially since the Africans were not able to form separate communities of their own. One can plausibly argue that AAVE as spoken today was imported to those states by later migrations from the southern states, especially through the Great Migration of the late nineteenth and early twentieth centuries (see below).

8.2.2 The eighteenth century

Agricultural industry became more lucrative for both Virginia and South Carolina by the end of the seventeenth century. However, indentured labor became more and more expensive, as job opportunities improved and labor wages increased in England, while word spread around there that the conditions of indenture in the colonies were harsh. This change made slave labor more attractive and less expensive as life-long investments. The planters then turned to predominantly African slave labor, importing more of it directly from Africa and less from the Caribbean. According to Rawley (1991), Virginia imported only one-tenth of its slaves, and South Carolina only one-seventh (less than 15%), from the Caribbean in the eighteenth century. If a (widespread) basilectal sociolect had already developed in Barbados or elsewhere in the Caribbean by the end of the seventeenth century (but see the above observation about seventeenth-century importations from Barbados!), these demographics make it rather plausible to assume that the role of the Caribbean sociolect(s) would not have been as central as has been suggested by the creole-origins hypothesis. The Caribbean vernaculars had to compete, rather unfavorably away from home, with the local norm(s) favored by the local colonial ecologies. The situation would have been different if no local vernacular had already been developing locally and if the Caribbean slaves did not constitute such a minority relative to the massive imports from Africa.

On the other hand, Campbell-Kibler (1998) observes that Virginian planters turned to the direct importations from Africa about 1690, 30 years sooner than the less affluent planters in South Carolina did.[8] This difference in the socio-economic developments of Virginia and South Carolina allowed for varying possible influence of the then emerging Caribbean vernaculars on the development of African American vernaculars in North America. Note also that the Virginia African American vernacular developed independently of Gullah. The socioeconomic history of the American Southeast, which is recognized in section 8.2.4 to be the cradle of AAVE, suggests that the Gullah-speaking area, in coastal South Carolina and coastal Georgia, had little influence if any on the development of today's AAVE.

One of the reasons why Gullah, identified by linguists as a creole vernacular, rather than AAVE developed in coastal South Carolina (and Georgia) is also discussed by Campbell-Kibler (1998): the harsher climate and working conditions of South Carolina's and Georgia's coastal swamps just made it more difficult to attract European indentured labor there. Besides, the greater familiarity of the Africans with the subtropical climate and with the swampy vegetation, as well as their alleged greater resistance to malaria, prompted planters in these coastal areas to rely more on African labor. Thus, all sorts of practical considerations, including the inability of the planters to prevent Native American slaves from escaping and the need to maintain peaceful relations with them, favored the African slave solution. With or without the slave importations from the Caribbean, the socioeconomic ecology of the rice fields in coastal South Carolina and Georgia (described below) was similar to that of the Caribbean and thus likely to produce new English vernaculars similar to Caribbean creoles. This conclusion is further supported by similarities between the white vernaculars of these regions: plantation English in coastal South Carolina and coastal Georgia is different from American White Southern English but reminiscent, at least prosodically, of Bahamian and Caribbean White English. (The latter is not noticeably different from Caribbean blacks' English.) Note that the same kinds of British populations served as indentured servants in all these English colonies in the seventeenth and eighteenth centuries.

By 1708, the African population in colonial South Carolina was almost equal to that of Europeans (4,100 Africans versus 4,080 Europeans), and in 1720, when South Carolina became a crown colony, the ratio was almost 2:1 (11,828 Africans versus 6,525 Europeans). The latter ratio remained constant until 1740 (39,155 Africans versus 20,000 Europeans), when it started declining (Wood 1974). However, both populations kept increasing to meet the labor demands of the agricultural industry, so that in 1790, they numbered 108,900 Africans and 140,200 Europeans, even though the Africans constituted about 44% of the total colonial non-indigenous population. 85–90% of the Africans were concentrated on the coastal plantations (often at the ratio of 10 Africans to 1 European), while the vast majority of European indentured servants were in the hinterlands.

Georgia, which was founded in 1733, developed pretty much on the pattern of South Carolina, from which its first African runaways and illegal slaves originated, totaling about 1,400 by 1745, according to Wood (1989: 60). He estimates that by 1790 "the new state of Georgia included 52,888 whites, plus 29,264 slaves and 398 free blacks," with the Africans constituting almost 36% of the total colonial non-indigenous population. However, although the Africans never constituted the majority of the total non-indigenous population, 85–90% of them were concentrated in the coastal area, where there lived about 10% of the European population (Coleman 1978). The social ecology in the coastal area was definitely favorable for Gullah to thrive, if it had been imported from South Carolina, or simply to develop.[9]

The proportion of Africans did not exceed that of Europeans either in Virginia, or in the Chesapeake in general, although the total population was the highest there.[10] According to Perkins (1988) and Fischer (1989), the Africans never exceeded 38% of the colonial population by the end of the eighteenth century.[11] Here too, there were more slaves scattered on the coastal land holdings than on the tobacco plantations in the hinterlands, where their proportion remained lower than that of indentured servants (Kulikoff 1986). However, unlike in

244 *Salikoko S. Mufwene*

South Carolina and in Georgia, most of the Virginia coastal holdings were generally small farms, which would not have favored the development of a Gullah-like sociolect, though one cannot rule out individual idiolects that would contain features associated with creoles.

Stereotypes of African speech based on such basilectal idiolects, which need not have been representative, flourished during the eighteenth century; and they apparently fed contemporary literary representations in which black characters are portrayed as speaking creole-like varieties. However, Brasch (1981) reports advertisements in local papers about runaway slaves of the time which correlate "good English" with being born or having lived long in Virginia and "poor, bad," or "unintelligible" English with recent arrivals. Kulikoff (1986: 317) quotes Jones as saying that "slaves born in Virginia 'talk good English, and affect our language, habits, and customs'" (Jones 1724/1956). This non-fiction evidence suggests that at least some, if not most, instances of these creole-like varieties may have been transitional interlanguages but not well-established sociolects.

We must remember that during the seventeenth century the non-indigenous population in Virginia, including people of African descent, grew largely by birth (Thomas 1997; Wood 1989), aside from immigrations. Slaves were then more expensive than indentured servants and there was generally less capital to afford both massively. The situation entailed that by the eighteenth century there was a significant founder population of locally-born and seasoned slaves who could serve as model speakers of colonial English to the African newcomers. Language transmission remained normal and the same kinds of English vernaculars were being transmitted from the local populations to the newcomers, with the children acquiring them natively. As emphasized below, communication between Africans and Europeans was regular, despite increasing discrimination across races. Thus, restructuring of colonial English among the Africans could not have been more drastic than among the Europeans, subject of course to substrate influence in both groups.

The tobacco-plantation system did not start until the eighteenth century in North Carolina, unlike in Virginia, from which most of its slaves originated and on whose model it developed. Rickford (1997) is correct in reporting that most of the slaves lived in the coastal area, where the plantations were developed later by the English colonists (rather than by the generally poor German, Scotch-Irish, and Welsh colonists who had settled earlier in the hinterlands): 29% of the Africans lived on plantations of 20 slaves or more, out of total populations of 53,184 Europeans and 19,800 Africans in 1750. The latter constituted 27.1% of the colonial non-indigenous population. The figures grew to 288,200 Europeans versus 105,500 Africans in 1790, but with the latter still representing almost 27% of the total colonial non-indigenous population. Like Virginia, North Carolina did not overall provide the kind of social ecology that fostered the development of a Gullah-like sociolect. The tobacco plantations were rather small, the Africans hardly ever represented the majority on them, and they interacted regularly with the indentured servants. Given the initial dependence of North Carolina on Virginia, my conclusions below in relation to Caribbean creole influence apply to North Carolina as well.

Overall, the demographics suggest varying linguistic developments in the colonies. Virginia hardly provided the kind of ethnographic contact ecology that could foster the development of a Gullah-like creole. Although I surmise that here and there on the coast some individuals may have developed isolated features which are akin to those of Gullah, it is doubtful that any Gullah-like basilectal sociolect emerged there, *pace* Sutcliffe (1998). On the other hand, the large rice fields of South Carolina and Georgia provided an ecology favorable to the development of Gullah as a consolidated sociolect.

In any case, although South Carolina imported a large proportion of its slaves from Barbados during the first two decades of the eighteenth century, it is not evident that Gullah's development was influenced by the prior development of a creole basilect in the Caribbean. As noted above, the original exodus from Barbados was from small farms that could not compete with the large plantations. It may also be assumed that in the interest of the local economy, most of the slaves sent elsewhere had been in Barbados just on transit, hence they had not had enough time to command the then evolving local vernacular. I surmise that the influence of most of those slaves imported from the Caribbean, a minority according to Rawley (1991), was no more significant than that of the slaves who were imported later and massively straight from Africa.

Similarities between Gullah and Caribbean creoles need not surprise us, because the contact settings of the input varieties (African languages and British English dialects) were similar in the rice and sugar-cane colonies. Differences between the new colonial vernaculars may well reflect variation in the ethnographic ecologies of the local basilectalization processes. This observation applies as much to differences between Gullah and Caribbean creoles collectively as to variation among the Caribbean varieties themselves (Mufwene 1996).

In any case this socioeconomic history suggests that the influence of Caribbean creoles on the development of AAVE seems to have been exaggerated. Aside from the fact that both Gullah and AAVE could still have developed independently of the Caribbean connection, Virginia imported few slaves from the Caribbean in the eighteenth century, namely 10% of its total slave imports, at least fewer than South Carolina, where they constituted close to 15% of its total imports.

A less disputable catalyst to the development of both AAVE and Gullah is the greater dependence of both Virginia's and South Carolina's agricultural industry on slave labor imported directly from Africa. The reasons for the development of Gullah are articulated in Mufwene (1996), including the rapid population replacement caused by both the high mortality rate in the slave population and the need to increase the labor population to keep up with the growing plantation industry. These facts had the consequence of gradually reducing the proportion of native or fluent speakers of colonial English while the implementation of a segregated-community life on the plantations favored rapid autonomization of the vernacular spoken by (descendants of) Africans, in ways similar to the indigenization of English today in Africa and Asia. The more the (descendants of) Africans interacted among themselves outside the work place, the more likely it was for their vernaculars to develop their own separate peculiarities.

However, one must remember that as much discrimination as there was in Virginia against (descendants of) Africans, rigid segregation was not instituted until much later in the nineteenth century (see section 8.2.4), because there was not as much demographic threat to the colonial European population as on the coastal South Carolinian and Georgian plantations. The relative integration of Blacks and poor Whites – both living primarily on small land holdings – favored the development of similar Black and White vernaculars, except for Appalachian English, which developed in relative isolation, in an ecology that did not involve African slave labor either. Note then that structural similarities between the latter vernacular and AAVE and/or Gullah further underscores the significance of colonial English as the source from which features of these different vernaculars were selected and re-articulated into new systems; substrate influence, as defined above, notwithstanding.

8.2.3   The pre-Reconstruction nineteenth century

One may consider the beginning of the nineteenth century as the period during which AAE vernaculars (both Gullah and AAVE) stabilized, or started to. According to Rawley (1991), the most significant volume of slave importations into North America was in the eighteenth century. By 1808, importation of slaves was made illegal, although the practice of slavery would continue until the Civil War (1861–5). To be sure, there were clandestine slave importations until the mid-nineteenth century, but the slave population continued to grow primarily by birth. The increasing number of native speakers and the attrition of non-native speakers enabled the vernaculars that had been developing till then among descendants of Africans to stabilize, or at least not to undergo any form of restructuring motivated by language contact.

This observation is consistent with the available linguistic evidence from the Ex-Slave Narratives (Schneider 1989) (despite their shortcomings, see note 22) and from the Ex-Slave Recordings, although they both are more revealing of structures of vernaculars of the second half of the nineteenth century. Perhaps stronger evidence must be identified in Black English Diaspora varieties, such as Samaná and African Nova Scotian English, which have also been invoked to argue against the development of AAVE by debasilectalization (e.g., numerous papers by Poplack and Sankoff, Poplack and Tagliamonte, Tagliamonte and Poplack since 1984). Granted that each of these varieties must have undergone minimal restructuring consistent with the stabilization process, nothing has been found so far which suggests that AAVE was more creole-like at the beginning of the nineteenth century.[12]

There were also catalytic economic changes in the nineteenth century, for instance in the textile industry, that made cotton agriculture a more lucrative investment, thanks to the invention of the cotton gin. Planters moved from the Chesapeake former colonies and the hinterlands of Georgia and South Carolina to develop cotton plantations in Alabama, Mississippi, and Arkansas. They brought or imported their slaves from the same regions, which entailed the spread of the relatively stable AAE vernaculars that had developed there, varieties that presumably were very similar, if not identical to each other, though all differed from Gullah. The cotton plantations were also smaller than the tobacco plantations of Virginia, much smaller than the rice fields of coastal South Carolina and Georgia, employing on average 20 or more slaves.[13] Although various forms of discrimination were already in place, which often led ex-slaves to rebel and negotiate conditions of their employment, there was still no rigid discrimination of the kind that would be implemented toward the end of the century in these states: racial segregation.

From a linguistic point of view the pre-Reconstruction nineteenth century provided much of the foundation of today's AAVE, fostering the distinction between, on the one hand, coastal South Carolina and coastal Georgia, where Gullah has been spoken, and, on the other hand, the rest of the United States, the domain of AAVE among African Americans. The sociohistorical facts continue to cast doubt on the determinative role of Caribbean English creoles in the development of AAVE especially, and apparently also on that of Gullah as well. The conclusion that AAVE and Gullah must have stabilized since the early nineteenth century is also consistent with literary evidence compiled by Brasch (1981), which indicates similarities in types of features between representations of African American vernaculars in fiction during that period and how it is spoken today.

An important mystery, which deserves more investigation, is the development of AAVE in territories covered by the Louisiana Purchase in 1803. The region had been francophone and to date there are still speakers of the French creole that developed there. Today's linguistic situation in Louisiana suggests gradual replacement of the local nineteenth-century French vernaculars, hence post-colonial language evolution under contact conditions. There are anecdotal reports of differences between rural Louisiana AAVE and varieties spoken elsewhere (see below), consistent in fact with reports by native speakers of regional differences within AAVE. However, very little has been investigated about the development of AAVE in Louisiana and why it has not diverged from other AAVE varieties more significantly than is the case.[14]

8.2.4   From the Reconstruction to date

The Civil War (1861–5) brought a new world order in North America, as it abolished slavery and undermined the plantation economy, although it did little that would improve the economic welfare of former slaves. In any case, it also eroded the one important difference that existed between former slaves and poor Whites, namely, freedom and citizens' rights in the eyes of the law versus slavery and lack of such rights. White supremacists then sought to re-articulate this social inequity in other race-based terms. They enacted the Jim Crow laws in the southern states in 1877, laws that disfavored African Americans in the competition for jobs and for welfare entitlements. The laws also led to the establishment of a generalized, most severe form of segregation that forced African and European Americans to live in separate neighborhoods and not to use the same public facilities. All these changes entailed limited interaction between African and European Americans, thus providing the first socio-economic ecology for linguistic divergence between the vernaculars of the two races (as noted first by Schneider 1995) outside the Gullah-speaking area, where segregation had been in place since the early eighteenth century.

We must, however, note that this rigid segregation of races in the American South followed two hundred years of common development. Similarities between AAVE and Southern White English vernaculars are undoubtedly the result of that long period of common history. On the other hand, at least part of the differences between the vernaculars are attributable to their speakers' separate histories over the past century, including the following factors:

1.   There were no more immigrations of Africans or Caribbeans into African American communities until after World War II. In addition, most of the

post-war immigrants (primarily from the Caribbean) were not integrated into the African American communities, a factor which precluded additional influence of African languages or Caribbean creoles on AAVE.[15] In places like New York, these late immigrants have typically developed their own African or Caribbean networks of communication, thus preserving their non-American accents. However, their children have had a choice between the AAE way, the educated middle-class English way, and, exceptionally, the non-American way.

2. On the other hand, the American population continued to grow significantly throughout the nineteenth century, owing largely to immigrations in the order of millions from each of the following parts of Europe: Germany (6.9 million), Italy (5.2 million), Ireland (4.7 million), Austria–Hungary (4.3 million), Canada (4.0 million), the Soviet Union/Russia (3.3 million), and England (3.1 million).[16] Compared with African Americans, the majority of the new European immigrants were relatively integrated into the extant European-American communities, although, as noted below, it is all a matter of degree.[17] By the Founder Principle, further restructuring of English was constrained by the local majority populations, especially since the immigrants increased the population by increments, with each addition being typically a minority relative to the established population. As in the case of African slaves in the seventeenth and the eighteenth centuries, the immigrants' children, regardless of whether they were born locally or immigrated with their parents, acquired the local vernaculars natively. Thus, they slowed down further restructuring of the extant European-American English vernaculars. As we see below, they did not prevent it totally, because other factors bore on the outcomes of these later population movements and contacts.

The increasing volume of immigrants, their social class and level of education (in several cases higher than that of the majority of seventeenth- and eighteenth-century colonists), and the actual patterns of settlements were likely to cause some changes that may have accentuated differences between the European and African American vernaculars. The fact that African Americans were generally not affected residentially by these later waves of European immigrations may be a potential factor in the divergence of African and European-American vernaculars in the twentieth century, which has attracted a lot of attention since Labov and Harris (1986) and Bailey and Maynor (1987, 1989) and to which a special issue of *American Speech* was devoted in (1989). See also Butters (1989).

3. One of the consequences of the Jim Crow laws was Northward and Westward migrations of African Americans from the vastly rural South, because the plantation industry was collapsing, and because they were losing political rights and could not compete fairly for the few jobs, aside from also being threatened or endangered by White supremacists. The emigrations started with the Black Exodus of 1879, when 20,000 African Americans moved to Kansas. They gained momentum with the Great Migration (1910–30),[18] during which almost a million African Americans left the South. By the 1970s, over six million had "outmigrated."

   However, the vast majority of these African Americans found themselves segregated in urban ghettoes, where they have socialized primarily among themselves and interacted with other populations only at work and, to some extent, in public places. These new living conditions enabled them to consolidate speech peculiarities they had brought from the southern states and thus to produce what was characterized by Labov (1972: xiii) both as a "relatively uniform grammar" cross-regionally and as a "whole range of language [varieties] used by black people in the United States: a very large range indeed, extending from the Creole grammar of Gullah spoken in the Sea Islands [and coastal marshlands] of South Carolina [and Georgia] to the most formal and accomplished literary style."

The sociohistorical facts support the hypothesis that AAE originated in the southeastern states, where, as reported by Bailey and Maynor (1989), Bailey and Thomas (1998), and by Rickford (1997, 1998), close to 90 percent of African Americans lived up to the end of the nineteenth century.[19] However, they also suggest the right kind of ecological explanations for other observations that have been made by either native speakers or some linguists. Consistent with Labov's (1972) observation that AAE consists of a "whole range of language" varieties, Troike (1973), for instance, calls for the study of regional variation in AAVE, which may highlight, among other things, differences between its northern and southern subvarieties. The apparent regional variation suggests that AAVE in northern and western cities was to some extent influenced by contacts with varieties previously spoken by the small minority of African Americans who had lived in the North (by the Founder Principle) or by other Americans that its speakers came to interact with. The questions are: (i) How much such influence is there? and (ii) Was the influence mostly in the sense of selecting from among options that were already available in the pre-migration systems?

Bailey (1997) and Bailey and Thomas (1998) are correct in noting that several of the features that have been stereotyped as peculiar to (White) Southern

English or to AAVE have either emerged or spread since the last quarter of the nineteenth century, because the histories of the two races which started to diverge at that time were likely to yield different, though still largely overlapping, linguistic characteristics. The fact that several of the new features continue to be correlated with nonstandard features of British English suggests also that the features may have been a latent part of the range of variants typical of colonial English, but they gained selective advantage thanks to socioeconomic ecological changes that started at the end of the nineteenth century. Perhaps the late nineteenth century was also the time when African and European Americans were particularly eager to identify some linguistic peculiarities as ethnic markers and thus made divergent selections of features from the pool of variants that they had shared until then. Such selections would have enhanced ethnic–dialectal differences that may have been minor at the dawn of the twentieth century.

African Americans also observe that they can tell a New Yorker from a Chicagoan, the latter from a Mississippian, etc. The variation may be primarily phonological and lexical, but it may extend to other structural aspects of AAE too. Consistent with the above observations, this one also suggests that slightly different kinds of restructuring took place in different cities or geographical areas, corresponding perhaps somewhat with different dialectal regions in North America.[20] All these observations also suggest that urban varieties of AAVE are twentieth-century phenomena, however little they differ structurally (and in the constraints that control several of their variables) from their nineteenth-century antecedents in the agricultural South.[21] While several previous studies and others in this volume have shown that AAVE could not have developed by debasilectalization from an erstwhile Gullah-like creole – a position that is consistent with the sociohistorical facts summarized in this chapter – it should be informative in the future to figure out what kinds of developments have produced these urban varieties and how they compare, for instance, with the twentieth-century developments which, according to Bailey (1997), have produced today's Southern White English vernaculars.

8.3   Evidence from the African American Diaspora on the Origins of AAVE

The divergence hypothesis, especially the above remarks by Bailey (1997), add a new twist to the question of the origins of AAVE. According to these observations, some of the features that now distinguish AAVE and European-American nonstandard vernaculars are recent, twentieth-century developments. Barring coincidental recent selections, what they share reflects their common history, in the case of American Southern English, or simply their common heritage from colonial English. Basically, they suggest that today's AAVE itself is a twentieth-century development. We thus depend very much on the Ex-Slave Recordings and, to some extent, on the Hoodoo Texts to determine how much AAVE has changed since the nineteenth century.[22]

Studies conducted so far suggest that little, if anything, has changed in AAVE's grammar. Aside from remaining controversial (see, e.g., Rickford 1992), changes such as those reported by Bailey and Maynor (1987, 1989) for usage of invariant *be* seem minimally qualitative, although they are significantly quantitative. Could there be changes in aspects of grammar that have retained little of our scholarly attention to date? Are what Howe and Walker (this volume) characterize as "recent and spectacular developments" regarding negative concord and use of *ain't* for *didn't* in AAVE among such grammatical innovations?[23] These remain open questions. Could AAVE have changed mostly phonologically and lexically? This too is an open question. After all, as Bailey and Thomas (1998) observe, phonological features alone have proved to be strong evidence to mark individuals as speaking a different variety.

If AAVE has changed since the late nineteenth or early twentieth century, do similarities between it and its congenors of the African American diaspora reflect only what was in African American vernaculars by the early nineteenth century? Are the other diasporic varieties any more conservative than AAVE itself is? What can we make of the fact that the differences among the diaspora varieties are not greater than they could have been? Or are the recent developments suggested by Bailey and Thomas (1998) really minor and was the substance of AAVE already in place by the end of the nineteenth century, and perhaps even as early as the early nineteenth century, as suggested by the sociohistorical evidence discussed here and by studies of the AAE diaspora materials?

More fundamental yet is the following question: How homogeneous was today's AAVE's ancestor in the early nineteenth century when some of its speakers emigrated to Samaná, to Nova Scotia, and to Liberia? What do conflicts among comparative studies of different features of the varieties and of AAVE tell us about the structural condition of AAE almost two hundred years ago?

It is also interesting that AAVE's features which are putatively recent developments have not made it more similar to other North American English vernaculars spoken particularly by European Americans, but have made it more different from them. This is compelling argument against the debasilectalization hypothesis, which has invoked interaction with European Americans as the primary reason why AAVE would be shedding off its "creole" features. Some of the evidence suggests that it would actually be developing in the opposite direction, basilectalizing further in some ways. After all, the social history suggests that since the late nineteenth century African and European Americans have not socialized more than they did before with each other, barring a few middle-class African Americans who have moved to ethnically integrated neighborhoods. Even in such cases, adult neighbors often do not socialize with each other.

8.4   Conclusions

The preceding sections have provided some sociohistorical reasons that make it unlikely that AAVE developed from a Gullah-like creole, least of all from Caribbean creoles. The slaves that were imported from the Caribbean to North America in the seventeenth century wound up generally in small communities where they were somewhat integrated among the vast majority of indentured servants with whom they worked and appear to have interacted in other ways. The homestead or small farm communities on which they lived could not foster the kind of segregation that would produce a creole, even in coastal South Carolina, by the end of the seventeenth century.

Quite significant about the seventeenth century is also the fact that the founder African population in British colonies actually started as indentured servants, with the same socioeconomic status as a large proportion of the European colonists in the Chesapeake. The very first Africans did not originate from the Anglophone Caribbean either, and they learned to speak colonial English. Also the slave population grew as much by birth as by importation. Importations were not massive, because slavery was then more expensive than indenture. The circumstances entail that the locally-born Africans spoke colonial English as fluently as the locally-born Europeans; and they and the seasoned slaves constituted a sizeable proportion of models to offset any influence that the Caribbean slaves who came later could have exerted on the development of the seventeenth-century ancestor of AAVE. It is also likely that Caribbean slaves did not then bring with them a basilectal creole sociolect.

Slavery conditions certainly changed during the eighteenth century, with the servile population growing more by importation, especially in South Carolina and Georgia, than by birth. However, the vast majority of slaves were imported directly from Africa: 90% in the Chesapeake and about 85% in South Carolina. Sound economic practice also suggests that at least a significant proportion of the slaves then imported from the Caribbean, especially from Barbados, would have lived only briefly there before coming to North America. Linguistically, their influence on the development of both Gullah and AAVE was as African as that of the majority imported directly from Africa. It is also very likely that a large proportion of the slaves who had lived long in the Caribbean before coming to North America had lived on small farms, thus they may not have spoken basilectal Creole in the first place.

What must also be borne in mind is that even if Caribbean (basilectal) creole vernaculars were brought over, the origins of their features were not necessarily non-English, as largely restructured as they may have been. This aspect of language contact in the New World complicates the picture. What kind of influence have Caribbean vernaculars exerted on the development of African American vernaculars which had been developing independently under similar ecological conditions at least in coastal South Carolina and Georgia? Convergence of features selected by Africans both in the Caribbean and in North America would of course have favored their shared peculiarities. However, do such similarities necessarily entail that North American vernaculars developed from their Caribbean kin? Moreover, what would have been the motivation for the Africans who preceded Caribbean slaves in North America to prefer Caribbean vernaculars to their own and why would the other newcomers have preferred the models of a minority over that of a majority?

The nineteenth century brought the importation of slaves from outside the United States to an early official end, in 1808, although slavery and clandestine importations of slaves continued till the end of the Civil War. That is, the restructuring which led to more divergence of colonial English into today's Gullah and AAVE then depended more on changing internal, local dynamics of inter-ethnic interaction than on influence from outside the United States. The evidence from offshoots of African American vernaculars in Samaná, Nova Scotia, and Liberia suggest that perhaps most of the features associated with these vernaculars today were already in place at the beginning of the nineteenth century. Hannah's (1997) discussion of the validity of the diasporic evidence also suggests that materials from offshoot varieties are useful mostly when they agree with today's features of AAVE (or Gullah), suggesting that a feature was part of the system by the early nineteenth century. However, one cannot make much of differences, because, like AAVE (and Gullah), these vernaculars may have changed somewhat, diverging a little bit in their present ecologies. We should perhaps be impressed by how much has remained the same, which sheds light on the role of non-integration in the dominant community in helping an enclave variety survive.

Quite noteworthy is also Rickford's (1998) recognition of some merits in assuming that AAVE had an independent development; i.e., it did not originate as a creole nor does it simply represent "the transfer and acquisition by Africans and African Americans of English dialects spoken by British and other White immigrants to America in earlier times" (1998: 192). That is indeed the position Mufwene (1996; in press) argues for: all varieties of English in North America are contact-based and developed concurrently. AAVE and Gullah shared with other North American vernaculars part of the pool of features from which those who developed them selected their respective linguistic peculiarities. In addition they had an overlapping pool of features from African languages. The impact of African languages remains open.

The obvious part of the above question is that if African languages did not play a role at all in their development, then AAVE and Gullah would not be as different as they are from the vernaculars spoken by European Americans – although even the nature of the differences themselves remains an open question outside the more obvious phonological items of divergence which Bailey and Thomas (1998) highlight. Much remains debatable, aside from what appear to be effects of convergence. We can, nonetheless, hypothesize that African languages influenced Africans in North America to re-articulate and integrate English features in somewhat different ways from their European counterparts.

Exactly the same kinds of observations apply to the development of Caribbean English creoles and the like. *Mutatis mutandis*, similar observations apply to the development of other North American vernaculars, especially in those cases where non-English-speaking Europeans and others were not fully integrated among English speakers. There should thus be more emphasis on principles that regulate selection of features and the integration of the latter into new systems, under specified ecological conditions. The invocation of influence from Caribbean English creoles is typically question-begging. In the first place, not much more is known about the origins of their features nor about the probable times of their formation, aside from the objections articulated above.

Like Tagliamonte (1996, and to appear), works by Poplack and Tagliamonte (1989), Smith and Tagliamonte (1998), Tagliamonte and Smith (1998), and other papers in this volume do well in highlighting features of Early Modern English that are likely to have been brought to North America and thus to have found their way into AAVE, Gullah, and the like. One of our common mistakes in the literature is to have compared these new vernaculars with Standard English rather than with the right varieties, that is, whatever evidence may be gathered from seventeenth- and eighteenth-century (nonstandard) English and contemporary nonstandard English vernaculars that have developed concurrently with AAVE and its creole kin but without the influence of African languages. Such comparisons should shed light on the nature of African substrate influence itself, especially now that our knowledge of African languages is more adequate than when Lorenzo Turner published *Africanisms in the Gullah Dialect* (1949). We can only hope that our knowledge of White nonstandard vernaculars will soon grow as much, to make possible more adequate discussions of the development of AAVE and the like.

Notes

1   In fact, if one agrees with Hjelmslev (1938), as I do, all languages are! They have been affected by contact to some extent (Mufwene 1998), a fact well taken into account in Chomsky's (1986) characterization of the core/periphery distinction in knowledge of language. Unlike the core, which is putatively determined by Universal Grammar *qua* biological endowment for language, facts of the periphery are claimed to originate partly in contacts with other languages. The question is whether we can always tell to what extent a linguistic system is mixed, and in what respects.

2   The diffuseness of colonial English was a consequence of both its heterogeneous metropolitan origins and the fact that several European indentured servants, who certainly passed as model speakers for several Africans, were themselves acquiring it as a second language and therefore spoke it with variable non-native features. Colonial English was itself a continuum of varieties in development when, like other immigrants whose native languages could not thrive in the new ecology, the Africans targeted it as their vernacular.

3   Communication mostly among the Africans themselves, especially on large plantations and after communities were segregated (see below), would favor the *normalization* of such deviations from native norms and the integration of Allsopp's "apports" within the emerging systems. Note that the term "normalization" is being used deliberately here, after Chaudenson (1979), to suggest the development of new norms.

4   Things are, of course, messier than presented here. Questions involving *gon* still require a copula, as in *is he gon come?* However, this is no conclusive evidence that *gon* is still a progressive form. It may also be interpreted as a non-verbal auxiliary which requires a copula in some constructions.

5   This is not to deny that the Africans were discriminated against in several ways. In fact, the history presented here should highlight the fact that slavery for life, as opposed to indenture, was a consequence of discrimination. Segregation as the practice of separate residential quarters/neighborhoods and public facilities is also a consequence of discrimination, which must have been there since the beginning. Integration here is simply in the sense of absence of segregation by race, although there was already one based on socioeconomic class, lumping all indentured servants together.

6   No working assumptions in today's linguistics encourage this kind of correlation between race and language acquisition or evolution. We know of no genetic racial peculiarities that bear on the divergence of linguistic developments.

7   The latter are aptly captured by Chaudenson's (1979) phrase "conditions de robinsonnade," after Daniel Defoe's (1719) *Robinson Crusoe*.

8   By 1690, few of the South Carolina planters were rich enough or had secured enough collateral for the kinds of loans that would enable them to commission full shiploads of slaves directly from Africa.

9   Georgia and North Carolina are what one may identify, after Chaudenson (1979), as second-generation colonies, whose rapid development was facilitated by an antecedent colony which provided both the model that they followed and a large proportion of the founder population. If South Carolina, founded from Barbados, had launched (immediately) into sugar-cane agriculture and had developed on the Barbadian model, then it too would be a literal second-generation colony and would have borne more of its linguistic influence. In any case, second-generation colonies are not bound to be like their antecedents if the socioeconomic conditions are not preserved. They were in the case of Georgia relative to South Carolina, and of North Carolina relative to Virginia (as explained below).

10 Rickford (1997) reports that Virginia had 42.9% "of all Blacks in the thirteen colonies in 1750." In fact if we focus on the southeastern colonies, in which slavery was the backbone of the economy, the Virginia Africans constituted 49.5% of the total population. However, Virginia had a very high percentage of the total European population in the same southeastern colonies too: almost 42%. In any case, the total number of slaves in a colony does not tell the full story, although numbers are relevant to whether or not a critical mass obtained that could foster the development of a separate vernacular and when individuals of similar geographical or ethnic backgrounds could interact primarily with each other and develop their own peculiarities. Among the important factors that bore on the restructuring of colonial English into African American vernaculars are the following: (i) the kinds and sizes of the communities in which the Africans lived; and (ii) how they were integrated in, or marginalized from, the larger or politically dominant colonial population (see section 8.2.4).

11 Wood (1989) estimates the proportion of people of African descent in Virginia at 41%. The lower ratio in the main text applies to the Chesapeake colonies, including Maryland, where the proportion of slaves was lower. Still, the overall state-wide proportions are misleading. It is the communities with the highest concentrations of Africans that matter and the kinds of interactions which they had with the European populations.

12 Singler (1998) also argues more explicitly that the Liberian English data suggests that the African American English vernaculars exported to the diaspora were heterogeneous. Although creole-like features are attested in the speech of some descendants of Liberian settlers, they do not necessarily argue for (a generalized) prior creole structure of AAVE. In fact, some of the features have their origins in Kru Pidgin English, whose development is independent of Liberian Settler or vernacular English.

13 The tobacco plantations employed 80 individuals on average, whereas several rice fields used 200 individuals or more, although there were a few small ones.

14 In a recent posting on the CreoList (8 August 1998), Tom Klingler of Tulane University reported hearing forms of African American English in Louisiana that

Salikoko S. Mufwene

he has not heard elsewhere. Charles DeBose of California State University at Hayward shared a similar observation with me in January 1995 in New Orleans, corroborating my own observation in the same city in November 1994. However, not every African American there speaks a form of AAVE that diverges from what is spoken elsewhere, and the differences reported so far are more prosodic than anything. (See also section 8.2.4.)

15 A large proportion of these immigrants have been college and graduate students, who, after graduation, have typically chosen to reside in relatively integrated middle-class neighborhoods, along with many economically successful middle-class African Americans.

16 Bodnar (1991: 534) estimates these figures for the 1820–1975 period. After 1975, volumes of immigrations shift in importance to those from outside Europe, with Mexico leading at 720,000. Fewer than 120,000 immigrants have come from Africa, and only 200,000 from Jamaica (Bodnar 1991: 537). Large proportions of the European immigrations took place by World War II. According to Bodnar, "From 1815 to the Civil War, 5 million people moved to the United States, about half from England and 40 percent from Ireland. Between the end of the war and 1890, another 10 million came, mostly from northwestern Europe – England, Wales, Germany, and Scandinavia. And finally about 15 million immigrants arrived in the relatively brief period between 1890 and 1914 . . . [consisting of] Poles, Russian Jews, Ukrainians, Slovaks, Croatians, Slovens, Hungarians, Romanians, Italians, and Greeks" (534–5). One may establish a correlation between, on the one hand, the time, volume, and place of immigration, as well as patterns of social integration within the majority English-speaking population, and, on the other hand, the development of some ethnic varieties of English, e.g., Italian, Jewish, and German.

17 As suggested in note 14, this observation oversimplifies a situation that is much more complex. Europeans looked integrated relative to the more conspicuous segregation of Africans but were not so unified either. Lack of absolute integration among them accounts for the development of varieties identified as Jewish, Italian, and German English. (This lack of absolute integration is well highlighted by Fischer's (1989) description of original patterns of settlements, in which he clearly shows which groups were directed to settle in the more, or less, comfortable parts of the colonies.) In a way, one may argue that we are just dealing with a continuum of new varieties of English whose divergence from each other may be correlated inversely with the degree of integration of its speakers with those of another. Race and socioeconomic class have worked concurrently, but not exclusively, to define boundaries. Local economic conditions influenced the dominant directions of later immigrations from Europe and what Bodnar (1991: 535) describes as "ethnic clustering."

18 The onset of this second exodus is said to have started in 1890. However, the term "Great Migration" is apparently restricted to the 1910–30 period, when the "outmigration" from the South was the most intense under the lure of World War I and post-war industry.

19   An interesting 1861 demographic map of the states that would later on form the present United States (except Hawaii and Alaska; McPherson 1991: 184) shows that outside the southern states, African Americans hardly exceeded 2% of the total population. The only exceptions were Maryland (25%), Delaware (20%), New Jersey (4%), and Missouri (10%). African Americans constituted 59% in South Carolina and 55% in Mississippi.

20   Interestingly, Bailey (1997) observes that the dialectal regions remain basically the same as those identified by Kurath (1949). Only the features that are stereotypical of the dialects have changed since the late nineteenth century, especially at the phonological level.

21   Bailey and Thomas (1998) show that phonologically this conclusion is correct. One may, however, dispute their position that the phonological features that AAVE shares with Caribbean creoles "reflect some sort of shared history" with them (106). They say it better in terms of "shared heritage" (97), which makes it possible to recognize parallel competition and selection of features of colonial English and of African languages into the structures of AAVE and its creole kin without necessarily suggesting creole origins for AAVE. Similarities in internal and external ecologies would have produced similarities in resulting structures.

22   The Ex-Slave Narratives have been criticized by several scholars as unreliable, chiefly because the texts have been edited by field workers or project coordinators in ways that either stereotyped the vernacular or simply distort its authenticity (see, e.g., Maynor 1988; Dillard 1993; Ewers 1996). Although they contain evidence of features heard in African American vernaculars in the 1930s, they probably require more scrutiny before being used as diachronic evidence.

23   The alternation of *ain't* and *didn't* may actually have to do with the ambiguity of the preterit form in North American English between the past tense meaning and the perfect tense meaning. The perfect meaning of *ain't* corresponding to "have not" may be the reason why *ain't* is used to negate verbs that would be in the preterit form in an affirmative sentence. Uses of *ain't* for *didn't* are attested in Gullah, which, as argued above, developed in a separate ecology from AAVE.

References

Allsopp, R. (1977) Africanisms in the idioms of Caribbean English. In P. F. Kotey and H. Der-Houssikian (eds), *Language and Linguistic Problems in Africa*, Columbia, SC: Hornbeam Press, 429–41.

Bailey, G. (1997) When did Southern American English begin? In E. Schneider (ed.), *Englishes Around the World, 1: General Studies, British Isles, North America: Studies in Honor of Manfred Görlach*, Amsterdam and Philadelphia: John Benjamins, 255–75.

Bailey, G., and Maynor, N. (1987) Decreolization? *Language in Society*, 16 (4), 449–73.

Bailey, G., and Maynor, N. (1989) The divergence controversy. *American Speech*, 64 (1): 12–39.

Bailey, G., Maynor, N., and Cukor-Avila, P. (1991) *The Emergence of Black English: Texts and Commentary.* Amsterdam and Philadelphia: John Benjamins.

Bailey, G., and Thomas, E. (1998) Some aspects of African-American vernacular phonology. In S. S. Mufwene, J. R. Rickford, G. Bailey, and J. Baugh (eds), *African-American English*, London: Routledge, 85–109.

Baker, P. (1997) Directionality in pidginization and creolization. In A. K. Spears and D. Winford (eds), *The Structure and Status of Pidgins and Creoles*, Amsterdam and Philadelphia: John Benjamins, 91–109.

Baugh, J. (1980) A reexamination of the Black English copula. In W. Labov (ed.), *Locating Language in Time and Space*, New York: Academic Press, 83–106.

Bodnar, J. (1991) Immigration. In E. Foner and J. A. Garraty (eds), *The Reader's Companion to American History*, Boston: Houghton Mifflin.

Boretzky, N. (1993) The concept of rule, rule borrowing, and substrate influence in creole languages. In S. S. Mufwene (ed.), *Africanisms in Afro-American Language Varieties*, Athens: University of Georgia Press, 74–92.

Brasch, W. (1981) *Black English and the Mass Media.* Lanham, MD: University of America Press.

Butters, R. (1989) *The Death of Black English: Divergence and Convergence in Black and White Vernaculars.* Frankfurt: Peter Lang.

Campbell-Kibler, K. (1998) History in the making of language: A critique of the literature on the development of African-American English. M.A. thesis, University of Chicago.

Carrington, L. (1993) On the notion of "Africanism" in Afro-American. In S. S. Mufwene (ed.), *Africanisms in Afro-American Language Varieties*, Athens: University of Georgia Press, 35–46.

Cassidy, F. G. (1986) Barbadian Creole – Possibility and probability. *American Speech*, 61: 195–205.

Chomsky, N. (1986) *Knowledge of Language: Its Nature, Origin and Use.* New York: Praeger.

Coleman, K. (1978) *Georgia History in Outline.* Athens: University of Georgia Press.

Corcoran, C., and Mufwene, S. S. (1998) Sam Matthews' Kittitian: What is it evidence of? In P. Baker and A. Bruyn (eds), *St. Kitts and the Atlantic Creoles: The Texts of Samuel Augustus Matthews in Perspective*, London: University of Westminster Press, 75–102.

DeBose, C. E. (1983) Samaná English: A dialect that time forgot. In *Proceedings of the Ninth Annual Meeting of the Berkeley Linguistics Society*, 47–53.

DeBose, C. E. (1988) *Be* in Samaná English. In *Occasional Paper 21, Society for Caribbean Linguistics*, University of West Indies.

Dillard, J. (1993) The value (linguistic and philological) of the WPA ex-Slave narratives. In S. Mufwene (ed.), *Africanisms in Afro-American Language Varieties*, Athens, GA: University of Georgia Press, 222–31.

Ewers, T. (1996) *The Origin of American Black English: Be-forms in the HOODOO Texts.* New York: Mouton de Gruyter.

Fischer, D. H. (1989) *Albion's Seed: Four British Folkways in America.* New York and Oxford: Oxford University Press.

Hannah, D. (1997) Copula absence in Samaná English: Implications for research on the linguistic history of African-American Vernacular English. *American Speech*, 72 (4): 339–72.

Hjelmslev, L. (1938) Etudes sur la notion de parenté linguistique. *Revue des Etudes Indo-Européennes*, 1: 271–86.

Holm, J. (1984) Variability of the copula in black English and its creole kin. *American Speech*, 59 (4): 291–309.

Jones, H. (1724/1956) *The Present State of Virginia: From Whence Is Inferred a Short View of Maryland and North Carolina*, ed. Richard L. Morton. Chapel Hill: North Carolina Press.

Kulikoff, A. (1986) *Tobacco and Slaves: The Development of Southern Cultures in the Chesapeake, 1680–1800*. Chapel Hill: University of North Carolina Press.

Kurath, H. (1949) *Word Geography of the Eastern United States*. Ann Arbor: University of Michigan Press.

Labov, W. (1972) *Sociolinguistic Patterns*. Philadelphia: University of Pennsylvania Press.

Labov, W., and Harris, W. A. (1986) De facto segregation of Black and White Vernaculars. In D. Sankoff (ed.), *Diversity and Diachrony*, Amsterdam and Philadelphia: John Benjamins, 1–24.

LePage, R., and Tabouret-Keller, A. (1985) *Acts of Identity: Creole-based Approaches to Language and Ethnicity*. Cambridge: Cambridge University Press.

Lovejoy, P. (1989) The impact of the Atlantic slave trade on Africa: A review of the literature. *Journal of African History*, 30: 365–94.

McPherson, J. M. (1991) Civil war: causes and results. In E. Foner and J. A. Garraty (eds), *The Reader's Companion to American History*, Boston: Houghton Mifflin, 182–5.

Mufwene, S. S. (1992) Africanisms in Gullah: A re-examination of the issues. In J. H. Hall, D. Doane, and D. Ringler (eds), *Old English and New: Studies in Language and Linguistics in Honor of Frederic G. Cassidy*, New York: Garland, 156–82.

Mufwene, S. S. (1993) Introduction. In S. S. Mufwene (ed.), *Africanisms in Afro-American Language Varieties*, Athens: University of Georgia Press, 1–31.

Mufwene, S. S. (1996) The Founder Principle in creole genesis. *Diachronica*, 13 (1): 83–134.

Mufwene, S. S. (1998) What research on creole genesis can contribute to historical linguistics. In M. Schmid, J. Austin, and D. Stein, *Historical Linguistics*. Amsterdam and Philadelphia: John Benjamins.

Mufwene, S. S. (in press) North American varieties of English as by-products of population contacts. In R. Wheeler (ed.), *Living English*, Westport, CT: Greenwood Publishing Group.

Perkins, E. J. (1988) *The Economy of Colonial America*. New York: Columbia University Press.

Poplack, S., and Sankoff, D. (1984) El inglés de Samaná y la hipótesis del origen criollo. *Boletín de la Academia Puertorriqueña de la Lengua Española*, *VIII*, 103–21.

Poplack, S., and Tagliamonte, S. (1989) There's no tense like the present: Verbal *-s* inflection in Early Black English. *Language Variation and Change*, 1 (1): 47–84.

262 *Salikoko S. Mufwene*

Poplack, S., and Tagliamonte, S. (1991) African American English in the diaspora: The case of old-line Nova Scotians. *Language Variation and Change*, 3 (3): 301–39.
Poplack, S., and Tagliamonte, S. (1994) -*S* or nothing: Marking the plural in the African American diaspora. *American Speech*, 69 (3): 227–59.
Poplack, S., and Tagliamonte, S. (1996) Nothing in context: Variation, grammaticization and past time marking in Nigerian Pidgin English. In P. Baker (ed.), *Changing Meanings, Changing Functions: Papers Relating to Grammaticalization in Contact Languages*, Westminster, UK: University of Westminster Press, 71–94.
Rawley, J. A. (1991) Slave trade. In E. Foner and J. A. Garraty (eds), *The Reader's Companion to American History*, Boston: Houghton Mifflin, 994–5.
Rickford, J. R. (1992) Grammatical variation and divergence in Vernacular Black English. In M. Gerritsen and D. Stein (eds), *Internal and External Factors in Syntactic Change*, Berlin: Mouton de Gruyter, 175–200.
Rickford, J. R. (1997) Prior creolization of African-American Vernacular English? Sociohistorical and textual evidence from the 17th and 18th centuries. *Journal of Sociolinguistics*, 1 (3): 315–36.
Rickford, J. R. (1998) The creole origins of African-American Vernacular English: Evidence from copula absence. In S. Mufwene, J. R. Rickford, G. Bailey, and J. Baugh (eds), *African-American English: Structure, History, and Use*, London: Routledge, 154–200.
Rickford, J. R., and Blake, R. (1990) Copula contraction and absence in Barbadian English, Samaná English and Vernacular Black English. In K. Hall, J.-P. Koenig, M. Meacham, S. Reinman, and L. A. Sutton (eds), *Proceedings of the Sixteenth Annual Meeting of the Berkeley Linguistic Society*, Berkeley: Berkeley Linguistics Society, 257–68.
Schneider, E. W. (1989) *American Earlier Black English*. Tuscaloosa, AL: University of Alabama Press.
Schneider, E. W. (1995) Verbal -*s* inflection in 'early' American Black English. In J. Fisiak (ed.), *Linguistic Change under Contact Conditions*, Berlin: Mouton de Gruyter, 315–26.
Singler, J. V. (1989) Plural marking in Liberian Settler English. *American Speech*, 64 (1): 40–64.
Singler, J. V. (1991) Copula variation in Liberian Settler English and American Black English. In W. F. Edwards and D. Winford (eds), *Verb Phrase Patterns in Black English and Creole*, Detroit: Wayne State University Press, 129–64.
Singler, J. V. (1998) Mississippi in American, Mississippi in Africa: The role of enclave evidence in reconstructing the history of African American Englishes. Presented at the Fifth International Conference on World Englishes. University of Illinois at Urbana–Champaign.
Smith, J., and Tagliamonte, S. (1998) *We was all thegither, I think we were all thegither: Was* regularization in Buckie English. *World Englishes*, 17 (2): 105–26.
Sutcliffe, D. (1998) Gone with the wind? Evidence for 19th century African American speech. *Links & Letters*, 5: 127–45.
Tagliamonte, S. (1996) Has it ever been PERFECT? Uncovering the grammar of early Black English. *York Papers in Linguistics*, 17: 351–96.

Tagliamonte, S. (to appear) The grammaticalization of the PRESENT PERFECT in English: Tracks of change and continuity in a linguistic enclave. In O. Fischer and D. Stein (eds), *Grammaticalization Processes in Older English*, Berlin: Mouton de Gruyter.

Tagliamonte, S., and Poplack, S. (1988) Tense and aspect in Samaná English. *Language in Society*, 17: 513–33.

Tagliamonte, S., and Poplack, S. (1993) The zero-marked verb: Testing the creole hypothesis. *Journal of Pidgin and Creole Languages*, 8 (2): 171–206.

Tagliamonte, S., and Smith, J. (1998) Roots of English in the African American diaspora. *Links & Letters*, 5: 147–65.

Tate, T. W. (1965) *The Negro in Eighteenth-Century Williamsburg*. Williamsburg, VA: The Colonial Williamsburg Foundation.

Thomas, H. (1997) *The Slave Trade*. New York: Simon & Schuster.

Thomason, S. G. (1983) Chinook jargon in a real and historical context. *Language*, 59: 820–70.

Thomason, S. G., and Kaufman, T. (1988) *Language Contact, Creolization and Genetic Linguistics*. Berkeley and Los Angeles, CA: University of California Press.

Tottie, G., and Rey, M. (1997) Relativization strategies in Earlier African American Vernacular English. *Language Variation and Change*, 9 (2): 219–47.

Troike, R. (1973) On social, regional, and age variation in Black English. *The Florida Foreign Language Reporter*, Spring/Fall: 7–8.

Turner, L. D. (1949) *Africanisms in the Gullah Dialect*. Chicago: University of Chicago Press.

Winford, D. (1992) Another look at the copula in Black English and Caribbean Creoles. *American Speech*, 67 (1): 21–60.

Winford, D. (1993) Back to the past: The BEV/Creole connection revisited. *Language Variation and Change*, 4: 311–57.

Winford, D. (1997) On the origins of African American Vernacular English – A creolist perspective, Part I: The sociohistorical background. *Diachronica*, 15 (2): 305–44.

Winford, D. (1998) On the origins of African American Vernacular English – A creolist perspective, Part II: Linguistic features. *Diachronica*, 15 (1): 99–154.

Wood, P. H. (1974) *Black Majority: Negroes in Colonial South Carolina from 1670 through the Stono Rebellion*. New York: Alfred A. Knopf.

Wood, P. H. (1989) The changing population of the Colonial South: An overview by race and region, 1685–1790. In P. H. Wood, G. A. Waselkov, and T. M. Hatley (eds), *Powhatan's Mantle: Indians of the Colonial Southeast*, Lincoln and London: University of Nebraska Press, 25–103.

Wood, P. H. (1991) Southern colonies. In E. Foner and J. A. Garraty (eds), *The Reader's Companion to American History*, Boston: Houghton Mifflin, 1009–10.

Glossary

acrolect   A prestige or standard variety on the **creole continuum** approximating the standard European **lexifier** (e.g. acrolectal Jamaican English).

affix   A **morpheme** that can only occur when bound to another **morpheme** (e.g. *–s* in *dogs*).

allomorph(s)   The alternate forms of a **morpheme**, the occurrences of which are conditioned by the environment (e.g. [z], [s] and [əz] are allomorphs of the plural marker *–s*).

anglicist hypothesis   See **English-origins hypothesis**.

aspect   A grammatical category referring to the duration or type of action predicated by the verb.

basilect   A variety on the **creole continuum** that is furthest from the standard European **lexifier** (e.g. basilectal Jamaican Creole English).

bisystemic   Consisting of two linguistic systems or grammars (see **codeswitching**).

calque   A type of influence resulting from language contact consisting of **morpheme-by-morpheme** translation (e.g. French *gratte-ciel* is a calque of English *skyscraper*).

clitic   A grammatically independent form that is **prosodically** weak and must attach to another element.

codeswitching   The alternation between two linguistic systems in the course of speaking.

constraint hierarchy   The ranking of factors within a **factor group** according to the magnitude of their effect on variability.

convergence hypothesis   The theory that African American Vernacular English is becoming more like mainstream varieties of American English.

copula   A linking verb which serves to connect a subject and a non-verbal **predicate**.

corpus   A body of linguistic data, consisting of recordings of continuous speech or texts.

creole   A language of mixed origins, whose **lexicon** typically derives from one language and whose grammatical structure derives from another language or group of languages; a **pidgin** that has become the native or primary language of a group of speakers.

creole continuum The set of linguistic varieties ranging between a **creole** and its standard European **lexifier**.

creolist hypothesis The theory that African American Vernacular English derives its distinctive features from a prior widespread **creole** (also *creole-origins hypothesis*).

decreolization The process whereby a linguistic variety loses its **creole** features, usually through contact with its standard European **lexifier**.

deictic A form that indicates spatial or temporal location in relation to the speaker (e.g. *here, there, now, then*).

diaspora The geographic dispersal of a community or group.

divergence hypothesis The theory that African American Vernacular English is becoming less like mainstream varieties of American English.

elision The deletion of sounds in connected speech.

enclave See **relic area**.

enclitic A **clitic** that attaches to the end of a word.

English-origins hypothesis The theory that African American Vernacular English derives its features from (nonstandard) British-origin dialects.

epenthesis The insertion of non-etymological sounds into a word.

expletive A construction which serves to indicate existence but which itself has no referential content (e.g. *there is/are* in English) (also *existential*).

factor group A set of factors or values hypothesized to condition linguistic variability.

functional category A closed set of syntactic constituents with largely grammatical rather than referential content (e.g. determiner, auxiliary, copula).

habitual An **aspectual** category referring to an action that occurs repeatedly or regularly (e.g. *We used to skate in the winter*).

historical reconstruction A method by which aspects of an earlier stage of a language or linguistic variety are inferred through comparison of related extant varieties.

hypercorrection The overuse of a standard or prestige linguistic form outside of its prescribed environment (e.g. *I* in *between you and I*).

inflection An **affix** that indicates a grammatical relationship but does not alter the basic meaning of its root (e.g. verbal *-s*, as in *He sings*).

interaction (i) A situation in which two or more **factor groups** act on a **variable** synergistically or antagonistically rather than independently or additively. (ii) The statistical associations among **factor groups**.

irrealis A set of verb forms referring to unrealized or potential events or processes (e.g. future, conditional, subjunctive).

iterative An **aspectual** category referring to an action, usually punctual, that occurs repeatedly or regularly (e.g. *He jumped five times*).

lexical category A syntactic constituent with referential content (e.g. noun, verb, adjective).

lexicalization A process whereby a group of **morphemes** comes to function as a single **morpheme**.

lexicon The linguistic system consisting of the words and morphemes of a language; vocabulary.

lexifier The language supplying the **lexicon** of a **pidgin** or **creole**.

likelihood In **variable rule analysis,** a formal measurement of how likely a given set of data is to have been produced by various configurations of **factor groups**.

lingua franca An auxiliary language used to facilitate communication between groups of speakers who do not share a common mother tongue.

loanword A word originating in one language that has been incorporated into another, recipient, language and is used natively by its speakers.

log likelihood The logarithm of **likelihood,** used as part of a statistical test within the **variable rule** program to ascertain whether the contribution of a **factor group** is significant.

mesolect An intermediate linguistic variety on the **creole continuum** between **acrolect** and **basilect**.

modal An auxiliary verb expressing the grammatical **mood** of the main verb (e.g. *can, must, will*).

monomorphemic Consisting of a single **morpheme**.

mood A grammatical category expressing the speaker's attitude toward the content of his/her utterance.

morpheme The smallest meaningful unit of language (e.g. *un-, yield,* and *–ing* in *unyielding*).

morpholexical Pertaining to lexical aspects of **morpheme** structure.

morphophonological Pertaining to phonological aspects of **morpheme** structure; also **morphophonemic**.

morphosyntactic Pertaining to the **morphological** and **syntactic** expression of grammatical relations.

multiple regression A statistical procedure in which the value of one, dependent, **variable** is explained by the effects of one or more independent **variables**.

multivariate analysis The simultaneous statistical analysis of the co-variation of several **variables**.

neutralization context A linguistic environment in which distinctions among **variants** cannot be detected.

noncount context A context in which there is no variability, and which therefore does not form part of the **variable context**.

onomastic Pertaining to the study of proper names.

operationalization In **variable rule analysis**, the conversion of a claim or hypothesis into a **factor group** for the purpose of statistically testing its effect on the choice of **variant**.

phonetic segment The smallest discrete segment of sound in connected speech.

phonotactic Pertaining to the organization of phonetic segments into syllables.

pidgin A language with no native speakers, used for restricted purposes (usually trade).

postvocalic Occurring after a vowel.

predicate The part of the sentence indicating properties of the subject, usually consisting of a verb, its object(s) or complements, and adverbials.

prescriptive Promoting the idea that there are correct and incorrect ways of speaking.

preterite The simple past tense.

proclitic A **clitic** that attaches to the beginning of a word.

prosody The rhythmic structure of spoken language.

relic area A geographical region in which linguistic varieties or features that have disappeared elsewhere are retained.

resyllabification The association of a **phonetic segment** with a syllable other than the one with which it was originally associated.

sibilant A fricative sound made with a groove in the tongue that produces a hissing noise (e.g. [s] or [z]).

singleton A form which occurs only once in a **corpus**.

stative An **aspectual** category referring to a state (as opposed to an event).

subcategorization The specification of permissible grammatical constituents in a particular environment.

substrate A language spoken by an indigenous subordinate group that comes in contact with the language of a dominant group.

superstrate A language spoken by a dominant group that comes in contact with the language of an indigenous subordinate group.

syntax The system governing the way words are combined to form sentences.

variable A unit of language that may be realized in two or more **variant** forms.

variable context The environment in which it is possible for **variant** forms to occur.

variable rule analysis   A **multiple-regression** analysis in which the dependent **variable** is the occurrence or non-occurrence of some linguistic **variant**, and the independent **variables** are aspects of the linguistic or social context; the analytical procedure is based on principles of maximum **likelihood**.

variant   One of the alternate realizations of a **variable**.

Index